# Clean Architecture with .NET

Dino Esposito

# Clean Architecture with .NET

**Published with the authorization of Microsoft Corporation by:**

**Pearson Education, Inc.,** Hoboken, New Jersey

**Copyright © 2024 by Dino Esposito.**

ISBN-13: 978-0-13-820328-3

ISBN-10: 0-13-820328-8

Library of Congress Control Number: 2024930932

1 2024

## Trademarks

## Warning and Disclaimer

## Special Sales

For information about buying this title in bulk quantities, or for special sales opportunities (which may include electronic versions; custom cover designs; and content particular to your business, training goals, marketing focus, or branding interests), please contact our corporate sales department at corpsales@pearsoned.com or (800) 382-3419.

For government sales inquiries, please contact governmentsales@pearsoned.com.

For questions about sales outside the U.S., please contact intlcs@pearson.com.

**Editor-in-Chief**
Brett Bartow

**Executive Editor**
Loretta Yates

**Associate Editor**
Shourav Bose

**Development Editor**
Kate Shoup

**Managing Editor**
Sandra Schroeder

**Senior Project Editor**
Tracey Croom

**Copy Editor**
Dan Foster

**Indexer**
Ken Johnson

**Proofreader**
Jennifer Hinchliffe

**Technical Editor**
Milan Jovanovic

**Editorial Assistant**
Cindy Teeters

**Cover Designer**
Twist Creative, Seattle

**Compositor**
codeMantra

**Graphics**
codeMantra

# Contents at a Glance

# Contents

**Chapter 3    Laying the ground for modularity                            47**

**Chapter 4    The presentation layer                                       65**

## Chapter 6   The domain layer                                                      133

## Chapter 7   Domain services                                                       169

## Chapter 8  The infrastructure layer                                        189

## PART III    COMMON DILEMMAS

## Chapter 9  Microservices versus modular monoliths                          219

## Chapter 11 Technical debt and credit 285

# Acknowledgments

As hair thins and grays, memories return of when I was the youngest in every meeting or conference room. In 30 years of my career, I witnessed the explosion of Windows as an operating system, the rise of the web accompanied by websites and applications, and then the advent of mobile and cloud technologies.

Several times, I found myself having visions related to software technology developments, not too far from what happened a few years later. At other times, I surprised myself by formulating personal projects halfway between dreams and ambitious goals.

The most unspoken of all is the desire to travel the world, speaking at international conferences without the pressure to talk about what is cool and trendy but only about what I have seen and made work—without mincing words and without filters or reservations. To do this, I needed to work—finally—daily on the development of real applications that contributed to some kind of business and simplified the lives of some kind of audience.

Thanks to Crionet and KBMS Data Force, this is now a reality.

After many years, I have a full-time position (CTO of Crionet), a team of people grown in a few years from juniors to bold and capable professionals, and the will to share with everyone a recipe for making software that is neither secret nor magical.

I have nothing to sell; only to tell. And this book is for those who want to listen.

This book is for Silvia and Francesco.

This book is for Michela.

This book is for Giorgio and Gaetano.

This book was made possible by Loretta and Shourav and came out as you're getting it thanks to Milan, Tracey, Dan, and Kate.

This book is my best until the next one!

# Introduction

I graduated in Computer Science in the summer of 1990. At the time, there were not many places in Europe to study computers. The degree course was not even set up with its own Computer Science faculty but was an extension of the more classical faculty of Mathematics, Physics, and Natural Sciences. Those with strong computer expertise in the 1990s were really cool people—in high demand but with unclear career paths. I started as a Windows developer. Computer magazines were popular and eagerly awaited every month. I dreamt of writing for one of them. I won the chance to do it once and liked it so much that I'm still doing it today, 30 years later.

My passion for sharing knowledge was so intense that five years after my first serious developer job it became my primary occupation. For over two decades all I did was write books and articles, speak at conferences, teach courses, and do occasional consulting. Until 2020, I had a very limited exposure to production code and the routine of day-by-day development. Yet, I managed to write successful books for those who were involved in real-world projects.

Still, in a remote area of my mind was a thorny doubt: Am I just a lecture type of professional or am I also an action person? Will I be able to ever build a real-world system? The pandemic and other life changes brought me to ultimately find an answer.

I faced the daunting task of building a huge and intricate system in a fraction of the time originally scheduled that the pandemic sharply cut off. No way to design, be agile, do testing and planning—the deadline was the only certain thing. I resorted to doing—and letting a few other people do—just what I taught and had discovered while teaching for years. It worked. Not just that. Along the way, I realized that the approach we took to build software, and related patterns, also had a name: clean architecture. This book is the best I know and have learned in three years of everyday software development after over two decades of learning, teaching, and consulting.

In our company, we have several developers who joined as juniors and have grown up using and experimenting with the content of this book. It worked for us; I hope it will work for you, too!

# Who should read this book

Software professionals are the audience for this book, including architects, lead developers, and—I would say, especially—developers of any type of .NET applications. Everyone who wants to be a software architect should find this book helpful and worth the cost. And valid architects are, for the most part, born developers. I strongly believe that the key to great software passes through great developers, and great developers grow out of good teachers, good examples, and—hopefully—good books and courses.

Is this book only for .NET professionals? Although all chapters have a .NET flavor, most of the content is readable by any software professional.

## Assumptions

This book expects that you have at least a minimal understanding of .NET development and object-oriented programming concepts. A good foundation in using the .NET platform and knowledge of some data-access techniques will also help. We put great effort into making this book read well. It's not a book about abstract design concepts, and it's not a classic architecture book either, full of cross-references or fancy strings in square brackets that hyperlink to some old paper listed in a bibliography at the end of the book. It's a book about building systems in the 2020s and facing the dilemmas of the 2020s, from the front end to the back end, passing through cloud platforms and scalability issues.

# This book might not be for you if...

If you're seeking a reference book or you want to find out how to use a given pattern or technology then this book might not for you. Instead, the goal is sharing and transferring knowledge so that you know what to do at any point. Or, at least, you now know what other guys—Dino and team—did in an analogous situation.

# Organization of this book

In all, modern software architecture has just one precondition: modularity. Whether you go with a distributed, service-oriented structure, a microservices fragmented pattern, or a compact monolithic application, modularity is crucial to build and manage the codebase and to further enhance the application following the needs of the business. Without modularity, you can just be able to deliver a working system once, but it will be hard to expand and update it.

Part I of this book, titled "The Holy Grail of modularity," lays the foundation of software modularity, tracing back the history of software architecture and summarizing the gist of domain-driven design (DDD)—one of the most helpful methodologies for breaking down business domains, though far from being an absolute necessity in a project.

Part II, "Architecture cleanup," is about the five layers that constitute, in the vision of this book, a "clean" architecture. The focus is not much on the concentric rendering of the architecture, as popularized by tons of books and articles, but on the actual value delivered by constituent layers: presentation, application, domain, domain services, and infrastructure.

Finally, Part III, "Common dilemmas," focuses on three frequently faced stumbling blocks: monoliths or microservices, client-side or server-side for the front end, and the role and weight of technical debt.

## Downloads: reference application

Part II of the book describes a reference application, Project Renoir, whose entire codebase is available on GitHub at:

*https://github.com/Youbiquitous/project-renoir*

A zipped version of the source code is also available for download at *MicrosoftPressStore.com/NET/download.*

> **Note** The reference application requires .NET 8 and is an ASP.NET application with a Blazor front end. It uses Entity Framework for data access and assumes a SQL Server (any version) database.

## Errata, updates, and book support

We've made every effort to ensure the accuracy of this book and its companion content. You can access updates to this book—in the form of a list of submitted errata and their related corrections—at:

*MicrosoftPressStore.com/NET/errata*

If you discover an error that is not already listed, please submit it to us at the same page.

For additional book support and information, please visit *MicrosoftPressStore.com/Support*.

Please note that product support for Microsoft software and hardware is not offered through the previous addresses. For help with Microsoft software or hardware, go to *http://support.microsoft.com*.

## Stay in touch

Let's keep the conversation going! We're on Twitter: *http://twitter.com/MicrosoftPress*

# The Holy Grail of modularity

# CHAPTER 1

# The quest for modular software architecture

*The purpose of software engineering is to control complexity, not to create it.*
*—Dr. Pamela Zave, Princeton University*

Software as we know it today, in the middle of the 2020s, is the waste product of a more profound learning and transformation process whose origins are deeply rooted within the history of logic and mathematics. Since the 17th century, some of the world's greatest minds focused on building a coherent, logical system that could allow for mechanical reasoning. The proof that it was not just dreaming came only in the 1930s with Kurt Gödel's Theorem of Incompleteness. From there, Alan Turing and John Von Neumann started engineering physical machines.

None of them, though, ever dreamed of anything near the software of today. Their goal was to mechanize the human way of reasoning, as simple and ambitious as that may still sound. The early "thinking" machines of the 1950s were iron monoliths made of valves, pistons, and cables—wired hardware, no more, no less. John Von Neumann had the intuition that instructions were better separated from hardware so that the same machine could do different things, such as mathematics and text processing. The popular "von Neumann architecture" ultimately refers to having a stored program whose instructions are fetched one by one and processed sequentially.

Software gained its own dignity and identity only at the end of the 1960s, about the time humankind landed on the moon. The first reported use of the term "software engineering" dates to the mid-1960s. Nobody ever managed to create the software; rather, it emerged as a side effect—or waste product—of more ambitious research. Separating hardware from software was the first step of modularization ever experienced in computer science.

It seems that humans have always approached solving problems using an end-to-end sequence of steps, with references and interconnections between states set and exchanged as needed to reach a solution. As spaghetti code has shown, software is no exception.

**Note** The quest for modularization started as early as software itself and soon moved from the level of application code to the level of application architecture.

# In the beginning, it was three-tier

The first historical example of a software architecture that expands beyond the realm of a single computer was proposed in the 1960s with the IBM 360 system. The idea was that a remote workstation could send the central mainframe a request to execute some non-interactive data-processing operation, called a *job*. Further refined in successive years, the model became universally known as *client/server architecture* after the paper "Separating Data from Function in a Distributed File System," written by a group of Xerox PARC computer scientists in 1978. Client/server was the canonical way of building business applications when I got my first job as a developer right after graduating from university.

 **Note** Von Neumann broke up the computer monolith into hardware and software components, and IBM and Xerox researchers broke the software monolith into client and server components.

We all heartily welcomed three-tier architecture in the late 1990s. At the time, the definition of an additional software tier, which took on some client liabilities and some server tasks, proved necessary to better handle the complexity of the (new) applications being built at a fairly rapid pace.

 **Note** In the previous paragraph, I deliberately placed the adjective "new" in parentheses because it referred to applications planned and built using the three-tier architecture before the commercial explosion of the internet. At the time, colossus line-of-business applications (for example, financial, telecom, government, utilities, healthcare systems, and so on) remained safely anchored to the existing mainframe-based client/server schema. Even today, mainframes remain hard at work carrying on high-volume, real-time transactions, such as credit card and ATM operations. Performance and cost-effectiveness are the crucial reasons for this, despite the emergence of cloud, edge computing, Blockchain, and massively distributed systems.

## Core facts of a three-tier system

Although the skeleton of a three-tier system should be very well known to everyone in the software space, I've included Figure 1-1 to illustrate it as a memento of the progressive breakup of monoliths observed in the software industry, at least until the commercial explosion of the internet.

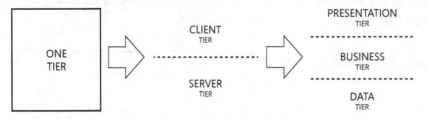

**FIGURE 1-1** First stages of the evolution from single-tier to multi-tier architecture.

The advent of multi-tier systems was hailed as a vast improvement over the monolithic applications of "prehistoric" software. Today, though—in the mid-2020s—the proposal of a multi-tier architecture is often blissfully dismissed as obsolete and badly tagged merely as a "monolith."

## Software monoliths

The current definition of a *software monolith* is different from what it was in the 1990s—a start-to-finish sequence of instructions with some input loop to keep it live and waiting for further instructions. Today, monolithic software is commonly intended to be an application made of multiple components combined in a single, self-contained deliverable. All the codebase lives in a single code solution and is deployed in a single step on a single production server, whether on-premises or in the cloud. Any constituent components become invisible from the outside once the application is deployed. Any disastrous bug could *potentially* take the entire application down, and any necessary improvements for scalability must be applied to the entire block. This can lead to significant rewrites of parts or pure vertical hardware-based scalability.

## Tier versus layer

Tiers were initially introduced to achieve physical separation between software components. In the client/server model, the remote workstation was wired to the central server. Later, the top tier became the presentation logic, whether made of masks, a console, or a graphical user interface (GUI). The business tier, or application tier, was another application responsible for accessing the database server.

In the common industry jargon, the terms *tier* and *layer* are often used interchangeably. In reality, they both refer to distinct pieces of a software application but differ significantly from a deployment perspective. A *tier* denotes a physical server, or at least a different process-execution space. In contrast, a *layer* is a logical container for different portions of code and needs a physical tier to be deployed.

 **Note** All layers are deployed to a physical tier, but different layers can go to different tiers.

When it comes to production, a debatable point is whether a multi-layer application should be mapped to a multi-tier architecture, with a one-to-one match between layers and tiers. Multiple tiers seem to give more flexibility and ease of maintenance and scalability, but this comes at the cost of spreading latency between tiers and subsequently making every single operation potentially slower. In addition, deployment is more expensive in a multi-tier scenario, as more resources (on-premises or in the cloud) are necessary.

In summary, tiers can provide a structure for scaling an application, but their mere presence doesn't guarantee faster performance. Efficient scaling involves not only the organization of tiers but also factors such as load balancing, code optimization, and the use of appropriate technologies for decoupling (for example, a bus). Tiers help by offering a logical separation of responsibilities, but their performance benefits are realized through thoughtful design, resource allocation, and performance tuning.

## The value of *N*

The term *multi-tier* (or *multi-layer*) refers to a number (*N*) of tiers (or layers) that conventionally equals three. So, is three the ideal number of tiers (or layers)? To answer this, consider Figure 1-2.

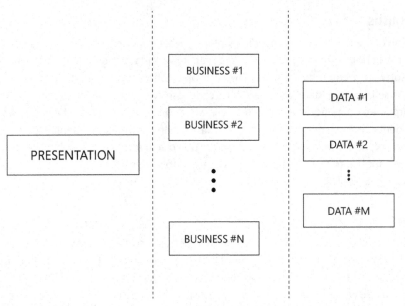

**FIGURE 1-2** Variable number of tiers in a massively distributed application architecture.

Tiers and layers have followed different scales. The popular approach based on microservices tends to increase the number of physical tiers up to hundreds. In contrast, the number of layers within a single tier rarely exceeds four, which is considered the ideal number by the canonical supporting architecture of the domain-driven design (DDD) methodology. As you'll see shortly, the four layers are:

- **Presentation**   This layer collects user requests and input to submit to processing layers down the stack.

- **Application**   This layer receives raw input from the presentation layer and orchestrates any necessary tasks.

- **Domain**   This layer contains reusable domain and business logic.

- **Infrastructure**   This layer deals with external services (for example, APIs and web services) and storage.

Compared to a three-tier architecture, a multi-layered architecture is more granular, because it splits in two an otherwise thick (and likely more convoluted) business tier.

## Multi-tiered systems today

Multi-tier architecture is a well-established pattern that still serves most business scenarios today. Let's reflect on the flavors of multi-tier we see today in the industry.

One flavor is the web application. For the purposes of this book, a *web application* is a line-of-business (LoB) application consumed through a client web browser application. This contrasts with a *website*, in which the stratification of what is referred to as the front end is quite simple in terms of domain complexity and workflows.

In action, a typical web application develops over two tiers: the client browser and the server (cloud) environment, sometimes referred to as the *back end*. How many tiers and layers exist within the back end? Classic ASP.NET and ASP.NET Core applications and Blazor server applications often count two tiers and multiple ($N > 3$) layers. One tier is the core application, and another is represented by the primary database server—for example, a relational database management system (RDBMS).

The challenge for everyone, then, is learning the good and bad of every possible application architecture pattern, making a thoughtful choice based on the specific business context, and, most of all, avoiding dogmatic disputes.

**Note** While researching the origin of the three-tier architecture, I ran into a curious fact I'd never heard before. In the United States during the 1930s, right after the repeal of the Prohibition Act, the government introduced a new distributed system for ensuring people's access to alcohol. Guess what? It was named the *three-tier* system, and the tiers were, from bottom to top, producers, distributors, and retailers.

## Layers, tiers, and modularization

Modularization is the primary reason for the introduction of multiple tiers and layers. Having been in this industry for more than 30 years now, I have observed many attempts to develop a universal approach to componentization (or should I say, *Legolization?*) in software development, from Visual Basic and Delphi components to ActiveX and COM, from JavaBeans to Web Forms server controls, and from old-fashioned web services to microservices. Frankly, my age-dependent disillusion leads me to state that none of them worked for more than a few people or for a limited amount of time. Still, I have no hope and no room for universality.

Behind known benefits such as the ability to reuse components, the parallelization of development, and ease of maintenance, the ultimate goal and primary benefit of modularization is *separation of concerns (SoC)*—a universal principle of software formalized in 1974 by Edsger W. Dijkstra in the paper "On the Role of Scientific Thought."

**Note** Although I have stated the core difference between a tier and a layer, from now on, for the sake of simplicity, I'll use the term *layer* to indicate tier or layer unless it becomes necessary to distinguish between the two.

## The presentation layer

Each of the layers briefly discussed here shares a common idea but a different implementation. In a desktop application, for example, such as legacy Windows Forms or Windows Presentation Foundation (WPF) applications, the presentation layer is the user interface. It contains a minimal amount of presentation logic to validate input and to adjust the user interface to reflect the current state of the application.

In contrast, in a web scenario, the user interface consists of a mixture of HTML, CSS, and JavaScript rendered in a browser. Alternatively, it can be a runnable piece of WebAssembly code, like the code generated by Blazor. Being run on a physically different machine, it is a real tier. The application, though, might also consist of a special presentation layer whose primary purpose is to route requests to some module to handle it. For ASP.NET Core applications, the presentation layer contains controller classes and, more generally, code that is directly connected to reachable endpoints.

## The business layer

In very abstract terms, the business layer processes information collected in the presentation layer with other information managed by the data layer. It is also the place where business rules are known and applied. In an ASP.NET Core scenario, the business layer is made by handlers that can respond to a controller request and return a response for the controller to package it back to the browser.

In recent years, a commonly recurring query in training sessions and workshops pertained to the optimal placement of specific code segments. For instance, questions often arose regarding the appropriate location for input validation code. Should it reside in the presentation or business layer? Alternatively, is it advisable to defer validation until it hits the database, possibly handled by a stored procedure or some surrounding code?

At its core, the business layer leaves such gray areas unclear. For this reason, a four-layer architecture emerged.

## The data layer

This is where information processed by the application is persisted and read. The thickness of the data layer is highly variable. It might coincide with a database server—whether relational or NoSQL—or it could be created by code that arranges raw calls to the storage server via dedicated object-relational mappers (ORMs) such as Entity Framework (EF) or Dapper.

Recently, the data layer has been abstracted into an infrastructural layer where persistence is just the primary (but not unique) responsibility. Seen as infrastructure, this layer is also responsible for emails and connections to external APIs.

> **Important** The primary purpose of a multi-layered architecture is to achieve separation of concerns (SoC) and to ensure that different families of tasks execute in a properly isolated environment. A crucial consequence of SoC, especially when applied across multiple layers, is that dependencies between layers must be strictly regulated. Discussing how to plan SoC across layers in the context of a web application written for the .NET stack is the main goal of this book.

## The DDD canonical architecture

In the early 2000s, the software industry faced a gigantic challenge: modernizing, or just migrating, existing business applications to seize new opportunities presented by the breakthrough of the internet. Attempting to adapt mainframe applications to handle the growing demand for e-commerce introduced monumental levels of complexity.

The three-tier architecture started creaking under the weight of this complexity—not so much because of its inherent inefficiencies, but rather due to the need to increase modularization to manage business and implementation requirements and (hopefully) scale. (It was at this time that the term *scalability* rose to prominence and gained its meaning as we know today—a system's ability to maintain a good level of service even if the number of requests grows unexpectedly.)

The domain-driven design (DDD) methodology systematized several practices and solutions that proved valid on the ground. Bundled with the design methodology, there was also a canonical supporting architecture.

> **Note** I don't use the phrase "monumental complexity" by chance. It is a quote from the stories I've heard from the people who devised DDD and an homage to all of them.

### The proposed supporting architecture

DDD proponents suggested a layered architecture to implement modules. This layered architecture generalized the three-tier architecture obtained in three steps:

1. Tiers were generalized to layers.

2. The business layer was broken in two, with an application layer for the orchestration of use cases and a domain layer for pure business logic. The domain layer in turn was composed of two elements: a collection of persistence-agnostic domain models and a collection of persistence-aware domain services. This is a key aspect of DDD.

3. The data layer was renamed the infrastructure layer, and the most common and important service it provided was persistence.

The resulting architecture—which also includes a presentation layer—is monolithic in its simplest form but has clear boundaries at any level and well-defined flows of data exchange. In some ways, it is even cleaner than the actual trumpeted clean architecture!

## The presentation layer

The presentation layer handles interactions with external systems that send input data to the application. This primarily includes human users, but also API calls from other running applications, notifications, bus messages, triggered events, and so on. Put another way, the presentation layer receives requests for tasks that will be processed down the stack, producing some effect on the domain. The presentation layer is also responsible for packaging results generated by internal layers in response to an accepted request and for sending it back to the requestor.

The presentation layer can take various technological forms. It might be a desktop application (for example, .NET MAUI, Electron, old-fashioned WPF, or Windows Forms), a mobile application, a minimal API, or a fully-fledged web application (whether ASP.NET Core, Blazor, Angular, React, or Svelte and friends). Also, the protocols involved may vary a bit, and include HTTPS, gRPC, and, in scenarios involving the internet of things (IoT), Message Queue Telemetry Transport (MQTT), Advanced Message Queuing Protocol (AMQP), and more.

Considering this, it is key to remember that despite the fact that the layer name (presentation) evokes the presence of some graphical front end, a visual interface is not necessary. Even when the bounded context is expected to be a plain web API, a presentation layer makes sense because, as mentioned, it represents a sort of reception and the gateway to internal functions and layers.

## The application layer

Whereas the presentation layer collects requests, the application layer coordinates any subsequent processing. The application layer, in fact, is where business workflows are launched and monitored. Any single request managed at the upper level finds a concrete executor in the application layer. A term that well describes the behavior of the application layer is *orchestrator*. A more elaborate job description is that the application layer is responsible for the implementation of the various use cases.

> **Important** In a classic three-tier scenario, the well-defined responsibilities described here are shared between all the tiers—presentation, business, and data—in percentages that vary between implementations based on the view and sensitivity of the involved teams.

The application layer goes hand-in-hand with the presentation layer and supplies one action method for each possible trigger detected by the presentation actors. When multiple versions of an application are necessary (say, one for web and one for mobile), each should have its own application layer unless the triggers and expected reactions are nearly the same.

## The domain layer

You can have multiple application layers—one per presentation layer. However, the domain layer must be unique and shared. That's the key principle of DDD: The domain layer is where all business rules and logic are coded.

The domain layer is made of two related parts:

- **Domain model** This is a plain library of classes that contains the definitions of all business entities plus any value objects, aggregates, factories, enumerations, and whatever else is helpful to provide a realistic representation of the business model. Ideally, this is coded as a distinct class library. Domain classes are empty and stateless crunching machines with the logic to process data according to business rules. A few important aspects of domain models are as follows:

  - One team is in charge of the domain model.
  - In the .NET space, the domain model is preferably shared as a NuGet package via a private company- or team-specific feed.
  - The domain model should have as few dependencies as possible on other packages or projects. Any dependencies that might arise (such as on helper third-party packages) should be evaluated bluntly and incorporated only if strictly necessary.
  - The domain model has no reference to the persistence layer (which is part of the infrastructure layer) and is completely database-agnostic.

- **Domain services** How do you query for data and load it into the empty and stateless crunching machines? That's what domain services do. These are database-aware classes that load into domain entity classes and run updates starting from those domain classes. Domain services have a dependency on the domain model and on the infrastructure layer (the persistence layer in particular).

## The infrastructure layer

The infrastructure layer is the container for persistence layer, external services such as email and messaging systems, and connectors to external APIs.

Data access is usually the primary service provided by the infrastructure layer. It includes all the possible combinations of read and write operations that the business needs. The most common scenario is when full persistence (read/write) is required. Other scenarios are possible as well, such as read-only, when data is read from existing external services, and write-only, when the infrastructure layer is used only to log events.

You isolate the components responsible for database access through the use of repositories. Interestingly, the use of repositories does not compromise SoC. The persistence layer, which is part of the infrastructure layer, is where repositories are collected. If you intend to use interfaces on top of repositories (for example, for testing purposes) then those interfaces can be placed in the domain service library. Another simpler approach, however, may be to place domain services and actual repositories in the persistence layer or even to build richer repositories that are not limited to CRUD methods but expose smarter methods. In this case, domain services blurs into the persistence layer.

Figure 1-3 shows the recommended way to set dependencies between the layers of a classic DDD architecture.

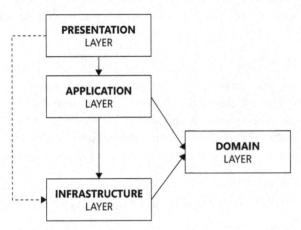

**FIGURE 1-3** Interconnections between layers in DDD layered architecture.

> **Note** The purpose of this chapter is to provide the big picture of application architecture and how the industry adopted modularity over the decades. It only scratches the surface of DDD and layered architectures. You will learn much more about the essence of DDD in Chapter 2, "The ultimate gist of DDD." The rest of this book covers the layers of the DDD-inspired architecture in detail, with code examples.

# Adding more to the recipe

The canonical DDD architecture was devised as a helpful reference. Its use is never mandatory. It first came with a strong flavor of object-orientation, but this aspect, too, was never a requirement. The object-oriented nature of DDD evolved over the years to incorporate some functional capabilities. Again, the resulting multi-layered pattern was just a recommendation, and simpler solutions (for example, CMS, CRM, coupled CRUD, and two-layer systems) were always acceptable as long as they could fit the requirements. More recently, two additional flavors have gained popularity: command/query responsibility segregation (CQRS) and event sourcing. I see both as additional ingredients for the original layered recipe.

## Add CQRS to taste

CQRS is simply a pattern that guides in the architecture of a specific component of a possibly larger system. Applied to a layered architecture, CQRS breaks up the domain layer into two distinct parts. This separation is obtained by grouping query operations in one layer and command operations in another. Each layer then has its own model and its own set of services dedicated to only queries and commands, respectively. Figure 1-4 compares plain layered architecture (left) with a CQRS-based version of it (right).

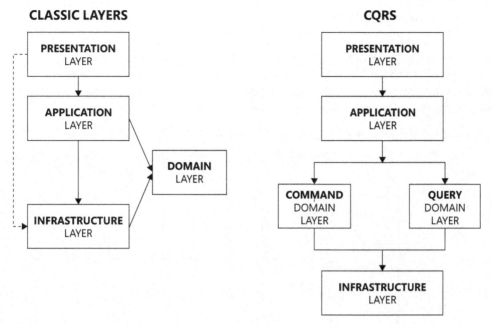

**CLASSIC LAYERS**

PRESENTATION LAYER

APPLICATION LAYER

DOMAIN LAYER

INFRASTRUCTURE LAYER

**CQRS**

PRESENTATION LAYER

APPLICATION LAYER

COMMAND DOMAIN LAYER

QUERY DOMAIN LAYER

INFRASTRUCTURE LAYER

**FIGURE 1-4** Visual comparison between classic layers and CQRS.

Unlike DDD, CQRS is not a comprehensive approach to the design of an enterprise class system. As mentioned, it's simply a guide. A DDD analysis based on ubiquitous language to identify bounded contexts remains a recommended preliminary step. (More on this in Chapter 2.) CQRS is just a valid alternative for the implementation of a particular module of the whole application.

Any operation against a software system is either a query that reads the status of the system or a command that alters the existing status. For example, a command is an action performed against the back end, such as registering a new user, processing the content of a shopping cart, or updating the profile of a customer. From a CQRS perspective, a task is mono-directional and generates a workflow that proceeds from the presentation layer to the domain layer, and likely ends up modifying some storage.

A model that only deals with queries would be much easier to arrange than a model that must deal with both queries and updates. A read model has a structure of classes more similar to data transfer objects (DTOs), and properties tend to be much more numerous than methods. The resulting model is therefore more anemic, as it loses all methods that alter the state of the object.

The application layer doesn't experience significant changes in a CQRS scenario. It's a matter of triggering the server task associated with the request. The same doesn't hold true for the infrastructure layer. This is where another flavor—event sourcing—kicks in.

## Add event sourcing to taste

Event sourcing takes CQRS command and query separation further by storing data as a series of immutable events, capturing every change to the system's state over time. These events provide a complete historical record of a system's evolution, enabling auditing, replay, and complex data analysis, including what-if analysis. Event sourcing is particularly valuable in systems where data changes are frequent or when a detailed historical context is essential, making it an evolution from the principles of CQRS.

In general, when the frequency of commands overwhelms the frequency of reads, you might want to consider a dedicated persistence subsystem within the infrastructure layer. Figure 1-5 shows a possible design.

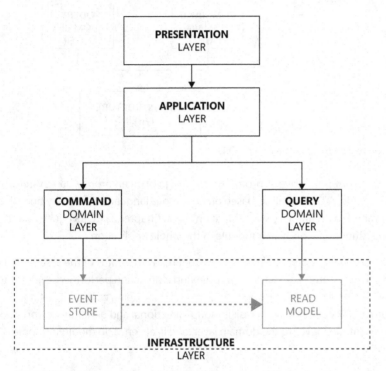

**FIGURE 1-5** The abstracted architecture of an event-sourcing system.

In the real world, we merely observe events. But for some reason, we feel the need to build a model to capture any information carried by events and store it. Models are immensely helpful when dealing with queries, but not so much for commands. For these, event-based systems are best. We could even take this further to say that event-based systems should be the norm and models the exception. Whenever we use a model, we're somehow working on a good-enough approximation.

The model of Figure 1-5 can even be extended to change the internal organization of the application layer. Usually, the logic necessary to implement use cases is written as a code-based workflow orchestrated by classes and methods in the application layer. However, when you opt for a full event-based view of the application, then all you do in the application layer is push a message describing the received request. The message is then delivered to a bus, where domain service handlers are listening.

Each handler reacts to events of interest by performing actions and pushing other messages to the bus for other listeners to react. As in Figure 1-6, the whole business logic of each task ends up coded as a sequence of messages rather than a sequence of code-based workflow activities.

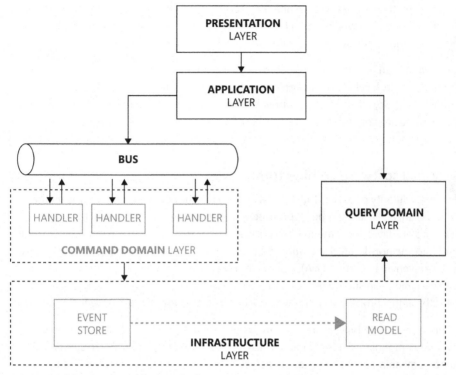

**FIGURE 1-6** Message-based business logic.

The biggest issue with events in software architecture is the concept of the "last-known good state" of a system, which has been mainstream for decades. It's being replaced by the "what's happened" approach that treats domain events as the core of the architecture.

Having events play such a central role in software architecture poses some new challenges and may even face some inertial resistance. Here are some of the reasons events have a deep impact on software architecture:

- **You don't miss a thing** By designing an event-based architecture, you give yourself the power to easily track nearly everything that takes place in the system. New events can be added almost any time, allowing for an increasingly more precise replica of the business space.

- **Extensibility of the business representation** Using a model to persist business use cases limits you to whatever can be stored and represented within the boundaries of the model. Using events instead removes most limits; as mentioned, adding or modifying business scenarios is possible and relatively inexpensive.

- **Well-positioned for scalability**   Used in combination with CQRS, event sourcing prepares the ground for any system to be scalable should the time ever come that scalability becomes crucial.

In abstract terms, the DDD layered architecture remains an extremely logical way of organizing individual applications. However, modern times have created new toppings for the final cake. As with any baking recipe, the correct amount of CQRS and event sourcing is "to taste."

For reasons that I can only try to guess, at some point in time, the layered architecture was considered not so much for its level of abstraction but as a concrete, horizontal, and object-oriented way of building applications. So, other flavors of application architecture with fancy names have emerged. As I see it, though, these are nothing more than different ways to dress software layers.

---

## Non-layered software architecture

The idea of modularity goes hand-in-hand with layers. Although the two concepts might seem a bit polarized, layers can be recognized everywhere. That said, though, the internal design details of a layer are sometimes so pervasive that they overflow the boundaries of the layer and become non-layered software architecture of its own. For example, this is the case with event-driven architecture (EDA). Essentially, EDA is what was shown in Figure 1-6, assuming that everything—including requests to the read model—passes from the bus or, more generally, through a broker component. (Look ahead to the left side of Figure 1-7.)

Another non-layered type of architecture is microservices. Chapter 9, "Microservices versus modular monoliths," is devoted to microservices. For now, it's crucial to simply grasp the intended meaning of the term, and to achieve this, one must have clear in mind the size of components. This means answering the question, "How large is micro?" If micro is large enough, we're back to a layered architecture. If micro is really small, we get close to EDA. In the context of a cloud-native architecture, microservices are relatively simple, and often stateless, handlers of events. The logic to orchestrate the activity of multiple microservices in a business action may exist in various places—the front end, in some GraphQL middleware, or in a gateway service. (See the right side of Figure 1-7.)

---

The main benefit of non-layered architecture is the inherent decentralization of functions compared to the monolithic nature of layered solutions. However, software always involves trade-offs. So, decentralization is not necessarily better in all cases, and monolithic solutions are not always dirty and bloated. How do architects decide which to use? Well, it depends!

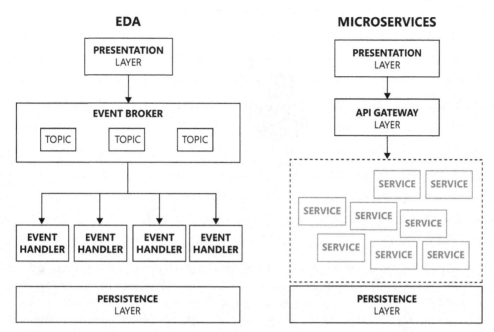

**FIGURE 1-7** Event-driven architecture versus microservices architecture.

## Different flavors of layers

Layered architecture often comes with different names and visions. Making sense of these is beyond me, but as I see it, at least a couple of these names are merely different flavors of layered architecture. This section discusses a few of these flavors: hexagonal architecture, clean architecture, and feature-driven architecture.

> **Note** All the architectural patterns discussed here (along with others you may encounter) share a common goal (modularity and separation of concerns) and a common tactic (software layers).

## Hexagonal architecture

Hexagonal architecture (HA) is based on the idea that the central part of an application is a core library that interacts with the outside world through well-defined interfaces. When compared to layered architecture, the application core in HA corresponds to the domain and application layers (implementation of use cases). The key factor in HA is that any communication between the core application and the rest of the world is set up via contracted interfaces, known as *ports*. Adapters serve as the interface between ports and various layers. At the minimum, there will be an adapter for the presentation layer and the persistence layer. (See Figure 1-8.)

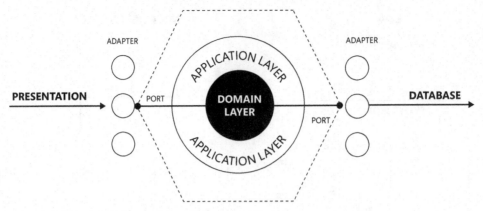

**FIGURE 1-8** Schema of a hexagonal, port/adapter architecture.

> **Note** Alistair Cockburn conceived and named the hexagonal architecture in 2005. Cockburn, who was also one of the authors of the Agile Manifesto, was close to the people who devised DDD, and his hexagonal architecture is essentially an attempt to mitigate possible pitfalls of object-oriented modeling, which is central to DDD. However, although hexagonal architecture originated about the same time as DDD and its layered architecture, it has little to do with it. Its main purpose was to achieve even more modularity by putting a port interface behind any real-world task the core application could execute.

The collection of input ports forms the API layer that the application defines so that the outside world (that is, the presentation layer) can interact with it. These ports are also known as *driver ports*. Ports placed on the other side of the hexagon are *driven ports* and form the interface that the application defines to communicate with external systems such as databases. Methods on the ports are all that application and domain services know. Similarly, adapters are implementations of the port interfaces that actually know how to package input data transfer objects and to read/write to the database.

> **Note** Because of the relevance that ports and adapters have in the hexagonal architecture, "port/adapter" is another popular name for HA.

## Clean architecture

Popularized by Robert Martin (a.k.a., Uncle Bob) around 2012, *clean architecture* (CA) is yet another flavor of layered architecture, which grabs from both DDD and HA. It brings nothing new to the table beyond an attempt to reorder and (arguably) clarify concepts. However, in the end, adding yet another pattern name and yet another style of diagram probably added confusion too. You're not too far from absolute truth by saying that CA is a way to call slightly different concepts by a new, unifying name.

CA renders itself with concentric circles rather than vertical bars or a hexagon. The outermost circle represents any possible communication with the outside world, whether via web front ends, user interfaces, or databases. The innermost circle is the domain layer—the repository of invariant business rules. The domain layer is surrounded by the layer of use-cases—namely, the application layer. Next, is the presentation layer, which is where input from outside users is conveyed. (See Figure 1-9.)

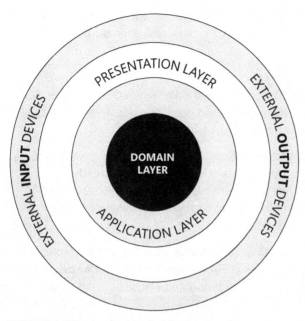

**FIGURE 1-9** Schema of a clean architecture.

It would be nice to compare the diagram in Figure 1-9 with the one in Figure 1-3. That diagram illustrates the same concepts vertically, groups output external devices under the name of infrastructure, and assumes (without rendering) the existence of input devices on top of the presentation block.

The acclaimed benefits of CA are the same as any other (properly done) layered architecture. They can be summarized as follows:

- Inherent testability of the business logic, which remains segregated from external dependencies on the UI, services, and databases

- Independence of the UI, as the architecture is not bound in any way to using ASP.NET, .NET MAUI, rich front ends, or whatever else; frameworks have no impact on the business rules

- Persistence agnosticism, as any knowledge of database details is restricted to the closest layer and ignored at any upper level

One final comment on the necessity of interfaces to cross the boundaries of each layer: In HA, those interfaces (ports) are, in a way, a mandatory and constituent part of the architecture itself. In CA and in general layered architecture, the use of interfaces is left to implementors. The use of interfaces—and coding against interfaces rather than implementations—is the universal principle of software low coupling. However, dropping interfaces while having their role clear in mind is a great sign of self-discipline and pragmatism.

**Note** Clean code is a universal attribute. You don't achieve clean code by using a specific technology stack (for example, .NET, Java, Android, Python, Go, or TypeScript) or a particular version.

## Feature-driven architecture

Feature-driven architecture (FDA) is a software architectural approach that emphasizes organizing the system's architecture around functional components that are crucial to the software's vitality. FDA is not exactly distinct from the architectural patterns we've explored thus far; it merely offers an alternative perspective on system design and building. FDA revolves around the identification of pivotal software features and orchestrates the architecture to prioritize their comprehensive support. A notable benefit of FDA is that it often results in a modular and component-based architecture.

The set of core features represents the smallest ever amount of complexity inherently related to the system. The real complexity is a combination of the organic feature complexity plus any sort of accidental complexity we add on top because of misunderstandings, technical debt, legacy code, or inaccurate design choices.

## Vertical slice architecture

A feature-driven approach to a system development usually goes hand-in-hand with vertical slice architecture (VSA). For example, a development team might adopt feature-driven architecture as a design approach and then use vertical slicing to implement and release those features incrementally, providing value to users at each step of development.

Reasoning by features doesn't have much impact on the architecture, which remains layered from use-case logic to domain logic to persistence. However, it does help organize development, including coding and testing. In fact, VSA involves implementing one slice after the next of functionality, each spanning the entire stack of layers, including the user interface, application logic, and data storage.

Designing a system in vertical slices means rebuilding the diagram in Figure 1-3 by putting vertical slices side by side, as in Figure 1-10.

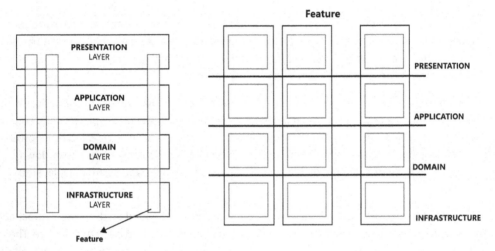

**FIGURE 1-10** Vertical slicing of features.

## Agility and trade-offs

Feature-driven thinking and VSA can help you better estimate the cost of development. VSA originates in relationship to Agile methodologies and is often used to build minimum viable products (MVPs) or develop incremental releases. The goal is to deliver a fully functional part of the software that can be used, tested, and demonstrated to stakeholders, while providing value to end-users early in the development process.

As the right diagram in Figure 1-10 shows, though, feature-driven design may fragment all the horizontal layers, creating some potential for code duplication. Furthermore, if one or more layers are deployed independently on their own app services, the costs may increase if you deploy each layer, for each feature, independently. To avoid that, some feature-specific pieces of the same layer (for example, the application layer) may be fused together, forming what DDD calls a *shared kernel*. (More on this in Chapter 2.)

In the end, a feature-driven approach sounds like a shortcut if applied at the architecture level, but it is an effective way to organize everyday development as well as files and folders in the code repository. The bottom line is that a DDD analysis is the ideal way to go because it proceeds through requested features and isolates them in a bounded context and shared kernel, providing the ultimate list of software components to code.

## Summary

If there was ever a time when architecture was negligible, that's no longer the case today. Especially for modern software, good architecture is a structural requirement, not a luxury.

If you ask around about what software architecture is most suitable for the current times, you will get one common answer: microservices. Objectively, microservices is an abused term that means little to nothing if not paired with a definition of the intended size of the components and the surrounding environment. As I see it, microservices are too often chosen for use as a pure act of faith in a pattern. You'll learn much more about microservices in Chapter 9; in brief, they fit nicely in a cloud-native, event-driven architecture if hosted within a serverless platform.

So, if not microservices, what else? A popular, ongoing debate today contrasts microservices with modular monoliths. The funny thing is that microservices emerged as a way to replace tightly coupled monolithic software applications. The breakdown was excessively granular and created other problems—essentially, how to gather sparse and small components. As popular wisdom passes down through proverbs, the virtue is in the middle. In this context, the middle way is a modular layered architecture.

This chapter provided a historical overview of tiers and layers and ended on the most abstract flavor of them—the layered architecture as defined in DDD and recently renamed *clean architecture*. The chapter mentioned DDD several times; the next chapter provides a summary of what DDD actually is.

# CHAPTER 2

# The ultimate gist of DDD

*Get your facts first, and then you can distort them as much as you please.*

*—Mark Twain*

Domain-driven design (DDD) is a 20-year-old methodology. Over the years, there have been several books, learning paths, and conferences dedicated to it, and every day, various social networks archive hundreds of posts and comments about it. Still, although the essence of DDD remains surprisingly simple to grasp, it is much less simple to adopt.

Today more than ever, software adds value only if it helps streamline and automate business processes. For this to happen, the software must be able to faithfully model segments of the real world. These segments are commonly referred to as *business domains*.

For a few decades, client/server, database-centric applications have provided an effective way to mirror segments of the real world—at least as those segments were perceived at the time. Now, though, working representations of segments of the real world must become much more precise to be useful. As a result, a database with just some code around is often no longer sufficient. Faithfully mirroring real-world behaviors and processes requires an extensive analysis.

What does this have to do with DDD? Ultimately, DDD has little to do with actual coding. It relates to methods and practices for exploring the internals of the business domain. The impact of DDD on coding and on the representation of the real world depends on the results of the analysis.

DDD is not strictly required per se, but it is an effective method for exploring and understanding the internal structure of the business domain. What really matters is getting an accurate analysis of the domain and careful coding to reflect it. DDD systematizes consolidated practices to produce an architectural representation of the business domain, ready for implementation.

## Design driven by the domain

Conceptually, DDD is about design rather than coding. It rests on two pillars: one strategic and one tactical. The original authors of DDD outlined the strategy pillar and suggested tactics to achieve it. Today, however, I believe strategic analysis is the beating heart of DDD.

# Strategic analysis

Any world-class software application is built around a business domain. Sometimes, that business domain is large, complex, and intricate. It is not a natural law, however, that an application must represent an intricate business domain to be broken down into pieces with numerous and interconnected function points. The strategic analysis can easily return the same monolithic business domain you started from.

## Top-level architecture

The ultimate goal of the DDD strategic analysis is to express the top-level architecture of the business domain. If the business domain is large enough, then it makes sense to break it down into pieces, and DDD provides effective tools for the job. Tools like ubiquitous language (UL) and bounded contexts may help identify subdomains to work on separately. Although these subdomains may potentially overlap in some way, they remain constituent parts of the same larger ecosystem.

Figure 2-1 illustrates the conceptual breakdown of a large business domain into smaller pieces, each of which ultimately results in a deployed application. The schema—overly simplified for the purposes of this book—is adapted from a real project in sport-tech. The original business domain—a data-collection platform—is what stakeholders attempted to describe and wanted to produce. The team conducted a thorough analysis and split the original domain into five blocks. Three of these blocks were then further broken into smaller pieces. The result is 10 applications, each independent from the other in terms of technology stack and hosting model, but still able to communicate via API and in some cases sharing the same database.

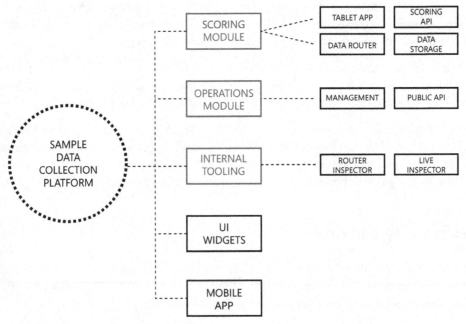

**FIGURE 2-1** Breakdown of a business domain.

## Business domain breakdown

Nobody really needs DDD (or any other specific methodology) to move from the dashed circle on the left of Figure 2-1 to the final list of 10 bold squares on the right. As hinted at earlier, DDD doesn't push new revolutionary practices; rather, it systematizes consolidated practices. With knowledge of the business and years of practice in software architecture, a senior architect might easily design a similar diagram without using DDD, instead relying on the momentum of experience and technical common sense. Still, although deep knowledge of a business domain might enable you to envision a practical way to break up the domain without the explicit use of an analytical method, DDD does provide a step-by-step procedure and guidance.

## Subdomains versus features

Recall the block labeled "Management" in Figure 2-1. This refers to a piece of functionality whose cardinality is not obvious. That is, whereas all the other blocks in Figure 2-1 reasonably map to a single leaf-level application, this one doesn't. Within the Management block, you could identify the functions shown in Figure 2-2.

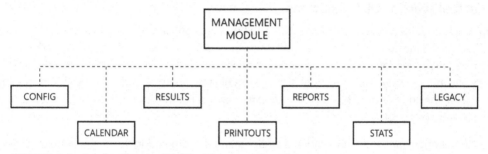

**FIGURE 2-2** Further functional split of the Management module.

The question is, are these functions just features in a monolithic application or independent services? Should this block be broken down further?

Determining the ideal size of building blocks is beyond DDD. That task requires the expertise and sensitivity of the architect. In the actual project on which this example is based, we treated the Management module as a whole and treated the smaller blocks shown in Figure 2-2 as features rather than subdomains. Ultimately, the DDD breakdown of subdomains hinges on the invisible border of local functions. All the blocks in Figure 2-2 are objectively local to the Management module and not impactful or reusable within the global, top-level architecture. Hence, in the actual project we treated them as features.

## The confusing role of microservices

These days, at this point of the domain breakdown, one inevitably considers microservices. I'll return to microservices in Chapter 3, "Laying the ground for modularity," and in Chapter 9 "Microservices versus modular monoliths." Here, however, I would like to make a clear statement about microservices and DDD: DDD refers only to top-level architecture and breaks the business domain in modules known as bounded contexts. A *bounded context* is an abstract element of the architectural design. It has its own implementation, and it can be based on microservices, but microservices are on a different level of abstraction than bounded context and DDD.

> **Note** The term *microservices* refers to physical boundaries of deployable units, whereas the term *bounded contexts* refers to logical boundaries of business units. Technically, though, a microservice might implement all business functions of a bounded context. When this happens, calling it "micro" is a bit counterintuitive!

With reference to Figure 2-2, the question whether blocks are features of a domain or subdomains relates to top-level architecture. Once it is ascertained that the Management block is a leaf subdomain—namely, a bounded context—its recognized features in the implementation can be treated as in-process class libraries, functional areas, lambda functions, or even autonomous microservices. The abstraction level, though, is different.

### The actual scale of DDD solutions

Many articles and blog posts that discuss DDD and bounded contexts presume that the entire enterprise back end is the domain that needs to be decomposed. So, they identify, say, Sales, Marketing, IT, Finance, and other departments as bounded contexts on which to focus. Such a large-scale scenario is fairly uncommon, however; companies rarely plan a big rewrite of the entire back end. But should this happen, the number of architects involved at the top level of the design, as large as that may be, would be relatively small.

DDD is a design approach primarily used for designing and organizing the architecture of software systems. It's not tied to a specific scale in terms of the size of the system. Instead, it focuses on the organization of domains and subdomains within the software. Since the beginning, it has been pushed as a method dealing with enterprise-scale applications, but it is also applicable and effective at a medium- and small-scale level.

## Tactical design

In general terms, strategy sets out what you want to achieve; tactics define how you intend to achieve it. Strategically, DDD provides tools to partition the business domain in smaller bounded contexts. Tactically, DDD suggests a default architecture to give life to each bounded context.

### The default supporting architecture

Chapter 1 presented the highlights of the default DDD supporting architecture—the layered architecture, whose inspiring principles are now at the foundation of clean architecture. The layered architecture evolved from the multi-tier architecture in vogue when DDD was first devised.

The DDD reference architecture, monolithic and OOP-friendly, is just one suggestion. It was ideal in 2004 but sufficiently abstract and universal to retain great value even now. Today, though, other options and variations exist—for example, command/query responsibility segregation (CQRS), event sourcing, and non-layered patterns such as event-driven patterns and microservices. The key point is that for a long time, with respect to DDD, applying the layered architecture and some of its side class modeling patterns has been the way to go, putting domain decomposition in the background.

## What's a software model, anyway?

Beyond the preliminary strategic analysis, DDD is about building a software model that works in compliance with identified business needs. In his book *Domain-Driven Design: Tackling Complexity at the Heart of Software* (2003), author Eric Evans, uses the object-oriented programming (OOP) paradigm to illustrate building the software model for the business domain, and calls the resulting software model the *domain model*.

At the same time, another prominent person in the software industry, Martin Fowler—who wrote the foreword for Evans' book—was using the same term (domain model) to indicate a design pattern for organizing the business logic. In Fowler's definition, the domain model design pattern is a graph of interconnected objects that fully represent the domain of the problem. Everything in the model is an object and is expected to hold data and expose a behavior.

In a nutshell, in the context of DDD, the domain model is a software model. As such, it can be realized in many ways, such as OOP, functional, or CRUD. In contrast, the domain model design pattern as defined by Martin Fowler is just one possible way to implement such a software model.

> **Important** In DDD, the outcome of the analysis of the business model is a software model. A *software model* is just the digital twin of the real business in software form. It doesn't necessarily have to be an object-oriented model written following given standards.

# DDD misconceptions

The name conflict with Fowler's design pattern—quite paradoxical in a methodology in which unambiguous language is key—sparked several misconceptions around DDD.

## The relevance of coding rules

The DDD definition details certain characteristics of the classes that participate in an object-oriented domain model: aggregates, value types, factories, behaviors, private setters, and so on. Having an object-oriented model, though, is neither mandatory nor crucial. To be crystal-clear, it's not the extensive use of factory methods in lieu of unnamed constructors, or using carefully crafted value objects instead of loose primitive values, that makes a software project run on time and budget.

Put another way, blind observation of the coding rules set out in the DDD tactics guarantees nothing, and without a preliminary strategic design and vision, may generate more technical issues and debt than it prevents. For example, using a functional approach in the design of the domain model is neither prohibited nor patently out of place. You're still doing DDD effectively even if you code a collection of functions or build an anemic object model with stored procedures doing the persistence work.

## The value of coding rules

When it comes to DDD coding rules, though, there's a flip side of the coin. Those rules—value types over primitive types, semantic methods over plain setters, factory methods over constructors, aggregates to better handle persistence—exist for a clear and valid reason. They enable you to build a software representation of the business model that is much more likely to be coherent with the language spoken in the business. If you don't first identify the language of the business (the ubiquitous language) and the context in which that language is spoken, the blind application of coding rules just creates unnecessary complexity with no added value.

## Database agnosticism

When you examine DDD, it's easy to conclude that the domain model should be agnostic of the persistence layer—the actual database. This is great in theory. In practice, though, no domain model is truly agnostic from the persistence.

Note, though, that the preceding sentence is not meant to encourage you to mix persistence and business logic. A clear boundary between business and persistence is necessary. (More on this in the next chapter.) The point of DDD is that when building an object-oriented software model to represent the business domain, persistence should *not* be your primary concern, period.

That said, however, be aware that at some point the same object model you may have crafted ignoring persistence concerns will be persisted. When this happens, the database and the API you may use to go to the database—for example, Entity Framework (EF) Core, Dapper, and so on—are a constraint and can't always be blissfully ignored. More precisely, blissfully ignoring the nature of the persistence layer—although a legitimate option—comes at a cost.

If you really want to keep the domain model fully agnostic of database concerns, then you should aim at having two distinct models—a domain model and a persistence model—and use adapters to switch between the two for each operation. This is extra work, whose real value must be evaluated case by case. My two cents are that a pinch of sane pragmatism is not bad at times.

## Language is not simply about naming conventions

DDD puts a lot of emphasis on how entities are named. As you'll soon see, the term *ubiquitous language (UL)* simply refers to a shared vocabulary of business-related terms that is ideally reflected in the conventions used to name classes and members. Hence, the emphasis on names descends from the need for code to reflect the vocabulary used in the real world. It's not a mere matter of choosing arbitrary descriptive names; quite the reverse. It's about applying the common language rules discovered in the strategic analysis and thoughtfully choosing descriptive names.

## Tools for strategic design

I've touched on the tools that DDD defines to explore and describe the business domain. Now let's look at them more closely.

You use three tools to conduct an analysis of a business model to build a conceptual view of its entities, services, and behavior:

- Ubiquitous language

- Bounded context

- Context mapping

By detecting the business language spoken in a given area, you identify subdomains and label them as bounded context of the final architecture. Bounded contexts are then connected using different types of logical relationships to form the final context map.

> **Note** In the end, DDD is just what its name says it is: design driven by a preliminary, thorough analysis of the business domain.

## Ubiquitous language

As emphatic as it may sound, the creation of the software model for a business domain may be (fancifully) envisioned as the creation of a new world. In this perspective, quoting a couple of (sparse) sentences about the genesis of the universe from the Gospel of John may be inspiring:

- In the beginning was the Word

- The Word became flesh, and dwelt among us

Setting aside the intended meaning of "the Word," and instead taking it literally and out of the original context, the *word* is given a central role in the beginning of the process and in the end it becomes substance. Ubiquitous language (UL) does the same.

## A domain-specific language vocabulary

As a doctor or an accountant, you learn at the outset a set of core terms whose meaning remains the same throughout the course of your career and that are—by design—understood by your peers, counterparts, and customers. Moreover, these terms are likely related to what you do every day. It's different if, instead, you are, say, a lawyer—or worse yet, a software architect or software engineer.

In both cases, you may be called to work in areas that you know little or nothing about. For example, as a lawyer, you might need to learn about high finance for the closing argument on a bankruptcy case. Likewise, as a software engineer in sport-tech, you would need to know about ranking and scoring rules to enable the application's operations to run week after week. In DDD, this is where having a UL fits in.

## Motivation for a shared glossary of terms

At the end of the day, the UL is a glossary of domain-specific terms (nouns, verbs, adjectives, and adverbs, and even idiomatic expressions and acronyms) that carry a specific and invariant meaning in the business context being analyzed. The primary goal of the glossary is to prevent misunderstandings between parties involved in the project. For this reason, it should be a shared resource used in all forms of spoken and written communication, whether user stories, RFCs, emails, technical documentation, meetings, or what have you.

In brief, the UL is the universal language of the business as it is done in the organization. In the book *Domain-Driven Design*, author Eric Evans recommends using the UL as the backbone of the model. Discovering the UL helps the team understand the business domain in order to design a software model for it.

## Choosing the natural language of the glossary

As you discover the UL of a business domain and build your glossary of terms, you will likely encounter a few unresolved issues. The most important is the natural language to use for the words in the glossary. There are a few options:

- Plain, universal English
- The customer's spoken language
- The development team's spoken language

While any answer might be either good or bad (or both at the same time), it can safely be said that there should be no doubt about the language to use when the team and the customer speak the same language. Beyond that, every other situation is tricky to address with general suggestions. However, in software as in life, exceptions do almost always apply. Once, talking DDD at a workshop in Poland, I heard an interesting comment: "We can't realistically use Polish in code—let alone have Polish names or verbs appear in public URLs in web applications—as ours is an extremely cryptic language. It would be hard for everyone. We tend to use English regardless."

> **Note** In the novel *Enigma* (1995), author Robert Harris tells the story of a fictional character who deciphers stolen Enigma cryptograms during World War II. Once the character decrypts some code, though, he discovers the text looks as if it contains yet another level of cryptography—this one unknown. The mystery is solved when another cryptogram reveals the text to be a consecutive list of abbreviated Polish names!

If the language of the glossary differs from the language used by some involved parties, and translations are necessary for development purposes, then a word-to-word table is necessary to avoid ambiguity, as much as possible. Note, though, that ambiguity is measured as a function that *approaches* zero rather than reaches zero.

# Building the glossary

You determine what terms to include in the glossary through interviews and by processing the written requirements. The glossary is then refined until it takes a structured form in which natural language terms are associated with a clear meaning that meets the expectations of both domain (stakeholder) and technical (software) teams. The next sections offer a couple of examples.

## Choosing the right term

In a travel scenario, what technical people would call "deleting a booking" based on their database-oriented vision of the business, is better referred to as "canceling a booking," because the latter verb is what people on the business side would use. Similarly, in an e-commerce scenario, "submitting an order form" is too HTML-oriented; people on the business side would likely refer to this action simply as "checking out."

Here's a real-world anecdote, from direct experience. While building a platform for daily operations for a tennis organization, we included a button labeled "Re-pair" on an HTML page, based on language used by one of the stakeholders. The purpose of the button was to trigger a procedure that allowed one player to change partners in a doubles tournament draw (in other words, as the stakeholder said, to "re-pair"). But we quickly learned that users were scared to click the button, and instead called the Help desk any time they wanted to "re-pair" a player. This was because another internal platform used by the organization (to which we didn't have access) used the same term for a similar, but much more disruptive, operation. So, of course, we renamed the button and the underlying business logic method.

## Discovering the language

Having some degree of previous knowledge of the domain helps in quickly identifying all the terms that may have semantic relevance. If you're entirely new to the domain, however, the initial research of hot terms may be like processing the text below.

As a registered customer of the I-Buy-Stuff online store, I can redeem a voucher for an order I place so that I don't actually pay for the ordered items myself.

Verbs are potential actions, whereas nouns are potential entities. Isolating them in bold, the text becomes:

As a **registered customer** of the I-Buy-Stuff online **store**, I can **redeem** a **voucher** for an **order** I **place** so that I don't actually **pay** for the ordered **items** myself.

The relationship between verbs and nouns is defined by the syntax rules of the language being used: subject, verb, and direct object. With reference to the preceding text,

- *Registered customer* is the subject

- *Redeem* is the verb

- *Voucher* is the direct object

As a result, we have two domain entities: (Registered-Customer and Voucher) and a behavior (Redeem) that belongs to the Registered-Customer entity and applies to the Voucher entity.

Another result from such an analysis is that the term used in the business context to indicate the title to receive a discount is *voucher* and only that. Synonyms like *coupon* or *gift card* should not be used. Anywhere.

## Dealing with acronyms

In some business scenarios, most notably the military industry, acronyms are very popular and widely used. Acronyms, however, may be hard to remember and understand.

In general, acronyms should not be included in the UL. Instead, you should introduce new words that retain the original meaning that acronyms transmit—unless an acronym is so common that not using it is a patent violation of the UL pattern itself. In this case, whether you include it in the UL is up to you. Just be aware that you need to think about how to deal with acronyms, and that each acronym may be treated differently.

Taken literally, using acronyms is a violation of the UL pattern. At the same time, because the UL is primarily about making it easier for everyone to understand and use the business language and the code, acronyms can't just be ignored. The team should evaluate, one by one, how to track those pieces of information in a way that doesn't hinder cross-team communication. An example of a popular and cross-industry acronym that can hardly be renamed is RSVP. But in tennis, the acronyms OP and WO, though popular, are too short and potentially confusing to maintain in software. So, we expanded them to Order-of-Play and Walkover.

## Dealing with technical terms

Yet another issue with the UL is how technical the language should be. Although we are focused on understanding the business domain, we do that with the purpose of building a software application. Inevitably, some spoken and written communication is contaminated by code-related terms, such as *caching*, *logging*, and *security*. Should this be avoided? Should we instead use verbose paraphrasing instead of direct and well-known technical terms? The general answer here is no. Instead, limit the use of technical terms as much as possible, but use them if necessary.

## Sharing the glossary

The value of a language is in being used rather than persisted. But just as it is helpful to have an English dictionary on hand to explain or translate words, it might also be useful to have a physical document to check for domain-specific terms.

To that end, the glossary is typically saved to a shared document that can be accessed, with different permissions, by all stakeholders. This document can be an Excel file in a OneDrive folder or, better yet, a file collaboratively edited via Microsoft Excel Online. It can even be a wiki. For example, with an in-house wiki, you can create and evolve the glossary, and even set up an internal forum to openly discuss features and updates to the language. A wiki also allows you to easily set permissions to control how editing takes place and who edits what. Finally, a GitBook site is another excellent option.

**Important** Any change to the language is a business-level decision. As such, it should always be made in full accordance with stakeholders and all involved parties. Terms of the language become software and dwell in code repositories. You should expect a one-to-one relationship between words and code, to the point that misunderstanding a term is akin to creating a bug, and wrongly naming a method misrepresents a business workflow.

## Keeping business and code in sync

The ultimate goal of the UL is not to create comprehensive documentation about the project, nor is it to set guidelines for naming code artifacts like classes and methods. The *real* goal of the UL is to serve as the backbone of the actual code. To achieve this, though, it is crucial to define and enforce a strong naming convention. Names of classes and methods should always reflect the terms in the glossary.

**Note** As strict as it may sound, you should treat a method that starts a process with a name that is different from what users call the same process as technical debt—no more, no less.

### Reflecting the UL in code

The impact of the UL on the actual code is not limited to the domain layer. The UL helps with the design of the application logic too. This is not coincidental, as the application layer is where the various business tasks for use cases are orchestrated.

As an example, imagine the checkout process of an online store. Before proceeding with a typical checkout process, you might want to validate the order. Suppose that you've set a requirement that validating the order involves ensuring that ordered goods are in stock and the payment history of the customer is not problematic. How would you organize this code?

There are a couple of good options to consider:

- Have a single Validate step for the checkout process in the application layer workflow that incorporates (and hides) all required checks.

- Have a sequence of individual validation steps right in the application layer workflow.

From a purely functional perspective, both options would work well. But only one is ideal in a given business context. The answer to the question of which is the most appropriate lies in the UL. If the UL calls for a validate action to be performed on an order during the checkout process, then you should go with the first option. If the vocabulary includes actions like check-payment-history or check-current-stock, then you should have individual steps in the workflow for just those actions.

> **Note** If there's nothing in the current version of the UL to clarify a coding point, it probably means that more work on the language is required—specifically, a new round of discussion to break down concepts one more level.

## Ubiquitous language changes

There are two main reasons a UL might change:

- The team's understanding of the business context evolves.

- The business context is defined while the software application is designed and built.

The former scenario resulted in the idea of DDD more than 20 years ago. The business model was intricate, dense, and huge, and required frequent passes to define, with features and concepts introduced, removed, absorbed, or redesigned on each pass.

> **Note** This type of iterative process usually occurs more quickly in the beginning of a project but slows down and perhaps almost stops at some point later. (This cycle might repeat with successive major releases of the software.)

The latter scenario is common in startup development—for example, for software specifically designed for a business project in its infancy. In this case, moving fast and breaking things is acceptable with both the software and the UL.

So, the UL might change—but not indefinitely. The development team is responsible for detecting when changes are needed and for applying them to the degree that business continuity allows. Be aware, though, that a gap between business language and code is, strictly speaking, a form of technical debt.

### Everyone makes mistakes

I have worked in the sport-tech industry for several years and have been involved in building a few platforms that now run daily operations for popular sports organizations. If tournaments run week after week, it's because the underlying software works. Sometimes, however, that software may still have design issues.

Yes, I do make mistakes at times, which result in design issues. More often, though, any design issues on my software exist because I'm pragmatic. To explain, let me share a story (with the disclaimer that this design issue will likely be sorted out by the time you read this).

Recently, my team adapted an existing software system for a different—though nearly identical—sport. One difference was that the new system did not need to support singles matches. Another difference was that points, rather than positions, would be used to order players in draws.

A segment of the domain layer and a few data repositories in the persistence layer used two properties—SinglesRank and DoublesRank. Initially, we didn't change anything in the naming (including related database tables). We simply stored doubles rankings in the DoublesRank property and left the SinglesRank property empty. Then, to use points instead of positions to order players in draws, I pragmatically suggested repurposing the otherwise-unused SinglesRank property—a perfectly effective solution that would require very minimal effort.

Just two weeks later, however, people began asking repeatedly what the heck the actual value of SinglesRank was. In other words, we experienced a gap between the UL and its representation in the code and data structures.

## Helpful programming tools

There are several features in programming languages to help shape code around a domain language. The most popular is support for classes, structs, records, and enum types. Another extremely helpful feature—at least in C#—is extension methods, which help ensure that the readability of the code is close to that of a spoken language.

An extension method is a global method that developers can use to add behavior to an existing type without deriving a new type. With extension methods, you can extend, say, the String class or even an enum type. Here are a couple of examples:

```
public static class SomeExtensions
{
    // Turns the string into the corresponding number (if any)
    // Otherwise, it returns the default value
    public static int ToInt(this string theNumber, int defaultValue = 0)
    {
        if (theNumber == null)
          return defaultValue;
       var success = int.TryParse(theNumber, var out calc);
       return success
          ? calc
          : defaultValue;
    }
    // Adds logic on top of an enum type
    public static bool IsEarlyFinish(this CompletionMode mode)
    {
        return mode == CompletionMode.Disqualified ||
              mode == CompletionMode.OnCourtRetirement ||
              mode == CompletionMode.Withdrawal;
    }
}
```

The first extension method extends the core String type to add a shortcut to turn the string to a number, if possible.

```
// With extension methods
var number = "4".ToInt();
// Without extension methods
int.TryParse("4", out var number);
```

Suppose you want to query all matches with an early finish. The code for this might take the following form:

```
var matches = db.Matches
                .Where(m => m.MatchCompletionMode.IsEarlyFinish())
                .ToList();
```

The benefit is having a tool to hide implementation details, so the actual behavioral logic can emerge.

### Value types and factory methods

Remember the misconceptions around DDD mentioned earlier in this chapter? I'm referring in particular to the relevance of coding rules.

DDD recommends several coding rules, such as using factory methods over constructors and value types over primitive types. By themselves, these rules add little value (hence, the misconception). However, in the context of the UL, these rules gain a lot more relevance. They are crucial to keeping language and code in sync.

For example, if the business domain involves money, then you'd better have a Money custom value type that handles currency and totals internally rather than manually pairing decimal values with hard-coded currency strings. Similarly, a factory method that returns an instance of a class from a named method is preferable to an unnamed constructor that is distinguishable from others only by the signature.

## The bounded context

Tweaking the business language and renaming classes and methods is tricky, but thanks to integrated development environment (IDE) features and plug-ins, it is not terribly problematic. However, failing to identify subdomains that are better treated independently could seriously undermine the stability of the whole solution.

No matter how hard you try, your UL will not be a unique set of definitions that is 100-percent unambiguous within your organization. In fact, the same term (for example, *customer*) might have different meanings across different business units. Like suitcases on an airport baggage belt that look alike, causing confusion among travelers, functions and names that look alike can cause problems in your solution.

Understanding differences between functions and names is crucial, and effectively addressing those differences in code is vital. Enter bounded contexts.

# Making sense of ambiguity

When analyzing a business domain, ambiguity occurs. Sometimes we run into functions that look alike but are not the same. When this occurs, developers often reveal an innate desire to create a unique hierarchy of highly abstracted entities to handle most scenarios and variations in a single place. Indeed, all developers have the secret dream of building a universal code hierarchy that traces back to a root Big-Bang object.

The reality is that abstraction is great—but more so in mathematics than in mere software. The great lesson we learn from DDD is that sometimes code fragmentation (and to some extent even code duplication) is acceptable just for the sake of maintenance.

> **Note** Code duplication can be just the starting point that leads to a model that is ideal for the business. Experience teaches us that when two descriptions seem to point to the same entity (except for a few attributes), forcing them to be one is almost always a mistake; treating them as distinct entities is usually acceptable even if it is not ideal.

## The cost of abstraction

Abstraction always comes at a cost. Sometimes this cost is worth it; sometimes it is not.

Originally, abstraction came as a manna from heaven to help developers devise large domain models. Developers examined a larger problem and determined that it could be articulated as many smaller problems with quite a few things in common. Then, to combat code duplication, developers righteously added abstraction layers.

As you proceed with your analysis and learn about new features, you might add new pieces to the abstraction to accommodate variations. At some point, though, this may become unmanageable. The bottom line is that there is a blurred line between premature abstraction (which just makes the overall design uselessly complex) and intelligent planning of features ahead of time. In general, a reasonable sign that abstraction may be excessive is if you catch yourself handling switches in the implementation and using the same method to deal with multiple use cases.

So much for abstraction in coding. What about top-level architecture? With this, it's nearly the same issue. In fact, you might encounter a business domain filled with similar functions and entities. The challenge is understanding when it's a matter of abstracting the design and when it's breaking down the domain in smaller parts. If you break it down in parts, you obtain independent but connected (or connectable) functions, each of which remains autonomous and isolated.

## Using ambiguity as the borderline

A reasonable sign that you may need to break a business domain into pieces is if you encounter ambiguity regarding a term of the UL. In other words, different stakeholders use the same term to mean different things. To address such a semantic ambiguity, the initial step is to determine whether you really are at the intersection of two distinct contexts. One crucial piece of information is whether one term can be changed to a different one without compromising the coherence of the UL and its adherence to the business language.

An even subtler situation is when the same entity appears to be called with different names by different stakeholders. Usually, it's not just about having different names of entities (synonyms); it often has to do with different behaviors and different sets of attributes. So, what should you do? Use coding abstractions, or accept the risk of some duplication? (See Figure 2-3.)

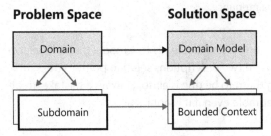

**FIGURE 2-3** Domain and subdomains versus domain models and bounded contexts.

Discovering ambiguity in terms is a clear sign that two parts of the original domain could possibly be better treated as different subdomains, each of which assigns the term an unambiguous meaning. DDD calls a modeled subdomain a *bounded context*.

> **Note** Realistically, when modeling a large domain, it gets progressively harder to build a single unified model. Also, people tend to use subtly different vocabularies in different parts of a large organization. The purpose of DDD is to deal with large models by dividing them into different bounded contexts and being explicit about their interrelationships.

## The savings of code duplication

From long experience in the code trenches, my hearty suggestion is that whenever you feel unsure whether abstraction is necessary, then by default, it isn't. In that case, you should use code duplication instead.

That said, I know that tons of articles and books out there (including probably a few of mine) warn developers of the "don't repeat yourself" (DRY) principle, which encourages the use of abstraction to reduce code repetitions. Likewise, I'm also well aware that the opposite principle—write every time (WET)—is bluntly dismissed as an anti-pattern.

Yet, I dare say that unless you see an obvious benefit to keeping a piece of the top-level architecture united, if a term has ambiguity within the business language that can't just be solved by renaming it using a synonym, you'd better go with an additional bounded context.

In coding, the cost of a bad abstraction is commonly much higher than the cost of duplicated code. In architecture, the cost of a tangled monolith can be devastating, in much the same way the cost of excessive fragmentation can be. Yes, as usual, it depends!

# Devising bounded contexts

A bounded context is a segment of the original model that turns out to be better modeled and implemented as a separate module. A bounded context is characterized by three aspects:

- Its own custom UL

- Its own autonomous implementation and technology stack

- A public interface to other contexts, if it needs be connected

As a generally observed fact, the resulting set of bounded contexts born from the breakdown of a business domain tends to reflect (or at least resemble) the structure of the owner organization.

## Breakdown of a domain

Here's an example taken from a realistic sport-tech scenario. If you're called to build an entire IT system to manage the operations of a given sport, you can come up with at least the partitions in subdomains shown in Figure 2-4.

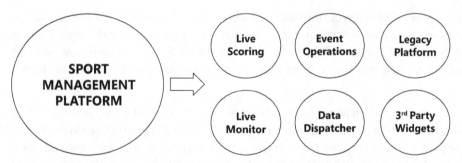

**FIGURE 2-4** Breakdown of an example domain model in a sport-tech scenario.

It's unrealistic to build the system as a single monolith. And it's not a matter of faith in the software creed of microservices; it's just that, with a decent analysis of the domain, processes, and requirements, you'll see quite a few distinct clusters of related operations (although maybe not just the six shown in Figure 2-4). These distinct blocks should be treated as autonomous projects for further analysis, implementation, and deployment.

In summary, each bounded context is implemented independently. And aside from some technical resources it may share with other contexts (for example, a distributed cache, database tables, or bus), it is completely autonomous from both a deployment and coding perspective.

## Shared kernels

Suppose you have two development teams working on what has been identified as a bounded context and you have an agreed-upon graph of functionalities in place. At some point, team 1 and team 2 may realize they are unwittingly working on the same small subset of software entities.

Having multiple teams share work on modules poses several synchronization issues. These range from just keeping changes to the codebase in sync to solving (slightly?) conflicting needs. Both teams must achieve coherency with their respective specs—not to mention any future evolutions that might bring the two teams into a fierce contrast. (See Figure 2-5.)

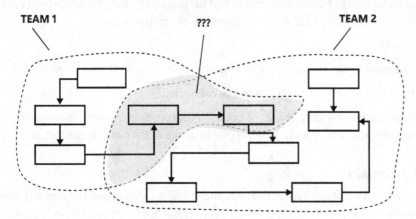

**FIGURE 2-5** Discovering a shared kernel.

There are three possible ways to deal with such a situation. The most conservative option is to let each team run its own implementation of the areas that appear common. Another option is to appoint one team the status of owner, giving it the final word on any conflicts. As an alternative, you could just let the teams come to a mutual agreement each time a conflict arises. Finally, there is the shared kernel option.

Shared kernel is a special flavor of bounded context. It results from a further breakdown of an existing bounded context. For example, the subdomain in Figure 2-5 will be partitioned in three contexts—one under the total control of team 1, one under the total control of team 2, and a third one. Who's in charge of the shared kernel? Again, the decision is up to the architect team, but it can be one of the existing teams or even a new team.

## Legacy and external systems

For the most part, bounded contexts isolate a certain related amount of behavior. Identifying these contexts is up to the architect team. However, certain pieces of the overall system should be treated as distinct bounded contexts by default—in particular, wrappers around legacy applications and external subsystems.

Whenever you have such strict dependencies on systems you don't control (or are not allowed to control), the safest thing you can do is create a wrapper around those known interfaces—whether a plain shared database connection string or an API. These wrappers serve a double purpose. First, they are an isolated part of the final system that simply call remote endpoints by proxy. Second, they can further isolate the general system from future changes on those remote endpoints.

In DDD jargon, the isolated wrappers around an external system are called an anti-corruption layer (ACL). Simply put, an ACL is a thin layer of code that implements a familiar pattern. It offers your calling modules a dedicated and stable (because you own it) programming interface that internally deals with the intricacies of the endpoints. In other words, the ACL is the only section of your code where the nitty-gritty details of the remote endpoints are known. No part of your code is ever exposed to that. As a result, in the event of breaking changes that occur outside your control, you have only one, ideally small, piece of code to check and fix.

## Coding options of bounded contexts

How would you code a bounded context? Technically, a bounded context is only a module treated in isolation from others. Often, this also means that a bounded context is deployed autonomously. However, the range of options for coding a bounded context is ample and includes in-process options.

The most common scenario—and the most common reason for wanting a bounded context—is to deploy it as a standalone web service accessible via HTTPS and JSON, optionally with a private or shared database. A bounded context, though, can easily be a class library distributed as a plain DLL or, better yet, as a NuGet package. For example, it is almost always a class library when it represents the proxy to an external system.

The public interface of a bounded context with other bounded contexts can be anything that allows for communication: a REST or gRPC gateway, a SignalR or in-process dependency, a shared database, a message bus, or whatever else.

**Note** Does the definition of a bounded context sound like that of a microservice? As you'll see in Chapter 9, there is a resemblance to the definition of *microservice* given by Martin Fowler: a module that runs in its own process and communicates through lightweight mechanisms such as an HTTPS API. In Fowler's vision, a microservice is built around specific business capabilities. The issue is in the intended meaning of the prefix *micro*. Size aside, I like to think of a bounded context as the theoretical foundation of a microservice. The same is true if we consider the alternative architecture of modular monoliths (see Chapter 9). A bounded context is also the theoretical foundation of a module in a monolith. I say "theoretical" for a reason: microservices and modular monoliths live in the space of the software solution, whereas bounded contexts exist in the space of the business domain.

# The context map

The outcome of a DDD analysis of business domain requirements is a collection of bounded contexts that, when combined, form the whole set of functions to implement. How are bounded contexts connected? Interestingly, connection occurs at two distinct levels. One is the physical connection between running host processes. As mentioned, such connections can take the form of HTTPS, SignalR, shared databases, or message buses. But another equally important level of connection is logical and collaborative rather than physical. The following sections explore the types of business relationships supported between bounded contexts.

Bounded contexts and their relationships form a graph that DDD defines as the *context map*. In the map, each bounded context is connected to others with which it is correlated in terms of functionalities. It doesn't have to be a physical connection, though. Often, it looks much more like a logical dependency.

## Upstream and downstream

Each DDD relationship between two bounded contexts is rendered with an arc connecting two nodes of a graph. More precisely, the arc has a directed edge characterized by the letter U (upstream context) or D (downstream context). (See Figure 2-6.)

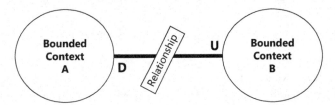

**FIGURE 2-6** Graphical notation of a context map relationship.

An upstream bounded context influences a downstream bounded context, but the opposite is not true. Such an influence may take various forms. Obviously, the code in the upstream context is available as a reference to the downstream context. It also means, though, that the schedule of work in the upstream context cannot be changed on demand by the team managing the downstream context. Furthermore, the response of the upstream team to requests for change may not be as prompt as desired by the downstream team.

Starting from the notion of upstream and downstream contexts, DDD defines a few specific types of relationships. Essentially, each relationship defines a different type of mutual dependency between involved contexts. These relationships are as follows:

- **Conformist**  A conformist relationship indicates that the code in the downstream context is totally dependent on the code in the upstream context. At the end of the day, this means that if a breaking change happens upstream, the downstream context must adapt and conform. By design, the downstream context has no room to negotiate about changes. Typically, a conformist relationship exists when the upstream context is based on some legacy code or is an external service (for example, a public API) placed outside the control of the development teams. Another possible scenario is when the chief architect sets one context as high priority, meaning that any changes the team plans must be reflected, by design, by all other contexts and teams.

- **Customer/supplier**   In this parent–child type of relationship, the downstream customer context depends on the upstream supplier context and must adapt to any changes. Unlike the conformist relationship, though, with the customer/supplier relationship, the two parties are encouraged to negotiate changes that may affect each other. For example, the downstream customer team can share concerns and expect that the upstream supplier team will address them in some way. Ultimately, though, the final word belongs to the upstream supplier context.

- **Partner**   The partner relationship is a form of mutual dependency set between the two involved bounded contexts. Put another way, both contexts depend on each other for the actual delivery of the code. This means that no team is allowed to make changes to the public interface of the context without consulting with the other team and reaching a mutual agreement.

## An example context map

Considering this discussion of bounded contexts and relationships, one might reasonably ask how these work in a realistic example. Figure 2-4 showed an example breakdown of a sport-tech data-collection business domain. Figure 2-7 shows a possible set of relationships for that scenario.

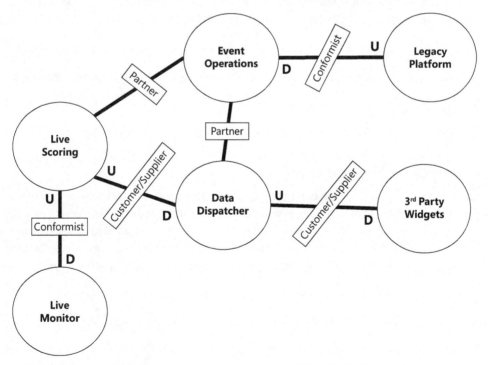

**FIGURE 2-7** An example context map for the bounded contexts identified in Figure 2-4.

Let's review the diagram proceeding from left to right:

- The Live Scoring context dominates the Data Dispatcher and Live Monitor contexts. So, any changes required for the Live Scoring context must be immediately accepted and reflected by the downstream contexts. This is reasonable, because the Data Dispatcher context is simply expected to route live information to takers and the Live Monitor context just proxies live data for internal scouting and analysis. Indeed, both relationships could be set to conformist, which is even stricter.

- The Live Scoring context partners with the Event Operations context. This is because in the architect's vision, the two modules may influence each other, and changes in one may be as important as changes in the other. A similar production system might have a partner relationship between the Live Scoring and Event Operations contexts, in which case it's often true that one team must conform to changes requested by the other (always for strict business reasons).

- The Event Operations context is totally dependent on the legacy applications connected to the system. This means that live data should be packaged and pushed in exactly the legacy format, with no room for negotiation.

- The Data Dispatcher context and the Event Operations context are partners, as both contexts collect and shape data to be distributed to the outside world, such as to media and IT partners.

- The Third-Party Widgets context contains widgets designed to be embedded in websites. As such, they are subject to conditions set by the Data Dispatcher context. From the perspective of the widget module, the dispatcher is a closed external system.

**Important** The person responsible for setting up the network of relationships is the chief architect. The direction of connections also has an impact on teams, their schedule, and their way of working.

## An example deployment map

The context map is a theoretical map of functions. It says nothing about the actual topology of the deployment environment. In fact, as mentioned, a bounded context may even be a class library coded in an application that turns out to be another bounded context. Often, a bounded context maps to a deployed (web) service, but this is not a general rule. That said, let's imagine a possible deployment map for the context map in Figure 2-7. Figure 2-8 shows a quite realistic high-level deployment scenario for a sport-tech data-collection platform.

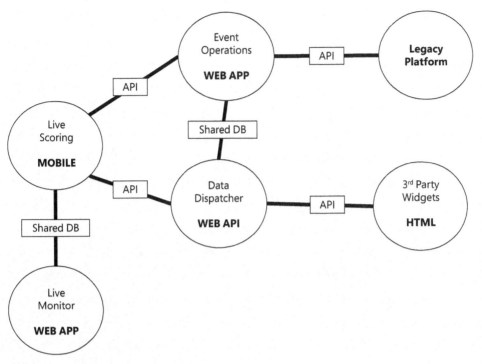

**FIGURE 2-8** An example deployment map.

## Summary

This chapter focused on DDD strategic design in a way that is mostly agnostic of software technology and frameworks. The strategic part of DDD is crucial; it involves discovering the top-level architecture of the system using a few analysis patterns and common practices.

The chapter covered the role of the UL, the discovery of distinct bounded contexts, and the relationships the chief architect may use to link contexts together. The map of contexts—the final deliverable of the DDD strategic analysis—is not yet a deployable architecture, but it is key to understanding how to map identified blocks to running services.

All these notions are conceptually valid and describe the real mechanics of DDD. However, it might seem as though they have limited concrete value if measured against relatively simple and small business domains. The actual value of DDD analysis shines when the density of the final map is well beyond the tens of units. Indeed, the largest map I've ever seen (for a pharmaceutical company) contained more than 400 bounded contexts. The screenshot of the map was too dense to count!

The next chapter draws some conclusions about the structure of a .NET and ASP.NET project that maintains clear boundaries between layers. In Part II of the book, we'll delve into each layer.

# CHAPTER 3

# Laying the ground for modularity

*The price of reliability is the pursuit of the utmost simplicity. It is a price which the very rich may find hard to pay.*
—Sir Tony Hoare, lecture at the 1980 ACM Turing Award in Nashville, TN, USA

In software development, the primary goal of introducing multiple tiers and layers is to achieve modularity, and the primary goal of modularization is to enhance software maintainability. *Modularization* involves breaking down a complex system into smaller, independent modules. Each module encapsulates a specific functionality and can be developed, tested, and maintained independently. Modularization works best when applied at the architecture level. When modules are well-isolated but clearly connected, it becomes much easier for the teams involved to understand what is going on and where to intervene to fix problems or add new features. Extensive use of modularization also helps to achieve two other crucial goals: reusability and scalability.

Having been in the software industry for more than 30 years, I have witnessed many attempts to develop a universal way of componentizing software development—from Visual Basic and Delphi components to ActiveX and (D)COM; from JavaBeans to Web Forms server controls; and from old-fashioned web services to microservices. Frankly, my age-related disillusion leads me to state that none of them worked, except perhaps for a few people and for a limited amount of time. There is no hope and no room for universality.

The only universal principle of software development is *separation of concerns* (*SoC*). SoC was formalized in 1974 by Edsger W. Dijkstra in the paper "On the Role of Scientific Thought," from which modularity is a direct emanation. In terms of software architecture, once you have a modular vision of a system, it's all about identifying logical layers and mapping them to physical tiers. Various software architecture patterns simply differ in how this mapping takes place.

You can apply modularization at any level, from coding a method within a class to implementing a systemwide feature such as a scheduler library, and from defining the pillars of an entire web application to envisioning the forest of services and standalone applications that form a business platform. (See Figure 3-1.)

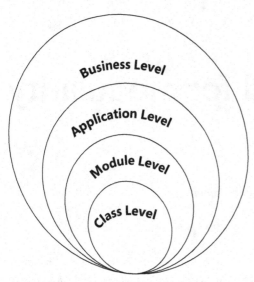

**FIGURE 3-1** All possible levels of modularization.

## Aspects and principles of modularization

Regardless of where you apply modularization, there are several key aspects and principles involved. These are nothing new; any student of computer science learns them early on. But seasoned professionals sometimes forget them when facing deadlines and last-minute changes. They include the following:

- Separation of concerns

- Loose coupling

- Reusability

- Dependency management

- Documentation

- Testability

## Separation of concerns

By far the most important aspect of any real-world software project of some complexity, separation of concerns (SoC) refers to the division of responsibilities within a software system. To achieve SoC, each module should have a clearly defined and focused purpose that addresses a specific aspect of the overall functionality. In theory, SoC—which is widely used—allows for better code organization and easier readability and comprehension.

The difficulty with SoC is identifying the exact position of the boundary and the area it fences in. In a software project, giving substance to expressions like "clearly defined and focused purpose" is a real sore point. A too-large area invalidates the SoC itself; a too-small one results in excessive fragmentation, which may add latency (thereby reducing performance), increase the cost of deployment, and make the code too verbose.

Ideally, you apply SoC at any of the levels shown in Figure 3-1, using different metrics at each level. At the class level, you focus on the micro actions of a method to forge the behavior of the entity class. At the module level, you identify and abstract away a common pattern of behavior and sandbox it into reusable (or just more readable) classes. This works for general-purpose modules such as an email sender or a task scheduler, as well as for business-specific modules such as rule validators and data importers.

## Loose coupling

Modules should interact with each other through well-defined interfaces or contracts, minimizing direct dependencies. Loose coupling ensures that changes in one module have minimal impact on other modules, promoting flexibility and ease of maintenance. Loose coupling also facilitates the replacement of modules and swapping modules with alternative implementations, which enhances modularity.

Loose coupling requires encapsulation. Encapsulation hides the internal complexity of a module and provides a clear boundary for communication and collaboration between modules. A module should ideally encapsulate its internal implementation details and expose a well-defined interface, or set of APIs, for interaction with other modules.

## Reusability

When done well, modularization results in the development of reusable modules that can be leveraged within the same project or wrapped up into closed packages (such as NuGet packages) for reuse across projects and teams. Well-designed modules with clear boundaries and encapsulated functionality can be easily extracted and reused, minimizing effort, limiting development time, and most importantly, promoting consistency.

**Note** One so-called "strength" of microservices—when the intended meaning of *microservice* is a very focused, small, autonomous, and independently deployable module—is that it can be created using any language or stack. So, any developer (or team) can select their pet stack (Python, C#, Java) to code their microservice. My take on this approach is that it breaks consistency and fragments the deployment. And while it might promote reusability, it does so for micro functionality only. So, microservices might offer a quick way to release software, but they can be limiting, and perhaps more expensive if the developer or team that created them leaves the company.

## Dependency management

Effective modularization requires the management of dependencies between modules to avoid unnecessary coupling and to ensure that each module relies only on the specific functionality it needs from other modules. At the application level, it usually suffices to select the minimal subset of necessary projects and packages. At a finer-grained level, though—when you are within a software component—dependency injection can help manage dependencies and promote loose coupling.

> **Note** In literature, the term *dependency injection* often appears related to inversion of control (IoC). According to the IoC principle—which precedes the concept of dependency injection and is considered more general—when an application needs to perform a certain behavior, the instructions for that behavior do not appear in the main code. Instead, they come from the outside, as a parameter. In other words, the control of the flow is "inverted." In contrast, dependency injection is a concrete pattern through which the inversion of control is achieved, thus removing hidden dependencies from the code.

## Documentation

Modularization involves building a map of references. So, it requires clear documentation of module interfaces, dependencies, and usage guidelines. This helps developers understand how modules interact, fostering collaboration and enabling the smooth integration of modules within a larger system.

## Testability

The clear separation of boundaries and the effective management of dependencies are the pillars of testable code. Along the course of my career, I've never emphasized the need for unit tests or the value of code coverage. And I always found test-driven design (TDD) to be a weird way to write code. At the same time, though, I've always stressed the absolute necessity of writing code that is testable. Indeed, I believe this is more valuable than actually running batteries of tests.

Designing for testability stems from modularization and facilitates unit testing and validation by isolating modules and their functionality. Each module can be tested independently, enabling faster feedback cycles, easier debugging, and better overall system stability. Testing at the module level also promotes reusability and modifiability because you can confidently modify or replace modules without worrying about affecting the entire system.

One practical approach I take and recommend is to write black boxes of code that do nothing but take and return expected data anytime you're implementing a process. At the end of the day, this is the second step of the canonical TDD practice: write a test for the method that fails, edit the method to barely pass the test, add more code to make it functional, and test indefinitely.

# Applying modularization

DDD strategic analysis and—even more—your domain expertise and abstraction capabilities enable you to identify the main concerns of the system. At the highest level, this probably results in several independent app services and database servers. Next, each app service—a web application—and any non-web services are addressed individually. This represents the second outermost circle of Figure 3-1: the application level.

I see two possible scenarios:

- The application is a mere algorithm so simple that it can be coded from start to finish, with or without a user interface and with nearly no external dependencies. It is just a self-contained module.

- The application is more complex, so anything like a layered architecture serves well for achieving modularity.

The modules of a layered application are the four layers presented in Chapter 1: presentation, application, domain, and data/infrastructure. These layers, which are discussed individually in greater detail in the second part of this book, map to four fundamental system functions:

- Interacting with the outside world

- Processing received commands

- Representing domain entities

- Persisting data

## The presentation layer: interacting with the outside world

The first duty of any application is to receive commands from the outside world and filter valid commands from those that, for whatever reason, are invalid. Typically, this interaction occurs via a user interface or API and, in terms of code, is handled at the presentation layer.

In a classic web scenario (such as ASP.NET), the presentation layer is not what the user views in the browser. Rather, it resides on the server. Its primary purpose is to route requests to some module that can handle them. For ASP.NET applications, the presentation layer consists of controller classes and, more generally, the code that is directly connected to reachable endpoints. For example, a minimal API has request handlers mapped directly to endpoints with no ceremony at all. In a rich client scenario— that is, a single-page application (SPA)—the presentation layer lives on the client browser and incorporates both interactions and routing to external server endpoints.

## The application layer: processing received commands

Every command needs a handler to process. This handler must be explicit and contracted—that is, it accepts a given input and returns a given output. The purpose of this is simple: to decouple the handling of request messages from the receiving environment.

In an ASP.NET Core scenario, the application layer consists of handlers that respond to a controller request and return a response to the controller for packaging back to the browser. The controller receives the input in the form of an HTTP request, but the application service processes that devoid of the HTTP context.

## The domain layer: representing domain entities

Any command handler has one main responsibility: to interact with the system infrastructure using domain entities as the currency. Essentially, *domain entities*—which are ideally database agnostic but must be populated with data—are where you code most business logic. The part of the business logic that relates to fetching and saving entities to the persistence layer belongs to another bunch of classes, which DDD refers to as *domain services*.

Ideally, domain entities are classes with read properties and methods to alter their state. Instantiation and persistence occur in the care of domain services or simple repositories—classes that just abstract basic create-read-update-delete (CRUD) operations.

## The data/infrastructure layer: persisting data

The data layer is where the module persists and reads information processed by the application. The thickness of this layer varies. It might coincide with a database server—whether relational or NoSQL—or it can be created by code (that is, repository classes) that arranges raw calls to the storage server via dedicated object/relational mappers such as Entity Framework or Dapper.

Recently, the data layer has been abstracted to an infrastructure layer, whose primary (but not only) responsibility is persistence. Seen as infrastructure, this layer is also responsible for emails and connection to external APIs.

# Achieving modularity

In the beginning, all software was built as a single block of code. The resulting monolithic architecture is characterized by a single, tightly coupled application in which all components and functionalities are bundled together. In a monolith, the entire system is built and deployed as a single unit.

This is not modular in the commonly accepted sense of the word in software. Modular in software refers to a design approach that involves breaking down a software system into multiple, self-contained, and possibly reusable units. In contrast, a monolith, seen from the outside, is made of just one module.

## More modularity in monoliths

Monolithic applications are typically developed on a single codebase and deployed as a single unit, with all components packaged together. Sharing code and logic is easy, and deployment is often really a matter of just one click within the integrated development environment (IDE) of choice.

What's wrong with monoliths, then?

It's the same old story from the ashes from which DDD was raised a couple of decades ago: managing business complexity effectively. When complexity grows, the codebase grows larger and development becomes more challenging, with increased dependencies and the need for careful coordination between team members. At the same time, updates and changes require redeploying the entire application, leading to longer deployment cycles and potential disruptions. Furthermore, making changes or updates can be complex due to the tight coupling between components. A modification in one part of the system may require regression testing of the entire application. Additionally, the complexity of the codebase can make debugging and issue resolution more challenging.

OK, so we have a problem. But what about the solution?

Making a monolithic application more modular is a common approach when you want to improve its maintainability and scalability and make development more efficient. This process typically involves breaking down the monolith into smaller, more manageable components that remain confined within the same deployable unit. The operation is based on the following points:

- Identifying the core functionalities

- Decoupling dependencies

Let's find out more.

## Identifying logical modules

In a monolith application that covers an inevitably large business domain, a deep understanding of the domain is crucial. Not just knowledge of the general domain, though—also having a deep understanding of the business processes is fundamental so you can identify the actual atomic tasks to be performed and decide how best to orchestrate them into a workflow.

To keep it really modular, connectable, and interoperable, each identified module should be given a clear and well-documented interface or API. These interfaces will specify how other modules can interact with and access the functionality of each module.

## Decoupling dependencies

In a modular architecture, components are isolated but should still be allowed to communicate. Like in a geographical archipelago, many islands form the unit, each isolated but connected through bridges and transport lines. You want to have connections, but not too many.

In software, dependencies between modules should be reduced so that each remaining module performs one—and only one—specific atomic task and supplies an interface for others to call it. Achieving this cleanup of the internal code may involve refactoring code, moving shared functionality into separate libraries, or using dependency injection to manage dependencies more flexibly.

## Scalability of monoliths

Moving from a monolith to a modular monolith doesn't fully address the main issue that often plagues monolithic applications: the level of scalability they can reach. Because a monolith is built and deployed as a single unit, when it comes to scalability, the safest option is vertical scaling. Vertical scaling means increasing the physical hardware resources available to the single instance of running code—in other words, more CPU, more memory, and more powerful database servers.

In contrast to vertical scaling is horizontal scaling, which means running the application on multiple servers simultaneously in combination with additional resources such as clustering and load balancing. Applied to monoliths, horizontal scaling may not turn out to be as efficient as planned.

When scaling up the application becomes an urgent need, it's because some parts of the application are slowing down the whole system. In a monolithic scenario, though, there is no way to separate a system's stable functionalities from those that are critical for ensuring a constant and decent level of service. The single block will be multiplied across servers, potentially resulting in the overprovisioning of resources and higher costs.

> **Note**  Horizontal scalability with monolithic applications is not always possible. For example, the presence of global data can lead to contention and locking issues in the shared state. Furthermore, proper load balancing is crucial for efficiently distributing incoming requests across multiple instances, and in a monolith, load balancing can be more challenging due to the complex nature of the application and the need to balance the load evenly. Finally, horizontal scalability in the case of monoliths is empirically limited to just a few instances before it starts being impractical or inefficient.

# Introducing microservices

To address these issues, companies often consider transitioning from a monolithic architecture to a microservices-based architecture. Microservices are designed to overcome many of the limitations associated with monoliths in terms of scalability and modularity. In a microservices architecture, individual services can be independently scaled, maintained, and updated, making it easier to take full advantage of horizontal scalability.

## Key aspects of microservices

A microservices architecture makes a point of decomposing a system into smaller, autonomous, and interoperable components. Microservices communicate with each other through well-defined APIs, often using lightweight protocols like HTTP or messaging systems. Each component focuses on a specific business capability and operates as a separate application independent from any other when it comes to development and deployment. A microservices architecture therefore promotes modularity by design.

Furthermore, microservices enable more efficient resource utilization, because only the necessary components are scaled rather than the entire application. Microservices can handle varying workloads and scale specific services horizontally as needed.

> **Note** Microservices aren't the only way to achieve modularity. Modularity is a higher-level architectural aspect, which teams are responsible for achieving. With microservices, achieving modularity is nearly free. But with development discipline and design vision, you can make any monolith modular enough to deliver nearly the same benefits innate in a microservices architecture.

## Technology diversity

Breaking up a codebase into smaller pieces may also lead to faster development cycles, as teams can focus on specific services without being hindered by the constraints of a monolithic codebase and the need to merge code with other teams. In addition, each team can use different technologies, programming languages, or frameworks. (See Figure 3-2.)

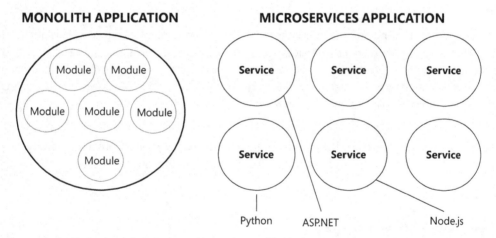

**FIGURE 3-2** Technology diversity in a microservices application.

Frankly, I'm not sure I would always place this aspect of microservices in the list of good points. Whether it's good or bad depends. Using different technology stacks breaks consistency, and having multiple technology stacks might be painful if teams change in number or composition. As usual, trade-offs guide any choice, and only actual results will tell whether a choice was good or bad.

If dedicated and permanent teams are allocated for each service, then it may be reasonable to give them the freedom to choose the most suitable tools and make them responsible for development, testing, deployment, and maintenance. Otherwise, a mix-and-match of languages and frameworks will likely turn into a maintainability nightmare.

**Note** In general, modularity is necessary. How you achieve it, however, is subject to specific business and project considerations. No one chose to write intricate and tightly coupled monoliths, but if you choose microservices on the hype of modernity and technology trends, you may run into trouble you might otherwise have avoided.

### Challenges of microservices

While microservices offer numerous benefits, they're not free of challenges. Microservices introduce significant complexity in several areas:

- Service communication

- Data consistency

- Distributed transaction management

- Security and logging

- Operational overhead

It's clear that embarking on a microservices architecture is not a decision to take with a light heart. Ultimately, the choice between microservices and monoliths depends on factors such as the size and complexity of the project, scalability needs, team structure, and the desire for flexibility and autonomy. If the benefits offered by a microservice architecture overtake their (objective) downsides, then it's OK. Otherwise, facing failure is more than just an option.

**Note** This chapter has looked at monoliths and microservices mostly from a modularity perspective. Chapter 9 returns to this same topic for a more thorough discussion.

# The simplest solution ever

Whatever problem you face, you should start with the simplest possible solution for that problem. This is the simplest solution ever (SSE) principle.

For example, although it's crucial to ensure that an application is fine-tuned for the expected workload, not all software systems need to scale indefinitely. Likewise, continuous delivery—a hallmark of the DevOps approach—is not essential if the system is expected to be updated via controlled upgrades or to receive a hotfix in case of emergency.

Ultimately, any new software project should be based on an architectural solution with these minimal characteristics:

- Modularity

- Maintainability

- Design for testability

We've already discussed modularity. Let's look more closely at maintainability and designing for testability.

# Maintainability

In software parlance, *maintainability* refers to the ease with which a software system can be modified, repaired, and enhanced over its lifetime. It is a measure of how well the application supports ongoing development, bug fixes, and the introduction of new features, while minimizing the risk of introducing errors or negatively affecting system stability.

If the level of maintainability remains constant over time, a pleasant side effect is that anybody who lays their hands on the codebase can quickly figure out where to look for things. If there's a bug to fix, the developer can quickly determine the areas of code to explore. If consistency exists in both the technology stack and the writing patterns, any such tasks become much simpler and effective.

Related points are the readability of the code, the reusability of the code, and the scalability of the code.

## Readability

Too often, readability is dismissed as a volatile recommendation to use clear and descriptive variable names, following consistent and sensible coding conventions, and organizing code into logical and modular components. While this is true and necessary, it is largely insufficient.

Readability increases considerably if at least a couple of SOLID principles are applied often. One is the single responsibility principle, which basically boils down to being extremely focused when coding any task and avoiding God objects and omniscient methods. The other is the open/closed principle. This principle states that code should be open to extensions but closed to changes. In other words, it refers to spotting blocks of code that can be abstracted into a reusable component that is generic—that is, it accepts one or more types of parameters—or supports the injection of interface-based behavior.

Applying both these principles on any line of code is unnecessary and even detrimental, but ignoring them entirely is bad as well. In any case, any time you succeed with the open/closed principle, you smooth the way to code maintenance.

Readability is also a product of a more pragmatic set of coding standards such as writing fluent code, extensively using value types in lieu of primitives, and leveraging C# extension methods to make any task look like schematic natural language.

## Reusability

I wouldn't suggest pursuing reusability as a primary goal or feeling bad if no derived classes exist in the codebase. This is because while code duplication may smell bad, it often saves lives.

On its own, code is merely an insentient collection of lines. As such, repeating it in multiple places is not necessarily an issue. Any repetition is isolated from all others and, if needed, each can be further extended without affecting others. If repetition is avoided at any cost, however, then you end up with a single piece of behavior that is called from many different places. That's all good until requirements change, and you need to break up that common piece into multiple units.

If repetition of lines of code may be acceptable, what should be absolutely avoided is repetition of code that expresses some logical behavior common in business. If you strive to spot repeated pieces of logical behavior and make them open/closed or just reusable, the codebase shrinks, and the effort to read and understand the code diminishes. Reusability is not much for big things—for that we have modularity and packages. Reusability is for small things like helper classes and HTML components.

## Scalability

Today, developers commonly plan overly sophisticated software architecture with the justification that you need scalability sooner rather than later. Paraphrasing the popular quote attributed to Donald Knuth, "Premature optimization is the root of all evil," we could state that premature arrangements for scalability are the root of most projects' evil.

Only the likelihood of some significant increase in traffic—not just hope or random numbers in some aleatory business plan—calls for developers to lay out the system in a way that makes it easier to accommodate higher volumes of traffic down the line. Even then, that should not occur until there is clear evidence of scalability issues.

Besides, there aren't really very many ways to pursue scalability. In fact, I'd say there's just one: planning the system so it is easier to reconfigure the deployment of certain pieces, or even a rewrite, when necessary. When it comes to scalability, the most important precaution you can take is to keep the system as modular as possible and with clear boundaries between modules.

> **Note** With modularity and maintainability comes everything else.

# Designing for testability

It is common to read about the need for unit tests for every single line of code. It is much less common, however, to read about the necessity of writing code to be easily testable.

Designing a system for testability involves incorporating certain principles and techniques during the design phase. Here are some aspects to consider (not surprisingly, they all touch on points I've covered already):

- **Mastery of the domain context**   Any method written should be the result of a deep and true understanding of the (correct and validated) user story.

- **Focus**   Every module, at all the levels shown in Figure 3-1, should focus on one—and only one—clear task.

- **Minimal dependencies**  Minimizing dependencies between modules reduces the impact of changes and facilitates independent testing. You can use techniques like dependency injection to decouple modules and enable the substitution of dependencies during testing.

- **Encapsulation**  Try to encapsulate internal implementation details within modules and expose only necessary interfaces to other components. This promotes modularity and allows for more focused testing, as the internal workings of a module can be hidden.

In addition, code testability is augmented by using one or more of the following programming practices:

- **Dependency injection**  This provides external dependencies to a class or method, making it easier to substitute real implementations with mock objects.

- **No global state**  Eliminating global variables or shared state between methods makes it easier to test each scenario more comfortably without having to know more than just what the method to test does.

- **Immutable data structures**  These make it easier to reason about the state of the system during testing and can prevent unexpected side effects.

Often associated with the theme of testability are two more, fairly divisive topics: design patterns and test-driven development (TDD). I have my views on these, as strong and unpopular as they may sound.

> **Important**  Following the principles of design for testability—not a pile of unit tests—is what really raises the quality of the code.

## Personal notes on design patterns

Design patterns, as we know them in the software development field, owe their origins to Christopher Alexander, an environment architect. In the late 1970s, he introduced the concept of a pattern language to enable individuals to express their inherent design sensibilities through an informal grammar. A pattern, he said, "is a recurring problem within our environment, for which a core solution is described. This solution can be applied countless times without ever being exactly the same."

In software, design patterns have come to be a well-established core solution that can be applied to a set of specific problems that arise during development. You can envision a design pattern as a comprehensive package, encompassing a problem description, a roster of actors involved in the problem, and a pragmatic solution.

How do you apply a design pattern? How do you recognize the need and the value of using a particular one? It's too superficial to just advocate the generic use of design patterns; I don't believe in their salvific use. Using design patterns per se doesn't enhance the value of your solution. Ultimately, what truly counts is whether your solution effectively functions and fulfills the specified requirements.

As a developer, you simply code armed with requirements and the software principles with which you are familiar. Along the way, though, a systematic application of design principles will eventually bring you to a solution with some structural likeness to a known design pattern, because patterns are essentially pre-discovered and documented solutions. Your responsibility is to assess whether explicitly adapting your solution to such a pattern offers any added value.

Ultimately, patterns can serve both as a goal when refactoring and as a tool when encountering a problem with a clear pattern-based solution. They don't directly enhance your solution's value but do hold value for you as an architect or developer.

 **Note** At the very least, every developer should be familiar with design patterns such as Adapter, Builder, Chain of Responsibility, Prototype, Singleton, and Strategy.

### Personal notes on TDD

My stance on TDD is clear and without much nuance. I don't care whether developers adopt TDD or not, as long as they push tested and reliable code to the repository. Whether you write unit tests—specific of the single developer activity—or not, and the order in which you write code and test, doesn't matter to me as long as the result is tested code that covers at least common business scenarios.

I don't believe in the salvific power of TDD either—which, in my opinion, remains a perfectly acceptable personal practice. Forcing it throughout a team or, worse yet, an entire company sounds like an arbitrary imposition that only makes people feel more uncomfortable.

## Summary

This chapter emphasized the role of modularization in software development in managing complexity, improving maintainability, and promoting reusability. Modularization involves breaking down a system into smaller, independent modules with well-defined boundaries, encapsulated functionality, and loosely coupled interactions. Through proper separation of concerns, encapsulation, loose coupling, and effective dependency management, modularization enhances the overall quality and scalability of software systems.

A discussion of breaking up software into modules inevitably involves the topic of microservices compared to monolithic architectures. As explained in this chapter, I'm not a big fan of microservices as a one-size-fits-all tool, nor am I an advocate of tightly coupled monolithic systems in which any update can quickly become an adventure—touch here and break there.

Instead, I am a fan of the SSE principle—a sort of software interpretation of Occam's razor. These days, my best suggestion is to start with modular—strictly modular—monoliths and then investigate what else can be done when you have evidence of heavy scalability issues. This is the approach we employed to design the platform to run daily operations in professional tennis and Padel since the international calendar resumed after early pandemic lockdowns. We're still running it successfully over a modular monolith with super-optimized database procedures, and every day we deliver thousands of touches on on-court tablets all the way through media takers, on various APIs up to betting companies. No bus, little cache, no serverless, no ad hoc cloud-native architectures—just plain ASP.NET and religious attention to modularity. As a final piece of wisdom, keep in mind that using an overkill approach to build software quickly results in technical debt.

This chapter ends the first part of the book. Part II—comprising the next five chapters—is devoted to covering the layers of a typical layered (monolithic) architecture that is modular and maintainable.

# Architecture cleanup

# CHAPTER 4

# The presentation layer

*Learn the rules like a pro, so you can break them like an artist.*

—*Pablo Picasso*

Abstractly speaking, the presentation layer is simply the segment of a computer system responsible for providing a user-friendly interface, representing data visually, ensuring a positive user experience, and facilitating communication with other layers of the software application. In more concrete terms, however, the presentation layer ultimately serves one main purpose: collecting external input and routing commands to the more operational layers of the system.

In any interactive application, all activity consists of requests sent by human or software agents to a known set of endpoints, and responses generated by those endpoints. The presentation layer acts as a gateway to receive requests and return responses.

Is *presentation* the most appropriate name for a layer that acts as a virtual front office? Probably not. But for historical reasons, this name is set in stone, even though gateway would probably be a more appropriate term for this layer in modern applications.

In most real-world cases, the presentation (or gateway) layer produces the user interface. In doing so, it assumes the responsibility of adding a sense of character and style to improve the experience of end users. Recently, the advent of single-page applications (SPAs) and the success of JavaScript-based frameworks such as Angular and React have moved the burden of building a canonical user interface to a dedicated team (and project). Yet, at some point, this distinct front end packs up and sends requests to some back-end system. The back-end system, however, still has its own presentation/gateway layer to collect requests and forward commands to generate responses, whether JSON or HTML. In brief, the purpose of this chapter is to illustrate the facts, features, and technologies of the (necessary) gateway that sits in between external input and invoked tasks.

> **Important** In spite of its name, the presentation layer is primarily about routing requests and controlling subsequent tasks. This gateway role is recognizable not just in server web applications but also in client-based single-page applications (SPAs) written using the Angular and React frameworks. Underneath the direct DOM-level interaction, in fact, some gateway code (mostly event handlers) handles the routing of requests to the back end.

# Project Renoir: the final destination

I've always been a strong believer in top-down development—and I've become even more so in recent years as the user experience has gained relevance and traction. To *really* be user-friendly, software applications must faithfully mirror real-world processes, and even improve them where possible and technologically appropriate.

When I talk to stakeholders, I try to mentally translate their words into items on an abstract menu long before I focus on the domain and data models. I usually like to start from the beginning, but to begin well, you need to envision the final outcome first. This part of the book is devoted to developing a sample project from scratch, called Project Renoir.

## Introducing the application

Project Renoir is a web application built on the .NET Core stack. It is restricted to a set of authorized users: admins, product owners, contributors, and simple viewers. It is centered around three fundamental business entities: product, release note, and roadmap. Depending on their role and assigned permissions, logged users can:

- Create and edit products

- Assign contributors to a product

- Create and edit release notes and roadmaps

- Navigate the list of available documents (release notes and roadmaps)

- Export and share documents

The sample project is not just another to-do list, nor is it some simplistic e-commerce system. Instead, it's a quick and dirty tool that anyone can use: a release note builder and reporter. The application's name, Project Renoir, is derived from its capabilities: ***Re**lease **No**tes **I**nstant **R**eporter*.

The rest of this chapter (on the presentation layer), and the next four chapters (on the application, domain, domain services, and infrastructure layers), are dedicated to the construction of Project Renoir using DDD analysis and a layered architecture. It will be a monolithic application with clear separation between layers—in other words, a *modular monolith*, as many like to say these days.

### Release notes in a nutshell

A release note document is a concise summary of changes, improvements, and bug fixes introduced in a new software release. It serves as a communication tool to inform users and, more importantly, stakeholders about modifications made to a software product. Release notes highlight key features, enhancements, and resolved issues, providing an overview of what users can expect from the new release. It may also include instructions, known issues, and compatibility information to help users work with the product more effectively.

Release notes can also serve another purpose: to document work done. By navigating release notes documents, one can track the history of an app's development, counting the number of fixes, hot fixes, and new features, as well as noting any maintenance that has been done within a specific range of time.

Too often, release notes are treated as an annoying chore, if not an afterthought. As a professional actively involved in the development of company-owned software products, I've long considered writing release notes to be so boring that it's actually enjoyable to pass the task on to someone else—at least I did until a key user disputed whether work we had done on a product had actually been completed, and our release notes hadn't been updated to prove that it had. Release notes matter!

## Who writes release notes?

Who's in charge of writing release notes? The release notes document is typically created by tech leads or by people within the product team such as a product manager, product owner, or members of the quality assurance (QA) team. Whoever takes the job, though, should strive to be empathetic and keep engagement and satisfaction high. That's why technical writers and even marketers are good candidates—especially when the communication doesn't have to be strictly technical or delve deeply into business rules and processes.

## Writing a release notes document

Release notes must be easily navigable for authors, company managers, members of the sales team, and stakeholders. Ultimately, a release notes document consists of free text content, usually saved as a plain rich text format file. What the release notes contain is up to you, although a few generally accepted guidelines do exist. Here's a common template:

- An introduction header and brief overview of the changes

- A clear explanation of affected users (if any)

- Changes to previous release notes

- A list of feature enhancements and new features added

- Fixed issues

I tend to use a slightly different template. Beyond the introductory header and explanatory notes to possible affected users, I usually just list development items and catalog them as fixes, new features, or ordinary maintenance. I also group these release notes items by area of impact—visuals, core functions, security, configuration, or performance.

My ideal release notes document—which is what Project Renoir is all about—contains a list of items queried from a table in a given time interval. These items are related to another key document to share with users and stakeholders: the product roadmap. A roadmap item is similar to a release note item except its feature descriptions are less granular. That is, roadmap items are macro features whereas release notes items are more like items assigned in task-management applications such as YouTrack, Asana, Trello, Monday, Jira, and others.

## Tools to create release notes

Nearly any task-management software—not to mention a variety of dedicated products—offers you the ability to create release notes from the list of assigned tasks. For example, you can create a release notes document on GitHub.com right from the main page of the repository. You simply click the Draft a New Release link and follow the prompts to generate release notes from known pushes. From there, you can edit and embellish the generated text.

To be honest, I don't particularly like this approach. It's what people do when they treat release notes like an afterthought. I much prefer for someone on the product team to invest some time composing a dedicated document for users and peers. I also like having a tailor-made, dedicated environment that stakeholders can access, too, to navigate the work done. This is the foundation for Project Renoir.

> **Note** Project Renoir is not meant to be a new task-management full-fledged application. Although we use it internally in our company, it has also arisen from the need to develop a (hopefully) attractive demo for the purposes of this book.

## The abstract context map

Chapter 2 explained that within the boundaries of the DDD methodology, ubiquitous language, bounded contexts, and context maps are the strategic foundation of any real-world application with some amount of complexity. This section presents a quick DDD analysis of Project Renoir.

### Ubiquitous language

To review, ubiquitous language (UL) refers to a shared language and set of terms used by all stakeholders involved in a project to ensure effective communication and understanding of the domain model. Table 4-1 lists the main UL business terms for Project Renoir and their intended meaning, and Table 4-2 lists the personas defined within the UL who are entitled to access and use the platform.

**TABLE 4-1** Dictionary of business terms in Project Renoir

| Business Term | Intended meaning |
| --- | --- |
| Product | A software product whose releases and roadmaps are managed by Project Renoir. |
| Release notes | A release notes document expressed as a list of release notes items. Each release note has a version number, date, and description. |
| Release notes item | A piece of work done in the context of a product release. Each item has a description, a category, and a delivery date. |
| Roadmap | A document that outlines features planned for inclusion in the product in list form. Each roadmap has a description and a time reference (for example, Summer 2024). |
| Roadmap item | A feature planned for inclusion in the product. Each item has an estimated delivery date and an actual delivery date to enable stakeholders to easily see how closely "promises" align with reality. |

**TABLE 4-2** Personas in Project Renoir

| Persona | Intended meaning |
|---------|------------------|
| Admin | The unlimited system account from which everything within the system can be checked and edited. In the case of Project Renoir, a multi-tenant application, the admin persona is the global administrator and can create new products and product owners. |
| Product owner | A role with full control over contributions to and releases of a specific product. |
| Contributor | A role that can create documents (notes and roadmaps) under the umbrella of a given product. A contributor can be active on multiple products, with different permissions on each. |
| Viewer | A role that is limited to viewing and possibly downloading available documents. |

## Bounded contexts

As noted in Chapter 2, a bounded context is a specific domain within a software system where concepts, rules, and language have clear boundaries and meaning. Project Renoir is too small to require multiple bounded contexts. In Project Renoir, both the business domain and the business language are unique, and there are no ambiguous business terms. So, Project Renoir can be a compact, stateless web module deployed to a single app service, easy to duplicate in case of growing volumes of traffic.

Still, it is helpful to treat the following parts as a distinct bounded context:

- **Main application**   The core web application, built as an ASP.NET Core application.

- **Domain model**   The repository of invariant business logic. It is built as a reusable class library and possibly published as an internal NuGet package to streamline reuse.

- **Infrastructure**   This contains the database server and all code and dependencies necessary to save and retrieve data. This context also acts as an anti-corruption layer for external services.

- **External services**   This describes any external web services used by the application such as those necessary to create PDF documents or send emails.

Recall that in DDD, the relationships and planned interactions between the different bounded contexts of a project are rendered in a diagram called the context map.

## Context map

Figure 4-1 shows a reasonable map for Project Renoir. Note that *reasonable* here doesn't mean *mandatory*. The actual relationships are chosen by the lead architect and match the availability of teams, the skills of the people in those teams, and the attitude of the lead architect with regard to exercising control over artifacts.

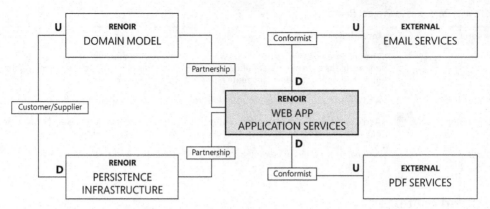

**FIGURE 4-1** The context map of Project Renoir.

The main application operates in partnership with the domain model and the infrastructure contexts. This is the only point that can be arguable. The ultimate decision should be made based on people, teams, and skills. The other relationships are much more established and harder to question.

Domain Model and Infrastructure work together, but the need (and purity) of Domain Model prevails in case of doubt, and preserving that should be the primary goal.

The use of Entity Framework (EF)—or any other object-relational mapping (O/RM) tool—as the gateway to databases represents a threat to the purity of the domain model. In fact, unless a completely different data model is used for persistence (and a costly set of adapters to go from the domain to the persistence model and back), serializing a domain model via an O/RM requires, at a minimum, that you leave default constructors and public setters in place for all entities so that dehydration of those entities can be performed. (See Figure 4-2.)

 **Important** The development of domain model and infrastructure contexts occurs in parallel to the extent possible, and the teams work together. In case of conflicts, though, the needs of the domain model (for example, preserving design purity) prevail.

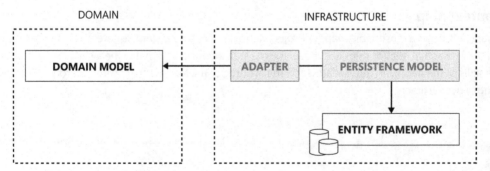

**FIGURE 4-2** The business-oriented domain model is converted into a persistence model tailor-made for the physical database structure managed by Entity Framework.

Finally, a conformist relationship is inevitable between the infrastructure context and the external services to which the application itself is a subscriber. For example, suppose SendGrid introduces breaking changes to the public interface of its API. In that case, all subscribers must conform to the new interface if they want to continue using the service.

# Designing the physical context map

With the big-picture aspects of Project Renoir clear in mind, let's create a physical context map. This will show the organization of the Visual Studio projects that, once assembled, will build the application. Figure 4-3 lists these projects and their dependencies.

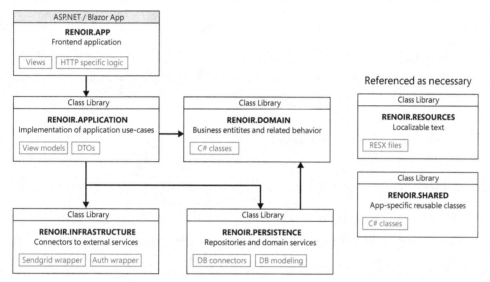

**FIGURE 4-3** The physical context map for Project Renoir.

## The front-end application project

Conceived as an ASP.NET Core application, Project Renoir is actually configured as a Blazor server application. All views are managed and rendered on the server and served as fast-to-render HTML to the browser.

The processing of incoming requests is assigned to MVC or code-behind classes of Razor pages, as appropriate. (This is determined on a case-by-case basis.) HTTP context information is exclusively managed at this level and never trespasses the boundary of controllers or code-behinds.

The front-end application references the application services class library—in fact, the application layer. Ideally, data exchange occurs through tailor-made data-transfer objects (DTOs) defined in the application class library. Any intermediate proxy, though, always represents a cost in terms of development time and sometimes in terms of performance too.

## The application services library

This class library project contains the entry points of each business task that users can request from the front end. The front-end application just formalizes commands out of raw HTTP requests and dispatches them to this logical layer. Any task is orchestrated from start to finish, distinct actions of the underlying process are spawned (sequentially or in parallel), and results are collected and merged as appropriate. Beyond implementing the actual business use cases, the library exposes all necessary DTOs to communicate in both directions with the presentation layer.

Note (again) that the application layer is not necessarily reusable across multiple front ends. If the overall application exposes multiple front ends for collecting data and requests such as web, mobile, or even an AI-based chatbot, each of these may need its own application layer or, at a minimum, its own personalization of the common application layer.

Figure 4-4 shows a presentation layer with multiple front ends. Two of these (web browser and mobile app) call directly into the same application layer API. The chatbot front end, however, calls into a dedicated API that, realistically, may take care of adapting the raw JSON feed captured by the chatbot into well-formed and semantically correct calls into the core application services.

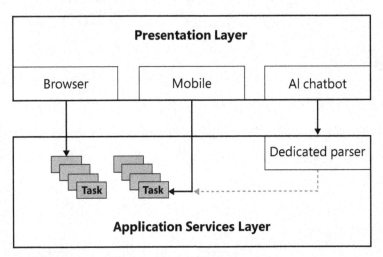

**FIGURE 4-4** Presentation layer with multiple front ends.

> **Note** The advent of large language models (LLMs), of which GPT (short for *generative pre-trained transformer*) is one of the most popular, has the true potential of a terrific breakthrough. GPT is a form of artificial intelligence (AI) that possesses a remarkable ability to comprehend and generate human language. Nicely enough, it can also turn its understanding into a formal JSON feed, ready for an endpoint to receive. The use of LLMs has the potential to spark a completely new breed of applications as well as a new development paradigm: conversational programming. For more information, we recommend *Programming Large Language Models with Azure OpenAI* by Francesco Esposito (Microsoft Press, 2024).

In Project Renoir, you'll code the application layer as a class library referenced directly from the front-end ASP.NET application. That can be easily wrapped up as a NuGet package for easier distribution across teams. Furthermore, with the sole cost of a (minimal) API layer, it can become an autonomously deployable service in a distributed application.

## The domain model library

The domain model is the nerve center of the application. As a class library—ideally wrapped up in an internal-use NuGet package—it defines all business entities.

The DDD philosophy calls for defining these entities as object-oriented classes that honor a number of constraints: factory methods over constructors, no property setters, very limited use of primitive types and, most of all, a set of methods that ensure the class can be used in software workflows in the same way the entity is treated in real business processes.

This library is referenced by the application layer and possibly by the front-end application. It may also be referenced by the persistence layer if no persistence model is defined (whether due to pragmatism, laziness, or attitude. The domain model library has no external dependencies except for the .NET Core framework and a few helper packages.

> **Note** For Project Renoir, you'll use a free NuGet package, Youbiquitous.Martlet, that contains several extension methods and facility classes. This will help you streamline programming and ensure that your code is as readable as possible. This kind of dependency is acceptable in a domain model. To access this package on NuGet, use the following link: *https://www.nuget.org/packages/Youbiquitous.Martlet.Core*.

## The infrastructure library

In a DDD-inspired layered architecture, the infrastructure layer serves as the depot of several services, such as data access and persistence, integration of external services (for example, the email platform and message queues), caching, logging, file system access, authentication, and cryptography.

Ultimately, it falls to the team leaders to decide whether to implement all these functions in a single project or to split them into multiple projects. This decision depends on various factors, including the need to manage scalability in a timely manner, team availability, and the skills of the team members involved. It also depends on the nature of the application and the number and weight of the required functions. The higher the impact of an infrastructural function, the more you want to isolate it to minimize the likelihood of breaking or slowing down other parts. If all you need is data access and an email service, however, everything can be packed up in a single class library project.

More for demo purposes than for actual needs, in Project Renoir, you'll separate infrastructure and persistence layers. Referenced by the application layer, the infrastructure layer sends emails and performs authentication. To achieve this, it references the persistence layer for physical access to databases.

### The persistence library

This is the only place in the whole application where database details (for example, connection strings, the number and design of tables, and so on) are known and managed explicitly. This layer references whatever (micro) O/RM or data access API (for example, raw SQL, ADO.NET, Mongo DB, Cosmos DB, or Dapper) you intend to use.

In Project Renoir, the persistence library will hold a reference to Entity Framework Core and the SQL Server connector. All application entities not strictly related to the business domain, or that don't have a direct link to nouns in the UL, will be coded in a dedicated, internal namespace of the persistence layer.

### Helper libraries

Very rarely, an application that supplies a web front end doesn't need to be localized. However, even if an application doesn't strictly require it, it's a good practice to use resource files and mnemonic monikers for any visual text. It also helps structure the verbal communication between the application and end users and removes ugly and always dangerous magic strings all over the place.

The immediacy of just putting some static text in a Razor view is unparalleled. At the same time, though, programming is the art of method much more than it is the art of getting straight to the point, no matter what. Furthermore, programming is the art of establishing a bridgehead in the domain of the problem to identify a working solution. The most effective way to achieve this is to go straight to the point *with* a method. Using resource files for visual text and packaging it in a separate helper library is just a good practice—one with significant potential and a minimal surcharge.

Along with a library of localizable strings, in Project Renoir, you will find a shared library with miscellaneous classes and functions. This is largely business-agnostic code that's good to have coded just once. In my programming style, most of the time, these are extension methods that are not general-purpose enough to make it to a NuGet package.

 **Note** Helper libraries may prove necessary to encapsulate somewhat reusable classes and functions in a sandbox to prevent them from spreading and hiding throughout the codebase.

## Business requirements engineering

Whether done up front or along the way, collecting and processing business requirements is a crucial and unavoidable activity. The internet literature is full of buzzwords and self-branded, loudly marketed recipes for this. I have nothing to sell here, but I'd love to link together some observables.

# Breakdown of software projects

I've been in software since the forgotten days of enterprise waterfall projects, in which a rigid sequential flow demanded that each phase of the project rely on the deliverables from the previous phase, and that each phase focus on specialized tasks with nearly no overlap.

## The waterfall model

Devised in a different software business era, the waterfall model is treated badly today—seen as a legacy antique at best and worthless junk at worst. However, the steps on which it is based are invariant and universal. A typical waterfall flow follows six steps:

1. Capture software requirements in a product requirements document.

2. Build models, schema, and business rules based on requirements.

3. Outline the software architecture based on the models, schema, and rules.

4. Write the necessary code based on the software architecture.

5. Test and debug the code.

6. Depending on test results, deploy the system to production.

What makes waterfall look obsolete today is not the constituent steps but the order in which they occur. Ultimately, the waterfall model is too rigid and formal (read: slow) for the time-to-market needs of the modern software business.

## The (non) sense of Agile

In 2001, a group of software developers signed what they called the *Agile Manifesto*. This document outlined a new software-development approach to combat the rigidity of the waterfall model. The 12 original principles laid out in the *Agile Manifesto* are pure common sense. They're impossible to disagree with. However, they are also too abstract to give specific guidance to working teams.

Since the release of the *Agile Manifesto*, Agile-branded methodologies have proliferated, each with the perfect recipe to take projects home on time and on budget. But the initial question remains largely unanswered: How do you realistically collect and make sense of requirements in a timely manner without jeopardizing the market appeal of the solution?

Since the formalization of DDD in 2004, a lot has happened in the software industry along a track that runs parallel with Agile. Whereas the term Agile deviated toward project management, the concept of *events within a business domain* emerged in software design as a method to replace the waterfall model.

Within a business domain, an *event* is a significant and relevant occurrence. Events represent notable changes or interactions within the domain, capturing important information that can trigger subsequent actions.

# Event-based storyboards

In the previous decade, a couple of correlated methodologies solidified around the concept of events in a business domain: event storming and event modeling. Although they each resulted from a different approach, both deliver the same output: a visual representation of the expected system's behavior, organized as a collection of flowcharts rooted in fundamental business events.

The overall look and feel of the output of event modeling and event storming resembles a storyboard. Indeed, event-based storyboarding provides a modern and effective way to summarize the first four steps of the waterfall model. Following a storyboarding session, you may be ready to begin conceptualizing the architecture and writing code. Along with proper coding strategies (for example, unit-testing, a test-driven development, and so on) and DevOps artifacts (that is, continuous deployment pipelines), storyboarding turns the old, multi-phase waterfall into a more agile, two-step version: storyboarding and development.

## Event storming

Event storming is a collaborative technique, usually conducted within the boundaries of a (preferably) in-person workshop, to facilitate exploration and comprehension of a business domain. Although it was conceived for the purposes of planning a software application, the technique can be applied to nearly any business-related brainstorming or assessment activity.

In an event-storming session, stakeholders, domain experts, software experts, and sales team members work together to identify and define relevant events that occur within the system. Discovered events are typically represented as sticky notes or cards arranged in chronological order on a timeline. For each discovered event, it is key to identify the trigger, whether it's a user action, another event, or some external factor.

In addition to events, event storming involves capturing the following:

- **Commands**   These represent actions or requests initiated by users or other systems.

- **Aggregates**   These are logical groupings of related events and data.

- **Policies**   These capture the business rules and constraints that must be respected.

The outcome of event storming is simply a mental model supplemented by photos of the whiteboard and written notes to keep some persistent memory of it. However, the knowledge acquired during event storming serves as a valuable reference for the development team throughout the software development life cycle. It also ensures a shared understanding among stakeholders, facilitates communication and collaboration, and provides a solid foundation for designing and implementing the system in a fully aligned manner.

## Event modeling

Shortly after the "invention" of event storming came an approach called *event modeling*. It allows for a deeper analysis at a level of detail closer to that of programming. Put another way, event storming focuses on uncovering and understanding the problem space, whereas event modeling aims to create a blueprint of the final application. The core of event modeling is in the definition of longer stories, built as the concatenation of business events in which changes of state and service boundaries are identified and marked out clearly.

The outcome of domain modeling is a structured representation of the essential concepts, relationships, and rules that define a specific problem domain. The primary outputs of domain modeling are as follows:

- **Domain model diagrams**   These visual representations use various notations to depict the entities within the domain and how they relate to each other. Common diagram types are class diagrams (in UML) and entity-relationship diagrams.

- **Entity definitions**   Each entity within the domain has defined its attributes and behavior through properties and methods. This provides a clear understanding of what information each entity should hold and how it can be manipulated.

- **Use cases**   A use case, or scenario, is the representation of a specific interaction that the application can have with its external actors. A use case illustrates how the application behaves in response to certain events or actions, typically from the perspective of an external user.

To some extent, event modeling can also be used to explore the problem space, but the opposite is not true. By the same token, event storming can explore areas of the business not strictly related to software development—for example, to validate a business idea or assess a production system.

The primary goal of domain modeling is to facilitate clear communication and shared understanding among developers, domain experts, and other project stakeholders. This shared understanding, in turn, serves as a foundation for developing software that accurately and effectively addresses the specific needs and requirements of the problem domain. It helps reduce ambiguity, improve the software's alignment with the real-world domain, and supports more efficient software development and maintenance processes.

> **Note**  Event modeling shines at exploring the problem space, whereas event storming focuses more on the exploration of the business processes. In this regard, event storming can explore areas of the business not strictly related to software development—for example, to validate a business idea or assess a production system.

## Fundamental tasks of Project Renoir

To assess the features of the sample Project Renoir, let's first identify the actions we want users of the application to complete. (See Figure 4-5.) It all starts from the product, for which it is critical to have release notes and roadmap documents that can be managed, explored, and shared by authorized users.

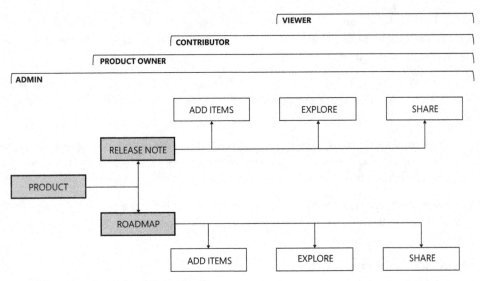

**FIGURE 4-5** Functions map of Project Renoir.

## User access control

In Renoir, there will be four distinct roles:

- **Admin**   Users with this role have superpowers; they can control and override every aspect of products and contributions. The creation of new products is a prerogative of admins too.

- **Product owner (PO)**   As shown in Figure 4-5, the PO has jurisdiction over the entire life cycle of product-specific release notes and roadmaps. This includes the power to nominate contributors and give individual viewers permission to view and share read-only versions of the documents.

- **Contributor**   Users with this role have permission to create, read, edit, share, and/or download documents for one or more products.

- **Viewer**   This role is for individuals inside and outside the organization who need permission to view, share, and/or download a specific document.

The entire Renoir application is available only to authenticated users.

## Product-related features

The product catalog lists software products for which release notes and roadmaps are issued and updated. The product catalog supports basic create, read, update, delete (CRUD) functions. When a product owner logs into the product catalog, they will see only those products to which they have been granted access.

From the documents manager section, product owners create, edit, review, and share release notes and roadmap documents. This user interface is also available to any contributors for which the PO has granted permissions spanning from read-only, to read-write, up to sharing and deleting.

From the export manager, it is possible to allow users to share documents via email, download them as Word files in HTML format, save them as PDF files, and print them. Users perform these actions from the export manager. The export subsystem is subject to strict, permission-based control.

# Boundaries and deployment of the presentation layer

The final Project Renoir application is deployed to an Azure app service to use the default in-process hosting model: ASP.NET Core applications. In-process hosting means that the application is hosted directly within an IIS application pool, running within the same process as the IIS worker process (w3wp.exe).

In contrast, out-of-process hosting involves running the application in a separate process from the IIS worker process. In this case, requests made to the IIS (acting as a reverse proxy server) are forwarded to the ASP.NET Core internal Kestrel web server.

## Knocking at the web server's door

The first thing that Project Renoir users see is a login page. This is an unavoidable step unless the user can present a valid and unexpired authentication cookie. The initial hit of the login page and any successive interaction involves a negotiation between the client browser and the IIS HTTP listener on the Azure side.

### The IIS middleware

In Azure app services, when the in-process hosting model is in place, the IIS middleware—a tailor-made IIS plugin—acts as a web server to handle incoming HTTP requests. Installed on top of an ASP.NET Core application, the middleware intercepts the request and performs initial processing tasks such as handling SSL/TLS, managing connection pooling, and managing the hosting environment.

When this initial processing is done, the IIS middleware then routes the request to the appropriate ASP.NET Core application. This routing is typically based on URL patterns and configuration settings. The middleware passes the request to the ASP.NET Core runtime, which then invokes the appropriate middleware pipeline and executes the necessary middleware components to handle the request.

### The ASP.NET Core middleware

The ASP.NET Core middleware pipeline consists of various components that perform tasks such as authentication, authorization, request/response transformations, logging, caching, and much more. Each middleware component in the pipeline can inspect, modify, or terminate the request/response as needed.

After the request has been processed by the middleware pipeline, the resulting response is sent back through the IIS middleware, which then delivers it to the client. In summary, the IIS middleware in ASP.NET Core acts as a bridge between the IIS web server and the ASP.NET Core application, facilitating the processing of HTTP requests and managing the hosting environment.

The crucial step in the ASP.NET Core middleware pipeline is the actual processing of the request that generates the response (for example, HTML, JSON, file content) for the caller. This is where the presentation layer of the overall application enters the game.

## The ASP.NET Core application gateway

Each request forwarded to a given ASP.NET Core application is managed by the built-in routing middleware, which examines the URL and matches it against a collection of configured route templates. Each route template specifies a pattern that defines how the URL should look to match a particular route. The overall table of routes results from URL patterns and route attributes placed on individual controller methods.

When a match is found, the routing middleware sets the endpoint for the request, extracts the relevant information from the URL (such as route parameters), and stores it in the request's route data so that subsequent middleware can use it if needed.

The endpoint represents the specific action to be executed to handle the request. Here's an excerpt from the startup class of a typical ASP.NET Core application that uses MVC and Blazor page endpoints:

```
app.UseEndpoints(endpoints =>
{
        endpoints.MapControllerRoute(
                name: "default",
                pattern: "{controller=home}/{action=index}/{id?}");

        // If necessary, place SignalR endpoints here
    endpoints.MapHub<YourSignalrHub>("some URL here");
});

// If server-side Blazor is used, reference the built-in here
// SignalR hub and fallback page
app.MapBlazorHub();
app.MapFallbackToPage("/_Host");
```

# ASP.NET application endpoints

There are three types of ASP.NET application endpoints: MVC methods, Razor pages (with and without the Blazor server layer), and direct minimal API. Interestingly, no ASP.NET Core application is limited to exposing endpoints of just one type. In fact, Project Renoir features all three of them. This is simply for the sake of demonstration. Exposing multiple flavors of endpoints is neither a requirement nor a random or arbitrary idea; whether you do so depends on the scenario. But technically speaking, it is doable.

## MVC methods

It's the classic model of ASP.NET applications to externally expose callable actions. Vaguely inspired by the MVC pattern, according to this model, requests are routed to controller classes that define actions to handle them. Controller classes have methods that trigger business logic and interact with models and views to generate responses.

Quite a bit of work is done by the runtime environment between the receipt of the request and the actual invocation of the actionable controller method. It's mostly for flexibility and neat separation of concerns between logic processing, data management, and response packaging. Controller methods allow for more complex routing, behavior customization, and easier unit testing, as the logic for handling requests is separate from the UI. Controllers provide a clear separation between the request-handling code and the views responsible for rendering the UI.

Sometimes, all this flexibility and rigorous structure comes at the cost of killing the immediacy of development. For this, there are Razor pages and, more recently, minimal API endpoints.

## Razor page code-behind classes

A Razor page is a page-based programming model in ASP.NET Core that combines both the UI and the code for handling requests in a single file. Razor pages were introduced to simplify the development of less complex scenarios where the UI and code logic are tightly coupled, such as basic CRUD operations or simple form submissions. They provide a more straightforward and compact approach, as the code for handling requests may reside directly within the Razor page file.

Razor pages allow a direct content request—the page—whereas controller methods handle requests by defining action methods to process the request and return a response.

A Razor page is a convenient choice for scenarios with tightly coupled UI and logic, while controller methods provide greater flexibility and separation of concerns, making them suitable for more complex applications. Especially if the overall project is also configured as a Blazor server application, the two types of endpoints can easily go hand in hand—even more so when you take further small precautions such as using code-behind classes.

A *code-behind class* is a separate file that contains the logic and event-handling code associated with a Razor page or a Blazor component, providing a separation between the component's UI markup and its code functionality. Conceptually, the code-behind class of a Razor page and the body of a controller method serve the same purpose: to trigger the orchestration of the process that will produce the final response for the client.

## Minimal API endpoints

Minimal API endpoints provide an even more lightweight and streamlined approach for handling HTTP requests. Minimal API is designed to simplify the development process by reducing the ceremony and boilerplate code required for traditional MVCs.

With minimal API, you can define routes and request handlers directly within the startup class of the web application by using attributes like `MapGet`, `MapPost`, and so on. A minimal API endpoint acts more like an event handler, with any necessary code being placed inline to orchestrate workflows, perform database operations, or generate an HTML or JSON response.

In a nutshell, minimal API endpoints offer a concise syntax for defining routes and handling requests, making it easier to build lightweight and efficient APIs. However, minimal APIs might not be suitable for complex applications that require extensive separation of concerns provided by traditional MVC architecture.

# Presentation layer development

Admittedly, in application development, the word *presentation* may sound a bit misleading. Although it evokes the visual and interactive elements of a user interface designed to convey information and engage users, with a web application, it is quite different.

The presentation layer of a web application is operational code that runs on the server. Its only concrete link to the user interface is the markup it produces. We all call it *front end* or *presentation*; we all act as if it is strictly UI-related. But in the end, the presentation layer runs and thrives on the server by way of the artifacts of controllers or Razor pages.

This section explores a few technical aspects and related technologies and, more importantly, how the presentation layer links to the downward layers to ensure separation of concerns.

## Connecting to business workflows

As the programming blocks of the presentation layer (for example, controller methods) process incoming HTTP requests, their main purpose is to trigger the workflow that ultimately produces a response. In terms of event modeling, each incoming request is an event that triggers a new instance of a process or advances a running one.

Internet literature is full of articles and posts that discuss the ideal thickness of controller (or code-behind) methods. Let's try to create some order and clarity.

### Fat-free controller methods

In an ideal world, every controller (or code-behind class) method is as thin as the following:

```
[HttpGet]
public IActionResult ReviewDocument(long docId)
{
    // Let the application layer build a view model
    // containing data related to the request.
    var vm = _doc.GetDocViewModel(docId);

    // Render out the given view template with given data
    return View("/views/docs/doc.cshtml", vm);
}
```

The controller receives input data from the body of the HTTP Get request that the ASP.NET machinery binds to method parameters. Within the body of the controller method, an instance of an application layer service class (_doc in the preceding snippet) fetches and massages any necessary data into a view model class. Finally, the view model class is passed as an argument to the View method in charge of merging the selected view template with view model data.

The schema is not much different in the case of HTTP Post requests.

```
[HttpPost]
        public IActionResult SaveDocument(ReleaseNoteWrapper doc)
        {
            // Let the application layer turn the content of the DTO
            // into a domain model object and save it.
            var response = _doc.SaveDoc(doc);

            // Render out the response of the previous operation
            return Json(response);
        }
```

The controller method receives any necessary data—the content of a document to save—through a tailor-made data-transfer object and passes it to the application layer for further processing. It receives back a command response—usually a custom class—with details on additional processing needed (if any). At a minimum, the response object will contain a Boolean to indicate the final success status of the operation.

## Dependency on the application layer

Ideally, any publicly reachable endpoint should have a connection to a method in the application layer that governs the execution of a specific task. Figure 4-6 illustrates the relationship between the presentation and application layers in the context of an ASP.NET Core web application.

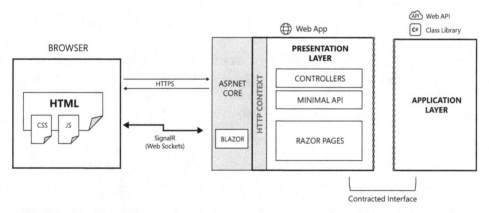

**FIGURE 4-6** From presentation layer to application layer.

The presentation layer is the only segment of a web application where HTTP context information—such as HTTP headers, logged users, or session or cookie data—is directly available. Any part of the HTTP context that business requires to be propagated beyond the boundaries of the presentation layer should be extracted from the envelope and passed as plain data.

```
public IActionResult SaveDocument(ReleaseNoteWrapper doc)
        {
            // Obtain the email of the currently operating user
            var currentUserEmail = User.Logged().Email;
```

```
        // Save the document along with a reference to the actual user
        var response = _doc.SaveDoc(doc, currentUserEmail);
        return Json(response);
    }
```

A contracted programming interface exists between controllers and application layers. The contract is ideally expressed through an interface, and the application services are provided to the controllers via dependency injection.

```
public class DocController
        {
            private IDocService _doc;
            public DocController(IDocService doc)
            {
                _doc = doc;
            }

            // More code
    :
        }
```

In summary, the presentation layer should merely be a pass-through layer that links external commands with internal use-case implementations. It should be as thin as possible and delegate work to other layers down the stack. In terms of dependencies, it should reference only the application layer, and data exchange between the presentation and application layers should take place via DTOs exposed by the application layer.

## Exceptions to the rules

Fortunately, the internal structure of a controller is not strictly ruled, and none of the aforementioned practices have the force of law. You should look at these practices as vectors that indicate a direction and stick to that, but feel free to simplify (in some cases even oversimplify) and apply shortcuts and bypasses as long as everything is done in full awareness of the context.

Typical exceptions to the rules for controllers are as follows:

- Programming directly to instances of application services rather than to interfaces.

- Being lax with DTOs and working with domain model objects at the presentation level as a shortcut. In this case, the presentation layer would set a dependency on the domain model library.

- Coding some very simple actions directly from the controller's method body. Common actions include basic CRUD operations coded in static repository methods, and logging/auditing operations such as tracking user agents and, if authorized, geolocation parameters.

To keep the controller class testable, many suggest injecting application services via interfaces and dependency injection. Using application services from within controllers promotes a clear separation of concerns, as controllers are responsible for handling HTTP requests and responses while application services handle the business logic. There's no question about using application services, but

I argue whether wrapping them in an interface brings concrete benefits—or just the need of using an additional DI layer. Many would argue that not using interfaces makes the controller less testable. True, but are you really willing to test controllers? If you rightly introduce application services, why testing controllers?

As for DTO and domain model objects, there are several reasons why using DTOs should be the first option: separation of concerns, testability challenges, tighter coupling between presentation and domain, and even potential security risks of unwanted data injection. DTOs, though, are yet another layer of code to add, maintain, and test. As usual, it's a trade-off.

## Connection through mediators

You can take one of two approaches to connect the presentation layer to the application layer:

- **Directly invoking methods**   With this approach, one component explicitly invokes the methods of another component to achieve a desired behavior. It's a straightforward and simple way to establish communication between components across layers.

- **Using mediators**   A mediator acts as a centralized hub to coordinate and control interactions between components instead of having those components communicate with each other directly. Instead of invoking methods on each other, parties interact with the mediator, which then relays the commands to the appropriate components. A benefit of this approach is that it decouples components from each other, promoting loose coupling.

In the .NET space, a popular mediator library is MediatR, available at *https://github.com/jbogard/ MediatR*. When MediatR is used in the presentation layer of an ASP.NET application, controller methods interact with the mediator and operate by packing messages, as shown in the following code. The controller knows nothing about the application layer or the code that will ultimately process the issued command.

```
[HttpPost]
        public async Task<IActionResult> SaveDocument(ReleaseNoteWrapper doc)
        {
            // MediatR reference inject via configuration
            await _mediator.Send(new SaveDocumentCommand(doc));
            return StatusCode(201);
        }
```

In MediatR, *messages* are defined as objects that represent requests, commands, or notifications. These messages are used to communicate between the requester and the handlers. The requester is responsible for initiating a request by sending a message to the MediatR pipeline, whereas handlers are tasked with processing messages received from the requester. Each message type can have multiple handlers associated with it. Handlers implement specific logic to handle the messages and produce the desired result.

```
public class SaveDocumentHandler : IRequestHandler<SaveDocumentCommand>
        {
            // Some code
        }
```

It should also be noted that MediatR also supports pub/sub scenarios and can be extended with custom behaviors and pipelines to add cross-cutting concerns, such as logging or validation, to the request/response processing flow.

However, like everything else in code and life, the mediator approach is not free of issues. For example:

- It adds complexity over operations that might otherwise be plain and simple. In fact, for every operation, you must write the actual routine plus the command and the handler class.

- Because the mediator is responsible for coordinating communication between multiple components, it may become more complex as the number of components and message types increases. This complexity can potentially affect the responsiveness of the mediator, especially if it needs to handle a large number of messages or perform complex logic for message routing.

- The mediator is a single point of failure. If it fails or becomes overloaded, it can affect the entire system's communication.

- The mediator itself must resort to optimization, caching, and scalability tricks when handling large volumes.

In the end, what do you really get in return for all this? Loose coupling between presentation and application layers? While there might be situations in which loose coupling at this level is a nice feature, in most common cases, the presentation and application layers work together and therefore must know each other. A plain separation of concerns is more than enough.

> **Note** In complex scenarios, instead of a mediator, you might want to consider using an enterprise-level message bus that supports commands and handlers but is more robust and offers better performance (plus advanced caching/storage features). Put another way, the mediator pattern (of which the MediatR library is a rich implementation) may serve as a bus within the context of a single application.

## Front-end and related technologies

Having established that the presentation layer of an ASP.NET web application is server-side code that is ultimately responsible for pushing out HTML markup, let's examine a few common corollary scenarios.

### Server-side rendering

A lot has happened since the trumpeted days when humankind discovered single-page applications (SPAs). Before that were the prehistoric days of plain old server-side rendering (SSR)—that is, platforms that generated HTML on the server and served it ready-for-display, at no extra cost beyond plain rendering, to client browsers.

On the wave of SPAs, new frameworks conquered the prime time, and terms like *front-end development*, and even *micro-front-end development*, became overwhelmingly popular. The net effect of doing more and more work on the client, combined with a substantial lack of programming discipline, was to reach incredible levels of convoluted code, tons of dependencies on never-heard JavaScript modules, and long waiting times for users upon first display.

Guess what? At some point, all proud proponents of API-only back ends and supporters of the neat separation between front end and back end started eagerly looking back at those days in which HTML could be generated on the server and become instantaneously available to users. No popular front-end frameworks today lack some SSR capabilities in production or on the roadmap. Hence, as of the time of this writing, the future of web development is (again) on the server—which is great news.

## Blazor server apps

As surprising as it may sound, in the .NET space, the oldest line-of-business applications are still built with Web Forms or Windows Forms. Companies that embarked on renewal projects for the most part used popular front-end technologies such as Angular and React. These frameworks, though, have dramatic startup costs—even higher in cases of teams with a strong ASP.NET background.

An excellent alternative for the visual part of the presentation layer in the .NET stack is Blazor—especially the server hosting model. It allows full reuse of ASP.NET skills, promotes C# to the rank of a full-stack language, and returns JavaScript to its original role as a mere scripting language. In this way, Blazor server becomes a technology for building better ASP.NET applications, specifically in terms of responsivity and rapid prototyping—responsivity because you forget page refreshes (except for full navigation to other URLs) due to the underlying SignalR transport, and rapid prototyping because of Razor pages and Blazor's excellent support for componentization. The Blazor version with .NET 8 fits well in this development trend. It is a strong candidate for handling visual presentation in the coming years due to the following features:

- Fast HTML-based initial loading

- Async background tasks

- Component-oriented

- No full-page refreshes

As I see things, pure client-only front ends are destined to become legacy. SSR is the (temporary) winner of the endless war between web technologies. A combination of ASP.NET controllers and Blazor pages is an extremely reasonable solution to employ in web applications.

## The Wisej model

Is there life in the front-end industry beyond Angular, React, and Blazor? An interesting commercial product to consider is Wisej (*https://wisej.com*)—a .NET development platform for building web applications using C#.

With Wisej, developers can create web applications that closely resemble desktop applications, including features like resizable and dockable windows, desktop-style menus, toolbars, and keyboard shortcuts. Wisej follows an SPA architecture, where all necessary UI components and logic are loaded once, and subsequent interactions happen without full page reloads in much the same way as with Blazor. The Wisej programming model closely mimics that of Windows Forms.

Any code you write in Wisej executes on the server, which can provide better performance and scalability compared to traditional client-side JavaScript-based web frameworks. Wisej also allows you to leverage the power of the .NET framework and use existing .NET libraries and components. Finally, Wisej integrates seamlessly with Microsoft Visual Studio, offering a design-time experience and leveraging features and tools such as IntelliSense, debugging, and code refactoring.

# API-only presentation

In addition to HTML markup, an ASP.NET presentation layer may provide clients with JSON payloads. The term *web API* is sometimes used to label API-only ASP.NET servers. It is purely a mnemonic difference; there's no difference between web API applications and plain ASP.NET applications that expose endpoints that return JSON. In both cases, you have controllers or minimal API endpoints.

## Exposing an API over the web

Technically speaking, a UI-less ASP.NET application that only (or mostly) exposes JSON endpoints is similar to a plain ASP.NET application with a visual front end. However, a web API library is subject to a few precautions:

- Support a non-cookie authentication

- Provide fewer runtime services

- Define routes more carefully

- Support a Swagger interface

Within a web API, authentication is preferably implemented using API keys or more sophisticated JSON web tokens (JWTs). API keys are simpler to implement and represent an excellent choice when the primary focus is authorizing rather than collecting and analyzing user-specific information. JWTs work more as a replacement for authentication cookies. They are issued upon successful login, are encrypted and signed, and are subject to expiration. Within a JWT, you might find claims about the user, such as their role and other carry-on information.

Finally, Swagger is an open-source software framework providing a standardized format to describe, test, and visualize RESTful APIs. Linked to the API ASP.NET pipeline, Swagger generates interactive API documentation and test endpoints. It is Swagger in any web API to be shared outside the development team.

## Minimal endpoints

Speaking of web APIs, the aforementioned minimal API endpoints return on stage. They're reachable URLs that perform some action and return some data but are not subject to the ceremony and flexibility of controllers. Minimal APIs do not facilitate authorization, but they don't deny it either. They are yet another option for having the system expose operations to external clients coded and executed in a really quick and direct way.

# Summary

Since their inception, web applications were built to do most of their work on the server. The client was used merely to display prebuilt markup with some little pieces of JavaScript to animate and make it more interactive. At some point—a decade after the explosion of e-commerce and the internet as we know it today—the industry switched to the SPA model in an attempt to add more interactivity and create a smoother and more pleasant user experience.

This attempt, made with all the best intentions, is now deteriorating. Why? Because huge and complex frameworks to support code written in "artificial" (because they're made-to-measure) programming languages form deliverables that are extremely slow to load and painful to develop and maintain.

The current reevaluation of server-side rendering is returning the community to square one—namely, to multi-page applications rendered on the server but with some improved mechanisms to provide rich, interactive experiences in the browser. So, the presentation layer of a web application (again) collects external input and renders the next visual interface. The presentation layer of a web application lives on the server, separated but well connected to other layers.

This chapter introduced the example application—Project Renoir—that will be developed further in the chapters to come. It also summarized the methods to convert a basic understanding of the application into concrete features and projects. Devised with DDD and layered architecture principles in mind, the stage of a reference application that fulfills the vision of a clean architecture is set. In the next chapter, you'll begin focusing on more Visual Studio aspects, functional diagrams, and code.

# CHAPTER 5

# The application layer

*Simplicity is prerequisite for reliability.*

*—Edsgar W. Dijkstra*

The classic three-tier architecture—presentation, business, and data tiers—leaves the burden of deciding what goes where to architects (and often to developers). If it's largely unquestionable where presentation and data access go, the content of the middle tier—and especially its boundaries—has never been clarified. Frankly, *business logic* is more of an umbrella term than a well-defined concept. It represents a group of related concepts such as rules, processes, and operations that define how an organization conducts business.

Such a definition—while perhaps quite clear at a fairly high level of abstraction—becomes blurry when planning project components. That's why, in my opinion, one of the most impactful changes brought by DDD is simply having split business logic into two distinct parts: application logic and domain logic. Domain logic is an invariant in the context of the whole and sits in a position of strength (technically as an upward node) in any relationship within a context map. It expresses how business entities are represented and behave. In contrast, application logic depends on the presentation layer and provides the end-to-end implementation of every single use case that can be triggered from the outside.

As a result, the application layer serves as the beating heart of modern systems designed to chase the ideal of a clean architecture. Within this layer, the intricate interplay of various components and functionalities comes to life, enabling the creation of applications that effectively mirror real-world processes.

This chapter delves into the application layer, exploring key concepts such as task orchestration, cross-cutting concerns, data transfer, exception handling, and deployment scenarios. First, though, it expands on the list of use cases for the Project Renoir application.

## An architectural view of Project Renoir

Project Renoir is a web application implemented in ASP.NET Core. The slice of reality that shines through it centers on three key entities: software product, release notes, and roadmap documents. All use cases therefore relate to creating, editing, and viewing instances of those entities.

Figure 5-1 presents an overall function-oriented view of the Project Renoir application. The login subsystem module is the barrier that users must overcome by providing valid credentials. When this occurs, each user is provided with a list of products to access, depending on what permissions the user has been assigned. Beyond that, each user will have their own menu for conducting CRUD operations on assigned products and documents.

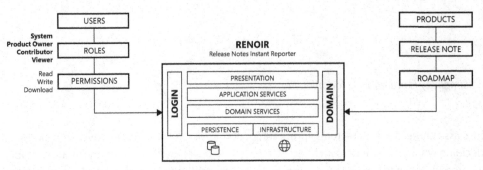

**FIGURE 5-1** An architectural view of the Project Renoir application.

## The access control subsystem

Users, roles, and permissions play a crucial role in managing and regulating user interactions and privileges within an application. In Project Renoir, an admin subsystem is responsible for preparing the application for first use by defining products and assigning the default product owner to each one. The product owner—a regular user with admin permissions for a product—is then free to create new users and give them any desired permissions.

> **Note** Upon creation, every user is only a guest in the system and cannot perform any operation other than logging in and observing an empty page.

## Authenticating users

Each user is identified by an email address and uses a password to authenticate. The user's profile may contain a photo, a display name, and perhaps a few personal notes. Each user record also has a flag to indicate a possible locked-out state. Locked-out users are allowed to attempt to log in but will be denied access. Only the system admin has the power to lock and unlock users.

Project Renoir supports cookie-based authentication, meaning that after credentials have been successfully verified, a unique user identifier is stored in a cookie, which the browser will present on any subsequent request. Project Renoir is envisioned as a document-sensitive application, so it is recommended to check the user lock status regardless of the evidence of a valid cookie. Because this approach requires direct access to the user record on every request, no claims will be saved to the cookie other than the identifier.

## Fixed user/role association

In general, a *role* defines a fixed set of permissions assigned to a user within a system. With roles, one can organize users into logical categories based on their operational requirements. For example, in an e-commerce system, common roles could include admin, customer, and vendor.

This basic pattern works only in relatively flat access-control scenarios, however. For example, in Project Renoir, the product owner role enables a user to perform several operations such as adding contributors and managing documents.

Should any product owner have access to all products? There is no answer that is absolutely right or wrong. It all depends solely on the business requirements. If it is acceptable that all users in a given role can perform all possible operations on the entire dataset, then the role can be assigned to the user once and become a constituent part of the user profile. Otherwise, a more flexible mechanism is necessary.

## Flexible user/asset/role association

The user profile is agnostic of role information, but a separate table keeps track of bindings set between users, assets, and roles. (See Figure 5-2.) As a result, when the user logs in with the same unique credentials, they are shown a list of assets they can work on, although with different roles. Typically, each role has an associated menu of permissible actions and possibly a dedicated controller to group them in a single place. Among this list of functions, there should be a few to edit the binding table and to create/remove bindings.

| User | | Asset | Role |
|------|------|-------|------|
| Email1 | Email1 | Product1 | Owner |
| Email2 | Email1 | Product2 | Contributor |
| | Email1 | Product3 | Contributor |
| | Email1 | Product4 | Viewer |
| USERS | USER-ASSET-ROLE bindings | | |

**FIGURE 5-2** Schema of a USER/ASSET/ROLE association.

**Note** To take this approach even further, consider adding a few more columns to the bindings table to set a start and an end date and/or a Boolean flag to denote the state (active/non-active) of the binding. The benefit is that you maintain a history of bindings and a full record of each user.

## More granular control with permissions

Permissions are access rights granted to a user that define what actions a user is allowed to perform (or not). Permissions are typically tied to specific assets or functions within the system. For instance, a new user might be added to the system with the product owner role but be denied the permission to add new contributors. Likewise, a user with the contributor role might be granted permission to add new contributors to the same asset. (See Figure 5-3.)

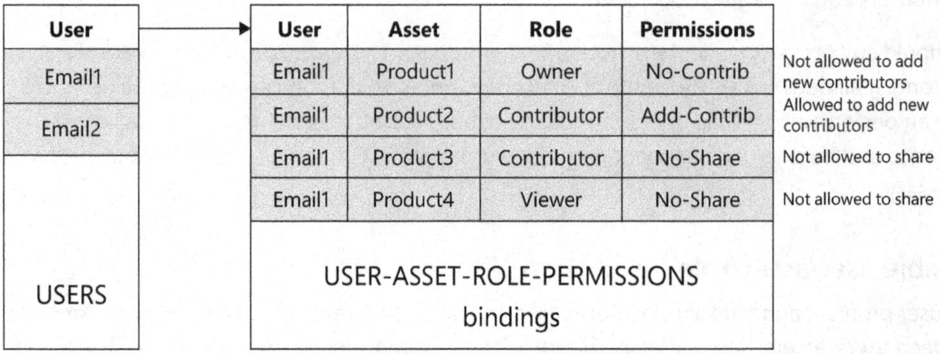

| USERS | | | | |
|---|---|---|---|---|
| **User** | **User** | **Asset** | **Role** | **Permissions** |
| Email1 | Email1 | Product1 | Owner | No-Contrib | Not allowed to add new contributors |
| Email2 | Email1 | Product2 | Contributor | Add-Contrib | Allowed to add new contributors |
| | Email1 | Product3 | Contributor | No-Share | Not allowed to share |
| | Email1 | Product4 | Viewer | No-Share | Not allowed to share |

USER-ASSET-ROLE-PERMISSIONS bindings

**FIGURE 5-3** Schema of a USER-ASSET-ROLE-PERMISSIONS association.

Permissions are more fine-grained than roles and allow for precise control over user actions. This ensures data security and gives customers the necessary flexibility. In summary, permissions are a way to override the characteristics of roles.

# The document-management subsystem

Project Renoir users work on products (software applications) and manage documents related to those products. The application layer implements the following use cases:

- **Product creation**   Only admin users are allowed to create and manage new products. An admin is also responsible for adding product owners. A product is fully described by code, a display name, and an optional logo. In addition, it can be given a start/end date range for support.

- **Document permissions**   Upon login, product owners see the list of products they can work on. An owner is entitled to create and edit new release notes and roadmaps as well as to assign and revoke contributors. A contributor operates based on the permissions received, as in Table 5-1. The granularity of a permission can be adapted as needed. For example, you can grant permission for all documents of a given type or just specific documents.

**TABLE 5-1** List of supported permissions in Project Renoir

| Permission | Description |
|---|---|
| CREATE | Allows the creation of a new document (release note or roadmap) |
| EDIT | Allows the modification of an existing document (release note or roadmap) |

| Permission | Description |
|---|---|
| DELETE | Allows the deletion of an existing document (release note or roadmap) |
| VIEW | Allows the viewing of an existing document (release note or roadmap) |
| DOWNLOAD | Allows the downloading of an existing document (release note or roadmap) |

- **Document sharing**  Documents are presented as a list of items. Bound to a product, a document has a code to identify its type (release note or roadmap), a date of release, a status, and various descriptors. A document item has a type column (for example, bug fix, internal feature, requirement, or new public feature) and a description of the feature. Sharing a document— whether as a printout, a PDF file, or perhaps a Word file—poses the issue of composing the rows of data into a single container with a human-readable structure. Figure 5-4 presents the persistence schema of a Project Renoir document.

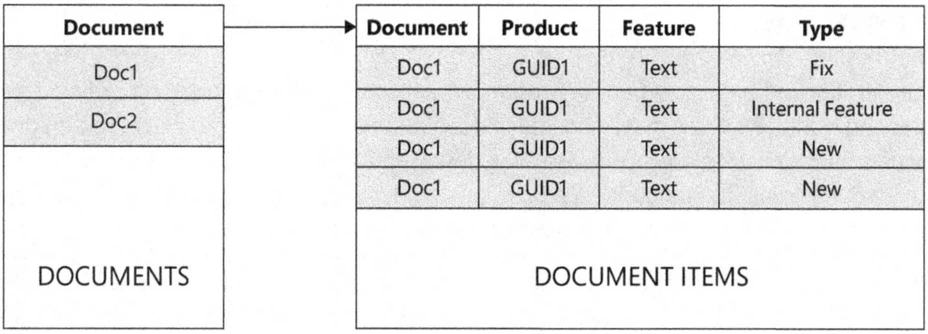

| Document | | Document | Product | Feature | Type |
|---|---|---|---|---|---|
| Doc1 | | Doc1 | GUID1 | Text | Fix |
| Doc2 | | Doc1 | GUID1 | Text | Internal Feature |
| | | Doc1 | GUID1 | Text | New |
| | | Doc1 | GUID1 | Text | New |
| DOCUMENTS | | DOCUMENT ITEMS | | | |

**FIGURE 5-4**  Persistence schema of a document in Project Renoir.

Project Renoir also introduces the concept of a document renderer—the actual implementation of a strategy pattern instance aimed at obtaining data records and returning a printable object. The default renderer uses a Razor template to produce a document that can be printed as HTML or PDF. Another renderer could perhaps build a Word document.

## Project Renoir in Visual Studio

Figure 5-5 shows the example Project Renoir solution live in Visual Studio. The solution comprises seven distinct projects: the startup ASP.NET Core web application and six class library projects. (These project nodes are collapsed in Figure 5-5.) As you can see, the projects follow a consistent naming convention, with a common prefix of Youbiquitous.Renoir followed by App, Application, DomainModel, Infrastructure, Persistence, Resources, and Shared.

The rest of this chapter focuses on the application layer and its main purpose: orchestrating tasks to provide a concrete implementation of use cases.

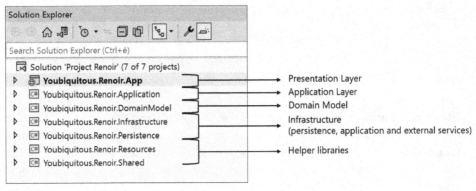

**FIGURE 5-5** Project Renoir at a glance in Visual Studio.

# Task orchestration

Task orchestration lies at the core of building complex applications that seamlessly coordinate multiple processes and workflows. From managing intricate sequences of operations to synchronizing diverse components, task orchestration encompasses the design and implementation of effective systems that are faithful to requirements and business processes, are relatively simple to modify as needed, and can easily be fixed in the event of errors or misinterpretation of business rules.

As the volume of traffic within a system grows, patterns of task orchestration also touch on the fields of efficiency and scalability of operations. However, unless you're researching ways to improve the capacity of a huge application (for example, Netflix or Amazon subsystems), task orchestration is fairly simple, as represented by a plain flow chart with at most a few chained operations in which the results of one are processed by the other. More often, a task is just a few isolated operations whose results are combined in some response object.

This section focuses on the abstract definition of a task and common practices rather than best practices (as *best* is quite problematic to define) for orchestrating tasks.

## What is a task, anyway?

In the current context of a layered software architecture, a *task* is a cohesive piece of functionality within an application—a specific unit of work that represents a meaningful action in the domain. It's a piece of code that receives some input and returns some output—as simple as it could be. Ideally, the task does its job relying on the minimum possible number of dependencies on other layers and services.

In the context of a layered architecture, a task is typically a standalone service class or a method in a cross-feature service class. The class lives in the application layer library. The task is triggered by a request from the outside—typically an HTTP request, a form post, or a scheduled action.

If the task is fully represented by its own service class, then the service class is envisioned as a sort of command handler, with just one publicly invocable method that triggers action and a few protected helper methods to do the actual job. In simpler scenarios, the task can just be one method in a cross-feature service class.

Abstractly speaking, a task encapsulates and coordinates interactions between the presentation layer and the domain layer to achieve a specific business goal. It serves as a bridge between the user interface and the domain logic. A task in the application layer is the ultimate implementation of a user story. A *user story* is a high-level description of a feature or functionality from the perspective of an end-user. It captures the who, what, and why of a particular requirement in a user-centric manner. A user story is intentionally concise. It does not go into the details of a possible technical implementation. Rather, it is a simple placeholder for conversations between the development team and stakeholders to clarify requirements and expectations.

Once a user story is defined, the development team breaks it down into units of works. A task in the application layer is one of these units of work—the root one that coordinates the functioning of most of the others. Other units of work not in the application layer typically relate to designing the user interface and coding data access logic.

A task triggered by some user-interface element to carry out a business operation is not necessarily a self-contained piece of code. Although we have defined a task as the centralized orchestrator of a business operation—and it is at the highest level of abstraction—in practice it may be split into various pieces. In other words, the task is always a single unit of work, but its implementation may not always be an end-to-end flow chart. Rather, it might be split across multiple subtasks invoked asynchronously. The following sections explore both scenarios—a distributed task and a self-contained task.

## An example distributed task

To make sense of tasks broken up into distinct and asynchronous subtasks, let's consider the classic checkout task of an e-commerce application. Typically, the checkout operation reaches its peak at the insertion of a new order record in the database. Before that, though, a lot usually happens. The application layer task triggers after all data has been collected. Here are some likely steps of a checkout flow chart:

1. Validate the input data to see if it coheres with business rules and expectations.

2. Check the payment history of the customer placing the request and raise flags to other subsystems in the event of non-clean records.

3. Check whether the ordered goods are in stock. Also check whether the store will run short of goods after serving the order and, if so, notify other parts of the system.

4. Proceed to payment and interact with any external payment gateway.

5. If all is well, create any necessary database records.

6. Email the customer to confirm order as appropriate.

All these steps are orchestrated by the Checkout task in the application layer. Given the complexity of the operations, it might be coded in a standalone CheckoutService class, as schematized here:

```
public class CheckoutService
{
    // Checkout flow chart (until payment)
    public static CheckoutResponse PreProcess(CheckoutRequest request)
    {
        if (Validate(request))
            return CheckoutResponse.Fail();

        CheckPaymentHistory(request.Customer);
        CheckGoodsInStock(request.Order);

        // Time to pay...
    }

    private bool Validate(CheckoutRequest request)
    {
        :
    }

    private void CheckPaymentHistory(Customer customer)
    {
        :
    }

    private void CheckGoodsInStock(Order order)
    {
        :
    }

    :
}
```

Let's take one step back and look at where in the presentation layer the task is triggered:

```
public class OrderController : Controller
{
    public IActionResult Checkout(CheckoutRequest request)
    {
        var response = CheckoutService.PreProcess(request);
        if (response.Success)
            return Redirect("/payment-gateway");
    }

    public IActionResult PostPayment(PaymentResponse paymentResponse)
    {
        var response = CheckoutService.Finalize(paymentResponse);
        return View("success", response);
    }
}
```

In a real-world e-commerce system, payment occurs outside the control of the application according to slightly different workflows depending on the payment gateway. In some cases, you need to redirect to a dedicated page and indicate via configuration your endpoint to call back after physical processing of the payment. If a redirect to some UI is required, the controller must become part of the orchestration. If the gateway exposes an API, then all can be coordinated by the application layer.

The payment gateway may return a direct JSON response or invoke an endpoint. In the former case, post-processing of the payment and actual creation of orders and confirmation emails take place within the application layer. In the latter case, a new request hits the presentation layer, which must then be forwarded to another segment of the checkout service—in the preceding example, the Post-Payment controller method.

## An example task in Project Renoir

In the example Project Renoir application, no use case requires interaction with external services except perhaps when (or if) a PDF printing service is used. Creating or editing a document is a simple matter of executing a data-driven sequence of operations—most of the time, within a SQL transaction. Thanks to the numerous data access APIs available in .NET Core (for example, Entity Framework, Dapper, and ADO.NET), the underlying database is abstracted away, and the task implementation is all in a self-contained method. Here's a possible outline:

```
public class DocumentService
{
    public static CommandResponse SaveChanges(ReleaseNote doc)
    {
        if (!doc.IsGoodToSave())
            return CommandResponse.Fail();

        return DocumentRepository.SaveReleaseNote(doc);
    }
}
```

It's admittedly a simple scenario, but not too far from many real-world situations. Most applications are line-of-business systems that, for the most part, need only to perform CRUD operations on database tables. For all these cases, a task matches up closely to a SQL transaction. Any method that implements a task coordinate calls to one or more repositories using the same database connection or distinct connections per operation. A use case implementation forms a bridge between presentation and infrastructure and moves data around, from user interface to persistence and back. Let's find out more about data transfer and data representation.

# Data transfer

For a massively distributed application made of relatively focused and small services, data transfer is fairly simple. It's all about plain-old C# classes (POCO) serialized as JSON across endpoints. In this context, the concept of a data transfer object (DTO) shines.

A DTO is a lightweight, immutable data container used to exchange information between different parts of a software application. DTOs promote simplicity and security in data communication—simplicity because a DTO is a POCO packaged with data and devoid of behavior, and security because it is inert data, rather than potentially harmful code, that is serialized and travels across the wire.

# From the presentation layer to the application layer

For every request to a web application, the presentation layer manages data from two sources—one explicit and one implicit. The explicit data source is the data the layer receives through query strings, route parameters, or the body of the request. It's packaged as plain text within an HTTP request. The implicit data source is the HTTP context that may hold information about the session state, HTTP headers, cookies, and the authentication state—namely, claims about the currently logged user. In observance of separation of concerns, no information in one layer should be directly accessible from another layer. At the same time, any information that must be forwarded should be rendered through plain DTOs.

## Implementing DTOs in C#

Conceptually, a DTO is a plain C# class, but C# offers three data structures to code a DTO:

- **Class** A *class* is a reference type that represents a blueprint for creating objects. Instances of classes are typically allocated on the heap, and variables of class types hold references to the actual objects. Classes support inheritance and are mutable by default, meaning you can change the values of their fields and properties after creating an instance. Finally, a class can contain methods, properties, fields, and events.

- **Struct** A *struct* is a value type. Instances of structs are typically stack-allocated, making them generally more lightweight than classes. Structs are suitable for representing small, simple data types like points, rectangles, or simple numeric types. They do not support inheritance but can implement interfaces. By default, structs are mutable, but you can create immutable structs using the readonly modifier. Structs are passed by value, meaning they are copied when passed to methods or assigned to other variables. The default equality comparison for structs is based on value comparison. Two structs with the same field values are considered equal.

- **Record** A *record* is a reference type like a class but optimized for immutability and equality comparison. Records provide a concise syntax for declaring properties and automatically generate value-based equality comparisons. Records are immutable by default, meaning their properties cannot be changed after creation. To modify properties, you must use the with keyword to create a new record with the desired modifications.

Which one should you use for DTOs? Any option is good, but records were introduced with C# 9 in 2020 to provide a tailor-made solution for modeling data-centric classes and DTOs.

## Disconnecting from the HTTP context

Usually, most information in the HTTP context of the current request lives and dies within the boundaries of the presentation layer. There are a few relevant exceptions, though.

The unique identifier (for example, email address or username) of the logged user often travels deep down the stack to reach the level of database repositories. This occurs when, for auditing purposes, you log the author of each relevant action. In Project Renoir, for example, you will need to keep track of the author of each version of each document. The name of the author is extracted as a plain string from the authentication cookie and propagated across the layers.

Any web application that uses session state does so because any stored information must then be consumed by some other layer down the stack. A good example is a shop application (for example, a ticketing platform) that needs to track the session ID of the user to retrieve the content of the shopping cart.

Another small piece of information to extract and propagate from the HTTP context may be the language in use, whether it comes from a dedicated culture cookie or the browser's settings. Finally, one more chunk of data to capture and propagate, if required, is the IP address of the caller.

As a rule, no information in the HTTP context should trespass the boundaries of the presentation layer. Hence, any information that must be consumed elsewhere should be extracted and explicitly passed as an argument, as shown here:

```
public IActionResult Checkout()
{
    var cart = (ShoppingCart) Session["ShoppingCart"];
    CheckoutService.PreProcess(cart);
    :
}
```

More realistically, you want to be very careful when it comes to session state in modern web applications. *Session state* refers to the storage of user-specific data on the server between HTTP requests. It's a simple and secure practice that was widely used during the first three decades of the World Wide Web. Today, however, it faces one huge drawback: conceived to live in the memory of one specific server, the session state is unreliable in a multi-server scenario, which is fairly common today.

Sticky sessions are an alternative. In this case, the load balancer that distributes traffic across the server farm also takes care of consistently routing user requests to the same server during the same session. Another alternative is to implement sessions through a distributed storage such as a SQL database or a cache platform (for example, Redis). A broadly accepted approach is simply to use a distributed cache instead of a session and perhaps use only a session ID as a unique identifier to index data in the cache.

## The input view model

In an ASP.NET web application, any user click or API invocation initiates a request handled by a controller class. Each request is turned into an action mapped to a public method defined on a controller class. But what about input data?

As mentioned, input data is wrapped up in the HTTP request, whether in the query string, any form of posted data, or perhaps HTTP headers or cookies. Input data refers to data being posted for the system to take an action.

Input data can be treated as loose values and mapped to primitive variables (int, string, or DateTime) or grouped into a class acting as a container. If a class is used, the ASP.NET model binding subsystem automatically matches HTTP parameters and public properties on the bound class by name.

```
// Parameters to build a filter on some displayed table of data are expressed as loose values
public IActionResult Filter(string match, int maxRows)
{
    var model = FilterTable(match, maxRows);
    :
}

// Parameters to build a filter on some displayed table of data are expressed as a class
public IActionResult Filter(Query query)
{
    var model = FilterTable(query.Match, query.MaxRows);
    :
}
```

The collection of input classes forms the overall input model for the application. The input model carries data in the core of the system in a way that precisely matches the expectations of the user interface. Employing a separated input model makes it easier to design the user interface in a strongly business-oriented way. The application layer will then unpack any data and consume it as appropriate.

### The response view model

Any request ultimately generates a response. Often, this response is an HTML view or a JSON payload. In both cases, you can spot a response DTO class that is calculated to finalize the processing of the request. If HTML must be served, the response class holds the data to be embedded in the HTML view. If JSON must be served, the response class just holds the data to be serialized.

In ASP.NET MVC, the creation of an HTML view is governed by the controller that invokes the back end of the system and receives some response. It then selects the HTML template to use and passes it and any data to an ad-hoc system component called the view engine. The view engine then mixes the template and data to produce the markup for the browser.

In summary, the application layer receives input model classes and returns view model classes:

```
public IActionResult List(CustomerSearchInputModel input)
{
    var model = _service.GetListOfCustomers(input);
    return View(model);
}
```

**Important** In general, the ideal data format for persistence differs from the ideal format for presentation. The presentation layer is responsible for defining the clear boundaries of acceptable data, and the application layer is responsible for accepting and providing data in just those formats.

## Are domain entities an option?

When it comes to plain CRUD actions on domain entities, is it acceptable to bypass input and view model classes and just use domain entities? Here's an example:

```
[HttpPost]
public IActionResult Save(ReleaseNote doc)
{
    var response = _service.Save(doc);
    return Json(response);
}
```

The Save method in some controller class receives data to save (or create) a release note document—a domain entity in the Project Renoir application. Built-in ASP.NET model binding does the magic of matching HTTP values to properties of the domain entities.

Is this approach recommended? Generally, it is not, for two reasons:

- It is not entirely secure.

- It generates dirtier code than necessary.

As far as security is concerned, by using a domain entity as the target of an endpoint, you delegate to the ASP.NET model binding subsystem the task of binding input HTTP data to properties of the entity. The state injected in the domain entity is not entirely under your control.

If the controller method is effectively invoked from the HTML page (and/or JavaScript code) you wrote, then all is well. But what if someone sets up an HTML form injection attack? An HTML form injection attack is when an attacker injects malicious content into the fields of an HTML form to manipulate the application's behavior or compromise user data. For example, an entity passed down to repositories could set fields you don't expect to be set or could pass dangerous parameters. This risk undoubtedly exists, but if you require proper validation and sanitize the entity's content before proceeding with storage or action, you reduce it nearly to zero.

Another reason to avoid putting domain entities at the forefront of a controller's methods is that conceptually, a domain entity is *not* a DTO. By design, a DTO has public `get`/`set` methods on properties and freely accepts and returns data via properties. A domain entity may be a different, much more delicate beast in which you hardly have public setters and resort to behavioral methods to alter the state. Hence, for model binding to work on domain entities, domain entities must open their properties setters, which may spoil the design of the business domain.

All this said, is this approach acceptable? Speaking pragmatically, yes, it is. But it all depends on how much pragmatism you (are allowed to) support.

> **Note** The point of having public setters in domain classes is broader than discussed so far, as it touches on the design of the persistence model used by Entity Framework (or other data access frameworks) to persist data to some storage. We'll return to this topic in a moment, and in much more detail in the next chapter.

# From the application layer to the persistence layer

The application layer receives DTOs from the presentation layer and orchestrates business tasks, such as handling database operations coded in repository classes and building response models for HTML views or JSON payloads. Data must flow from the application layer toward more inner layers, performing various calculations, and return to be massaged in view-oriented models.

## Exchanging data with repositories

By design, a repository class encapsulates the logic required to access well-defined aggregates of data. Repositories centralize common data access functionality while decoupling the infrastructure used to access databases from all other layers. Ideally, you aim at having one repository class per aggregate root.

*Aggregate root* is a DDD term that refers to the principal (root) entity of a cluster of domain entities that are better treated as a single unit of data for the purpose of CRUD operations. For example, in Project Renoir, the `ReleaseNote` entity is an aggregate root that encompasses the `ReleaseNoteItem` entity. Put another way, you don't want to give a release-note item its own independent layer of CRUD operations because the business domain itself doesn't recognize an item if it is not bound to a release note. Subsequently, any CRUD operation that involves a release-note item necessarily passes through the release note aggregate root. (More on this in the next chapter.)

**Note** By design, the methods of a repository class accept and return data as lists, or instances, of domain entities.

In the case of update operations, it is essentially up to you to either pass pre-built domain entities to repositories for them to blindly process or just pass loose values and have repositories create any necessary domain entities. The more work you delegate to repositories, the harder it gets to produce a generic structure of repository classes that would dramatically reduce the number of necessary classes.

In the case of queries, the application layer obtains data from the persistence layer expressed as domain entities. This data may flow into rendering models without concerns. If the rendering model produces HTML, then its server-side Razor views process it to prepare inert HTML for the browser. If the rendering model produces JSON, the domain entity is serialized into inert data and reduced to a plain DTO.

**Note** For JSON payloads obtained from the serialization of domain entities, you may face additional issues. By nature, domain entities are inherently intricate, with classes that refer to each other following the connections of the real-world business domain. When it comes to serialization, you risk obtaining quite large chunks of data or, worse, data incurring in cycles. Therefore, it is recommended that you always export relevant data of domain entities to ad hoc DTOs before serializing them as JSON.

## Persistence model versus domain model

Abstractly speaking, the domain model is a plain software model expected to mirror the business domain. It is not strictly related to persistence but serves the supreme purpose of implementing business rules. Yet, at some point, data must be read from storage and saved. How does this happen?

If you save data using, say, non-O/RM frameworks (for example, a stored procedure or ADO.NET), then no confusion arises around the role of the domain model. Moreover, its design can follow the characteristics of the business domain without conflicts or constraints. If you use an O/RM, however, things might be different—especially if the O/RM you use is a fairly powerful and invasive one, like Entity Framework. An O/RM needs its own model of data to map to database tables and columns. Technically, this is a *persistence model*.

What's the difference between a domain model and a persistence model? A domain model that focuses on logic and business rules inevitably has classes with factories, methods, and read-only properties. Factories, more than constructors, express the logic necessary to create new instances. Methods are the only way to alter the state of the entities according to business tasks and actions. Finally, properties are simply a way to read the current state of an instance of the domain model.

A domain model is not necessarily an entity relationship model. It can be simply a collection of sparse and loose classes that just contain data and behavior. In contrast, a persistence model matches the target database exactly. Its classes must honor relationships between tables and map to columns via properties. Furthermore, classes of a persistence model have no behavior and are effectively plain DTOs.

If the persistence model and the domain model are not the same thing, are both necessary? Technically speaking, you should have both, and you should introduce mapper classes to go from, say, the ReleaseNote entity rich class to the anemic class that represents how the release-note data is laid out on some (relational) database table. This is often a huge pain in the neck. Some middle ground is possible, though: using a partially pure domain model.

The domain model is initially designed to be pure and business-oriented with value types, factories, behavior, and private setters. At some point, Entity Framework stops saving and loading the domain model, complaining that it misses a default constructor or a public setter. By simply releasing the constraints as they show up and isolating the database mapping in a distinct partial class, you can have an acceptable compromise: a sufficiently elegant and independent domain model that also works well as a persistence model. (More on this in the next chapter.)

## Dealing with business logic errors

Any service class method in the application layer is invoked to execute either a command or query for some segment of the current application state. In the latter case, all it is expected to return is a response object, empty or in a default state, in case of failure. If the requested operation is a command, it should return an application-specific object that represents the response to the execution of a command. Project Renoir uses a class like the following:

```
public class CommandResponse
{
    public bool Success { get; }
```

```
    public string Message { get; }
    :

    public CommandResponse(bool success = false, string message = "")
    {
        Success = success;
        Message = message;
    }
    public static CommandResponse Ok()
    {
        return new CommandResponse(true);
    }
    public static CommandResponse Fail()
    {
        return new CommandResponse();
    }
}
```

This class can be extended and expanded in many ways—for example, to receive an exception object and to carry additional strings representing IDs, URLs, or even error codes. It serves two main purposes: reporting an error message and reporting a flag that clearly indicates whether the operation was successful.

# Implementation facts

The ASP.NET platform moved toward a revisited model-view-controller (MVC) pattern around 2010. Since the beginning, controllers—the beating heart of the presentation layer—have been designed as a fairly thick and highly flexible layer of code. As a result, every request involves a long trip through middleware to reach the final destination of an action method. In ASP.NET Core, nearly all middleware services are optional, and the developer is in full control of the length of the pipeline that connects an HTTP request to some action method.

Once within the boundary of an action method, a broadly accepted practice is to offload work related to the implementation of the use case to an application service. But how should you physically code an application layer?

## Outline of an application layer

Earlier in this chapter, Figure 5-5 showed the Project Renoir solution in Visual Studio, in which it was evident that the application layer was a separate class library project. In this class library project, one can expect to have a collection of application service classes. Each method in these classes delivers the end-to-end implementation of a use case.

Application service classes (and, why not, solution folders) serve the sole purpose of grouping use-case workflows into coherent and consistent aggregates. The granularity that counts is that of public methods rather than public classes. This said, in general, you might want to aim at having a one-to-one relationship between controller and application service classes so that, say, DocumentController offloads its use cases to an instance of DocumentService and its methods.

## An application service blueprint

Let's try to build a skeleton for an application service that serves as the blueprint for any classes in the application. In Project Renoir, all application service classes inherit from a common base class: `ApplicationServiceBase`. The inheritance is set up for the sole purpose of easily sharing a subset of features among all application service classes.

```
public class ApplicationServiceBase
{
    public ApplicationServiceBase(RenoirSettings settings) :
        this(settings, new DefaultFileService(settings.General.TemplateRoot))
    {
    }

    public ApplicationServiceBase(RenoirSettings settings, IFileService fileService)
    {
        Settings = settings;
        FileService = fileService;
    }
    /// <summary>
    /// Reference to application settings
    /// </summary>
    public RenoirSettings Settings { get; }

    /// <summary>
    /// Reference to the app-wide file service
    /// (i.e., required to load email templates from files)
    /// </summary>
    public IFileService FileService { get; }

}
```

This example base class shares two functions with all its inheritors: application settings and file services. We'll return to application settings in a moment. For now, let's focus on the file I/O service.

## Abstracting file access

The `IFileService` optional interface abstracts access to the file system in case plain text files must be read from and saved to disk. A possible use case for the file service is reading email templates or any sort of configuration data from disk files deployed as part of the web application.

```
public interface IFileService
{
    string Load(string path);
    void Save(string path, string content);
}
```

If your application makes intensive use of files, you can extend the interface as much as needed. As long as text files are all you need, you can start from the following minimal implementation:

```
public class DefaultFileService : IFileService
{
    private readonly string _root;
    public DefaultFileService(string root = "")
```

```
    {
        _root = root;
    }

    public string Load(string path)
    {
        var file = Path.Combine(_root, path);
        if (file == null)
            return null;

        var reader = new StreamReader(file);
        var text = reader.ReadToEnd();
        reader.Close();
        return text;
    }

    public void Save(string path, string content)
    {
        throw new NotImplementedException();
    }
}
```

Any implementation of IFileService lives in the infrastructure layer as a system service to man-age the file system visible to the application, but it is mostly managed by the application layer.

## Implementing a use-case workflow

To form a clear idea of the code that goes into an application layer class, let's focus on a common scenario: the password reset. If a user forgets a password, they click a link on the login page to initiate a controller method like the one that follows:

```
public partial class AccountController
{
    [HttpGet]
    [ActionName("recover")]
    public IActionResult DisplayForgotPasswordView()
    {
        var model = SimpleViewModelBase.Default(Settings);
        return View(model);
    }

    // More code
}
```

The user then enters the email address where they want to receive the link to reset the password and posts the form. The following action method captures this:

```
public partial class AccountController
{
    private readonly AuthService _auth;
    public AccountController(HospiSettings settings, IHttpContextAccessor accessor)
        : base(settings, accessor)
    {
```

```
        // Alternatively, add AuthService to DI and inject the reference in the constructor
        _auth = new AuthService(Settings);
    }

    [HttpPost]
    [ActionName("recover")]
    public IActionResult SendLinkForPassword(string email)
    {
        var lang = Culture.TwoLetterISOLanguageName;
        var response = _auth.TrySendLinkForPasswordReset(email, ServerUrl, lang);
        return Json(response);
    }

    // More code
}
```

The _auth variable references an instance of the application layer class in charge of account-related use cases. The class is named AuthService. The password-reset workflow is orchestrated from within the TrySendLinkForPasswordReset method. This method receives as loose values the email address of the requesting user, the root URL of the current application, and the ISO code of the language set on the current thread. The method returns a command response object with a Boolean flag to denote success or failure and an optional error message to present to the user.

```
public async Task<CommandResponse> TrySendLinkForPasswordReset(
        string email, string server, string lang)
{
    // 1. Get the user record using the email as the key
    // 2. Generate a token (GUID) and save it in the user record
    var user = UserLoginRepository.PrepareAccountForPasswordReset(email);

    // 3. Prepare the text of parameters to be inserted in the email text
    var parameters = EmailParameters.New()
            .Add(EmailParameters.Link, $"{server}/account/reset/{user.PasswordResetToken}")
            .Build();

    // 4. Finalize and send email
    var message = _emailService.ResolveMessage<PasswordResetResolver>(lang, parameters);
    var response = await _emailService.SendEmailAsync(email, "subject ...", message);
    return response;
}
```

In Project Renoir, the message resolver is an abstraction for a component capable of retrieving the actual email template from a disk file (via FileService) or a database table. The template accepts parameters provided through an aptly built dictionary. The email service is another infrastructure service that works as a wrapper around the actual email API, which, in Project Renoir, is SendGrid.

In a nutshell, any method of an application layer class implements all the steps necessary to carry out a given business operation by orchestrating the behavior of one or more repositories and infrastructural services. It returns plain data for query actions and a command response for update actions.

## Addressing cross-cutting concerns

In the pursuit of building maintainable and extensible applications, developers often encounter cross-cutting concerns. These are aspects of software that transcend individual components, affecting multiple layers and functionalities. Because all workflows are triggered from the application layer, all references to cross-cutting functions should also be accessible from this layer. Typical cross-cutting concerns are logging, permissions, error handling, and caching. Before exploring any of these, though, let's talk about sharing global application-wide settings.

# Propagating application settings

Application settings are configurable parameters and options that can be adjusted within the application to control its behavior, appearance, and functionality. These settings should not be confused with user settings. Application settings are global, are loaded once, and remain constant until they are changed by the development team and the application is restarted.

In ASP.NET Core applications, settings are loaded upon application startup. Data is collected from several sources—mostly, but not limited to, JSON files—and arranged in a data structure accessible to the rest of the application.

## Merging data from various sources

In ASP.NET Core, settings are first composed in a graph object with a dedicated API to inspect and set. You use a path-based addressing pattern to reach any desired element in the graph. The graph is generated by merging data from a variety of data sources. Here's an example taken from the startup class of the Project Renoir project:

```
private readonly IConfiguration _configuration;
public RenoirStartup(IWebHostEnvironment env)
{
        _environment = env;
        var settingsFileName = env.IsDevelopment()
                ? "app-settings-dev.json"
                : "app-settings.json";

        var dom = new ConfigurationBuilder()
                .SetBasePath(env.ContentRootPath)
                .AddJsonFile(settingsFileName, optional: true)
                .AddEnvironmentVariables()
                .Build();

    _configuration = dom;
}
```

The _configuration member accesses the graph built from the contents of the settings JSON file and all available environment variables. Of course, more JSON files could be added, as can data from any valid setting providers you have or build.

It's a matter of preference and attitude but, for what it's worth, my personal stance is that accessing loaded settings via the members of the IConfiguration interface is annoying and uncomfortable.

There are two alternative approaches to it: using the IOptions<T> interface and direct binding. Both approaches allow you to work with application settings as strongly typed objects. The difference is in an extra layer of abstraction that IOptions<T> applies around actual settings.

## Settings-related classes

Whether you use direct binding or IOptions<T>, you need to define type T as a hierarchy of C# classes that model the application settings of which the application must be aware. In Project Renoir, we have the following root class:

```
public class RenoirSettings
{
    public const string AppName = "RENOIR";
    public RenoirSettings()
    {
        Languages = new List<string>();
        General = new GeneralSettings();
        Run = new RunSettings();
    }

    public GeneralSettings General { get; set; }
    public List<string> Languages { get; set; }
    public RunSettings Run { get; set; }
}
```

GeneralSettings and RunSettings are similar classes that just focus on a subset of the application settings—project information in GeneralSettings and operational behavior (for example, functions to mock in debug mode, extra logging enabled, and so on) in RunSettings. The Languages property indicates the languages supported by the user interface.

The content of the configuration DOM is mapped to the hierarchy of settings classes using either the IOptions<T> approach or direct binding:

```
public void ConfigureServices(IServiceCollection services)
{
    // Need IOptions<T> to consume, automatically listed in DI engine
    services.Configure<RenoirSettings>(_configuration);

    // Direct binding, explicitly added to the DI engine
    var settings = new RenoirSettings();
    _configuration.Bind(settings);
    services.AddSingleton(settings);
}
```

As a result, whether through IOptions<T> or direct binding, the application settings are finally available through the dependency injection (DI) system of ASP.NET Core.

## Injecting settings in application services

Linked to the DI system, settings are injected into the controllers and from there passed to all application services. The ability for application services to access global settings is crucial for orchestrating tasks in a manner that is consistent and coheres with business requirements.

Here's an excerpt from an example application service—the one that takes care of authentication in Project Renoir. The service is invoked directly from the `AccountController` class:

```
public class AccountService : ApplicationServiceBase
{
    public AccountService(RenoirSettings settings) : base(settings)
    {
    }

    public AuthenticationResponse TryAuthenticate(AuthenticationRequest input)
    {
        // More code
    }

    :
}
```

The singleton object with all settings injected during startup becomes available to any application service class that inherits from `ApplicationServiceBase`. Should settings be required down the stack (for example, in repositories or in domain services), any needed data will be passed as loose values. The following code snippet illustrates this point:

```
public CommandResponse TryConfirmAccount(ConfirmAccountRequest input)
{
    return AccountRepository
            .ConfirmAccount(input.Email, Settings.Run.ConfirmTokenLifetime);
}
```

The service method responsible for handling the click that confirms the creation of a new account receives the default expiration time to check whether the link the user received is still valid. The token lifetime is globally indicated in the settings and passed as a loose value.

## Hot reload of application settings

So far, application settings—whether loaded through `IOptions<T>` or direct binding—are immutable until the app service is restarted in production or the debug session is restarted if you are working in `localhost` from within Visual Studio. But what if you want to be able to replace the singleton settings object within the DI system on the fly, without stopping execution?

Whatever route you explore to achieve this must take into account the fact that after the ASP.NET Core DI container has been finalized, no embedded registrations can be changed. No matter what you manage to do in your code (for example, recalculating settings on the fly), there's no way to replace the instance that has been stored in the container via `IOptions<T>` or direct binding. Here are some possible workarounds, however:

- Use `IOptionsSnapshot<T>` instead of `IOptions<T>`. To do this, simply rename the interface. `IOptionsSnapshot<T>` simply uses a transient instance rather than a singleton to load settings. As a result, settings are recalculated for each and every request. At the cost of this extra performance hit, you can always have up-to-date settings.

- Use `IOptionsMonitor<T>` instead of `IOptions<T>`. The monitor variant internally manages the change of the configuration DOM and ensures that you always get the most up-to-date values.

- Replicate the same underlying pattern of the `IOptionsXXX` interface in your direct-binding logic.

Code wise, the main difference between `IOptionsXXX` interfaces and direct binding logic is that in the former case, the controller doesn't receive the settings reference directly, but rather receives a wrapper to it:

```
public AccountController(IOptions<RenoirSettings> options)
{
    // Dereference the settings root object
    Settings = options.Value;
}
```

If the interface is `IOptionsMonitor`, you use `CurrentValue` instead of `Value`. How does this mechanism circumvent the limitation of the ASP.NET DI container that doesn't allow changes past the startup phase? Quite simply, it wraps the actual settings in a container class. The container class reference is added as a singleton to the DI system and never changes. Its content, however—the actual settings—can be programmatically replaced at any time and be instantaneously available. By manually coding this artifact yourself, you can also hot-reload settings in the case of direct binding. (See the Project Renoir source code for more details.)

# Logging

Logging is crucial for tracking application behavior, diagnosing reported issues, and monitoring performance. It provides valuable insights into errors, events, and user interactions, aiding in effective troubleshooting and ensuring a stable and reliable application. For any application, you should always seriously consider building an application-wide logging infrastructure that handles exceptions raised in production and audits steps taken during various application tasks. In ASP.NET Core, logging is performed by tailor-made logger components. All logger instances pass through the system-provided logger factory—one of the few services added to the DI system by default.

> **Note** In ASP.NET Core applications, only the exceptions processed through the `UseExceptionHandler` middleware are automatically logged. This is less than the bare minimum for any application as it leaves the application completely devoid of logging when in production, where a different middleware is typically used.

## Registering loggers

Unless you override the default web host builder in program.cs—the bootstrapper of any ASP.NET Core application—a few loggers are automatically registered. (See Table 5-2.)

**TABLE 5-2** List of default ASP.NET loggers

| Logger | Storage and description |
|---|---|
| Console | Displays events in the console window. No actual storage takes place through this provider. |
| Debug | Writes events to the debug output stream of the host platform. In Windows, this goes to a registered trace listener and commonly ends up being mirrored in a dedicated view of the integrated development environment (IDE). In Linux, any log is written to a system file log. |
| EventSource | Writes events on a tailor-made logging platform specific to each hosting platform. On Windows, this uses the Event Tracing for Windows (ETW) tool. |
| EventLog | Writes events to the Windows Event Log (registered only on Windows). |

The default configuration likely won't work for most common applications. In the startup phase, you can edit the list of registered logging providers at your leisure. The following code from the `ConfigureServices` method of the startup class clears out all default loggers and adds only selected ones:

```
services.AddLogging(config =>
{
    config.ClearProviders();
    if(_environment.IsDevelopment())
    {
        config.AddDebug();
        config.AddConsole();
    }
});
```

You may have noticed that in the preceding code snippet, the Console and Debug loggers are added only if the application is configured to run from a host environment labeled for development purposes. The net effect of this code is that the application has no logger registered to run in production mode.

## Production-level loggers

Both the Debug and Console loggers are useful during the development phase, albeit with different target outputs. The Debug logger is specialized for use with debuggers, while the Console logger is designed to display log messages directly in the command-line interface. Both allow developers to quickly see log messages while working on the application locally. Neither of these loggers is well-suited for the production environment, however. Fortunately, there are alternatives.

The loggers shown in Table 5-3 provide more comprehensive and powerful logging and monitoring services for production environments, offering deeper insights into application performance and user behavior. They are not part of the .NET Core framework and require a separate NuGet package and an Azure subscription.

**TABLE 5-3** Production-level loggers provided by Microsoft

| Logger | Storage and description |
|---|---|
| AzureAppServicesFile | Writes logs to text files created in an Azure App Service application's file system. |
| AzureAppServicesBlob | Writes logs to a blob storage in an Azure Storage account. |
| ApplicationInsights | Writes logs to Azure Application Insights, a service that also provides tools for querying and analyzing telemetry data. (More on this in a moment.) |

> **Note** As weird as it may sound, ASP.NET Core doesn't come with a logging provider capable of writing logs to plain disk files. To achieve that, you must resort to a third-party logging provider such as Log4Net, NLog, Serilog, or one of many others. While each library has its own documentation, using most third-party loggers requires only a couple more steps than using a built-in provider—specifically, adding a NuGet package to the project and calling an `ILoggerFactory` extension method provided by the framework.

Application Insights is designed for production environments. It enables you to gain valuable insights into how your application is performing in the real world, helping you to identify and resolve issues proactively. With Application Insights, you can collect, store, and analyze various types of data—not just explicitly written log records—including exceptions, request metrics, and custom telemetry data. Application Insights also provides sophisticated querying and visualization capabilities, making it a robust solution for monitoring and troubleshooting applications at scale.

Here's how to set up Application Insights telemetry in the startup class:

```
public void ConfigureServices(IServiceCollection services)
{
    // Telemetry
    var key = "...";
    if (_environment.IsDevelopment())
        services.AddApplicationInsightsTelemetry(key);
    else
        services.AddApplicationInsightsTelemetry();

    // More code
}
```

If you deploy your application to an Azure app service, you can configure your Application Insights subscription in the Azure portal. Otherwise, you need to explicitly provide the instrumentation key. Note, however, that a local emulator of Application Insights is available free of charge, which allows you to first test the functionality and migrate to the live service (and hence start paying) later.

In summary, a scenario in which you use console and debug logging in development and Application Insights in production is quite reasonable. In production, you can automatically log unhandled exceptions, various telemetry, and any other data you programmatically indicate through the logger.

> **Note** You don't need to host your application on Azure to use Application Insights. You do need to have a valid Azure subscription for the Application Insights resource, but your application can be hosted anywhere else and just log to Azure.

## Configuring loggers

You can configure a running logger for one key aspect: the relevance of messages. Expressed through the LogLevel property, relevance is measured on a scale from 0 to 6, where 0 merely traces activity, 5 blocks critical errors, and 6 means no logging. In between, there are levels for debug messages (1), informational messages (2), warnings (3), and errors (4).

You commonly set the log level from within a JSON property in the settings file, as shown here:

```
"Logging": {
   "LogLevel": {
     "Default": "Warning" // Logs only warnings and errors
   }
}
```

This script is interpreted as "ignore all log messages of a level below warning for any categories of message and all registered providers." Of course, you can be more specific by assigning different log levels per category and provider, like so:

```
"Logging": {
   "LogLevel": {
      "Default": "Warning"
   }
},

"Console": {
   "LogLevel": {
     "Default": "Information",
      "Microsoft.AspNetCore": "Warning"
   }
}
```

This script is read as "ignore all log messages of a level below warning for any categories of message and all registered providers but the Console provider. For this one, instead, start logging at the Information level but ignore informational messages that are tagged as coming from Microsoft.AspNetCore."

The logger configuration doesn't need to be mapped to the root application settings objects. All you need to do is place one or more calls to the following line, changing the name of the section as appropriate (Logging, Console, and so on):

```
services.AddLogging(config =>
{
   config.ClearProviders();
   config.AddConfiguration(_configuration.GetSection("Logging"));
```

```
    if(_environment.IsDevelopment())
    {
        config.AddDebug();
        config.AddConsole();
    }
});
```

Application Insights gets its own settings automatically if you add an `ApplicationInsights` section in the JSON file with exactly the same syntax as for other loggers. The default behavior of Application Insights, however, is to capture only logs above warning level from all categories.

## Logging application facts

Logging providers work by writing messages to their respective storage destinations. A log, therefore, is a related set of messages identified by name. The application code writes to a log through the services of the `ILogger` interface.

You can create a logger in a couple of different ways. One way is to do so right from the factory. The following code snippet shows how to create a logger and give it a unique name. Typically, the logger logs within the scope of a controller.

```
public class DocumentController : Controller
{
    private ILogger _logger;

    public DocumentController(ILoggerFactory loggerFactory)
    {
        _logger = loggerFactory.CreateLogger("Document Controller");
        _logger.LogInformation("Some message here");
    }
}
```

In this case, the `CreateLogger` method gets the name of the log and creates it across registered providers. The `LogInformation` method is just one of the many methods that let you write to the log. The `ILogger` interface exposes one logging method for each supported log level—for example, `LogInformation` to output informational messages and `LogWarning` and `LogError` for more serious messages. Logging methods can accept plain strings, format strings, and even exception objects to serialize.

The other way is to simply resolve the `ILogger<T>` dependency through the DI system, thus bypassing the logger factory, like so:

```
public class DocumentController : Controller
{
    private ILogger _logger;

    public DocumentController(ILogger<DocumentController> logger)
    {
        _logger = logger;
    }
```

```
    // Use the internal member in the action methods
    ...
}
```

The log that gets created in this case uses the full name of the controller class as a prefix. Here's how to log a message when a (managed) exception occurs:

```
try
{
    // Code that fails
}
catch (Exception e)
{
    // Apply logic to determine the message and logs as error
    var text = DetermineLogMessage(e);
    _logger.LogError(text);
}
```

Creating a logger for each controller can be annoying and even error-prone. Let's see how to abstract things and save the logger in a common controller base class instead.

## Embedding loggers in a base controller

It's a good practice to have all controller classes of an application be created by inheriting from a base class. In this way, some common pieces of information can be easily packaged up in one place so they're easily accessible from any action method.

```
public class RenoirController : Controller
{
    public RenoirController (AppSettings settings,
                IHttpContextAccessor accessor,
                ILoggerFactory loggerFactory)
    {
        Settings = settings;
        HttpConnection = accessor;
        Logger = loggerFactory.CreateLogger(settings.General.ApplicationName);
    }

    // Helper properties: server base URL
    protected string ServerUrl => $"{Request.Scheme}://{Request.Host}{Request.PathBase}";
    // Helper properties: current culture
    protected CultureInfo Culture => HttpContext
                    .Features
                    .Get<IRequestCultureFeature>()
                    .RequestCulture
                    .Culture;
    // Helper properties: standard logger
    protected ILogger Logger { get; }
}
```

 **Note** Along with application settings and HTTP access, logging is another functionality to enable at the base controller level.

# Handling and throwing exceptions

In the complex world of software, exceptions are inevitable. Robust exception handling is vital for maintaining system stability and ensuring graceful error recovery. This section delves into the intricacies of exception handling within the application layer, covering topics such as exception propagation and fault tolerance.

## Exception-handling middleware

ASP.NET Core's exception-handling middleware acts as a safety net, using your custom logic to capture any unhandled exceptions to arrange an appropriate error user interface:

```
app.UseExceptionHandler("/app/error");
```

The `UseExceptionHandler` middleware simply routes control to the specified URL that is responsible for any user interface and displayed error information. Although you can access and attach any context information to the view, during development, it is preferable to use another middleware, as shown here:

```
if (settings.Run.DevMode)
    app.UseDeveloperExceptionPage();
else
    app.UseExceptionHandler("/app/error");
```

The `UseDeveloperExceptionPage` automatically provides stack-trace information and a snapshot of the HTTP context at the time of the exception. This information is invaluable during development to track down unexpected behavior. A common pattern for forking middleware is the following, slightly different version of the preceding snippet:

```
if (environment.IsDevelopment())
    app.UseDeveloperExceptionPage();
else
    app.UseExceptionHandler("/app/error");
```

Overall, I prefer to take full control of the conditions that determine the switch. This is easier done with a custom setting than with system information. There are two types of scenarios you want to be able to address properly:

- Testing the production error page

- Temporarily enabling development-style functions on a production system to diagnose a reported issue

Of the two, only the former can be done by simply changing the target environment from Visual Studio. The latter requires more control and hot reloading of settings.

## Accessing exception details

The error handling page (/app/error in the preceding snippet) is a single-entry point that receives no additional parameter and is left alone to try to figure out what has gone wrong. Here's a possible implementation of the method in the controller class:

```
public IActionResult Error()
{
    var exception = HttpContext.Features.Get<IExceptionHandlerFeature>()?.Error;
    var model = new ErrorMainViewModel(Settings, exception);

    // NOTE: You're recovering here, so log-level may be less than error
    // and the message may be customized
    Logger.LogWarning(exception.Message);

    return View(model);
}
```

The HTTPContext.Features service can retrieve the last error set. From there, you retrieve the logged exception and pack it for the subsequent Razor view.

## Custom exception classes

Using an application-specific or team-specific base exception class gives you the flexibility you need to structure the error page and make exceptions easier to locate in potentially long system logs. A custom exception class might be more than a thin layer of code that simply presents a different name. For example, here's the one in Project Renoir:

```
public class RenoirException : Exception
{
    public RenoirException(string message) : base(message)
    {
        RecoveryLinks = new List<RecoveryLink>();
        ContinueUrl = "/";
    }

    public RenoirException(Exception exception) : this(exception.Message)
    {
        ContinueUrl = "/";
    }

    // Optional links to go after an exception
    public List<RecoveryLink> RecoveryLinks { get; }

    // Default URL to go from an exception page
    public string ContinueUrl { get; private set; }

    // Add recovery URLs (with display text and link target)
    public RenoirException AddRecoveryLink(string text, string url, string target = "blank")
    {
        RecoveryLinks.Add(new RecoveryLink(text, url, target));
        return this;
    }
```

```
    public RenoirException AddRecoveryLink(RecoveryLink link)
    {
        RecoveryLinks.Add(link);
        return this;
    }
}
```

Displaying an error page that recovers from an exception is not sufficient. If the error is tolerable and the user can continue within the application, it would be nice to supply a list of clickable links.

## When to bubble, reformulate, or swallow

Often, multiple operations are coordinated within the methods of an application layer class. But what if one of the methods—a given step in a workflow—fails and throws an exception?

In some cases, you might want the whole workflow to fail. In others, you might prefer that the workflow continue until the end and report which steps didn't complete successfully. This means that any thrown exception has three possible outcomes:

- It bubbles up until it is captured by the application error safety net.

- It is captured and rethrown (reformulated) with a different name and/or message.

- It gets swallowed and disappears as if it never happened.

Let's explore a few scenarios, starting with the most common situation—the code spots some inconsistent situation and throws an exception, the current module stops execution, and the burden of recovering shifts to the caller:

```
public bool TrySaveReleaseNote(Document doc)
{
    if (doc == null)
        throw new InvalidDocumentException()
            .AddRecoveryLink(...)
            .AddRecoveryLink(...);

    // More code
}
```

Swallowing an exception is as easy as setting up an empty try/catch block, as shown here:

```
try
{
    // Code that may fail
}
catch
{
}
```

Usually, code assistant tools signal an empty `try/catch` as a warning, with reason. However, swallowing exceptions may be acceptable if it is done with full awareness and not just to silence a nasty bug. Reformulating an exception looks like this:

```
try
{
    // Code that may fail
}
catch(SomeException exception)
{
    // Do some work (i.e., changing the error message)
    throw new AnotherException();
}
```

Especially within the application layer, though, you often want to silence exceptions but track them down and report facts and data within a response object. For example, suppose the application layer method triggers a three-step workflow. Here's a valid way to code it:

```
public CommandResponse ThreeStepWorkflow( /* input */ )
{
    var response1 = Step1(/* input */ );
    var response2 = Step2(/* input */ );
    var response3 = Step3(/* input */ );

    var title1 = "Step 1";
    var title2 = "Step 2";
    var title3 = "Step 3";
    return new CommandResponse
            .Ok()
            .AppendBulletPoint(response1.Success, title1, response1.Message)
            .AppendBulletPoint(response2.Success, title2, response2.Message)
            .AppendBulletPoint(response3.Success, title3, response3.Message);
}
```

The bullet point method acts as an HTML-oriented string builder and creates a message made of bullet points of different colors, depending on the status of the related `CommandResponse` object. (See Figure 5-6.)

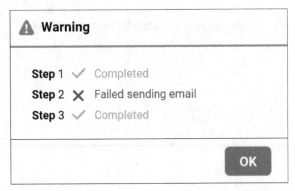

**FIGURE 5-6** An example message box for a multi-step workflow in which exceptions have been silenced.

# Caching and caching patterns

Caching is a technique that stores frequently accessed data in a temporary memory location rather than the original source for faster access. Typically, a cache saves data in memory, reducing the need to query a database for every request. The use of a caching mechanism improves system responsiveness and results in reduced processing time and network load.

## In-memory cache

In ASP.NET Core, the most basic form of caching is built upon the IMemoryCache interface and is nothing more than a cache stored in the memory of the web server. A memory cache is just a sophisticated singleton dictionary shared by all requests. Items are stored as key-value pairs.

The memory cache is not limited to plain read/write operations but also includes advanced features such as item expiration. Item expiration means that each stored item can be given a (sliding or absolute) expiration and is removed at some point. This keeps the size of the cache under control and mitigates data staleness.

When in-memory cache applications run on a server farm with multiple servers, it is crucial to ensure that sessions are sticky. Sticky sessions, in fact, guarantee that requests from a client are always directed to the same server. To avoid sticky sessions in a web farm, you need to switch to a distributed cache to avoid data consistency issues.

## Distributed cache

A distributed cache is a cache shared by multiple application servers and stored externally from those servers. A distributed cache provides two key benefits:

- It enables efficient data sharing by centralizing global data in a single place regardless of the number of servers in a web farm or cloud environment.

- It reduces redundant data fetching from primary sources such as databases.

Furthermore, by offloading cache memory to an external process, it optimizes response times for a more efficient application experience.

ASP.NET Core provides the IDistributedCache interface to unify the programming model for caches regardless of the actual store. No realistic implementation of this interface is provided as part of the ASP.NET Core platform. However, a few free NuGet packages exist, as do commercial products such as Redis and NCache. In addition, you can use the AddDistributedSqlServerCache class, which employs a SQL Server database as its backing store. Redis and NCache store data in memory and are significantly faster than a SQL Server-based cache.

Today, in-memory cache is just not an option anymore. A distributed cache like Redis is the de facto standard for any situation in which an intermediate cache proves necessary. However, the local or distributed nature of the cache is only one facet of the whole problem. *Local* and *distributed* refer to the store location of the data. In contrast, *caching patterns* refers to how cached data is retrieved by the application layer code. There are two caching patterns: cache aside and write-through.

**Note** To be precise, ASP.NET comes with a class that provides in-memory distributed cache: AddDistributedMemoryCache. However, it doesn't really work as a real distributed cache because data is saved in the memory of each server. It exists only for testing purposes.

## The cache-aside pattern

The cache-aside pattern is an extremely popular approach. With this pattern, when the application needs to read data from the database, it checks the cache to see if the data is available in memory. If the data is found in the cache (in other words, you have a *cache hit*), the cached data is returned, and the response is sent to the caller. If the data is not available in the cache (that is, you have a *cache miss*), the application queries the database for the data. The retrieved data is stored in the cache, and it is then returned to the caller.

A cache-aside cache pattern only caches data that the application requests, making the cache size quite cost-effective. Furthermore, its implementation is straightforward, and its performance benefits are immediately visible. That said, it is worth mentioning that with the cache-aside pattern, data is loaded only after a cache miss. Hence, any requests that end up in a cache miss take extra time to complete due to additional round trips to the cache and database.

**Note** Despite its apparent unquestionable effectiveness, the cache-aside pattern is not applicable everywhere. In situations in which requested data may vary significantly, keeping previously requested data in cache incurs a cost beyond resources and performance. In such (rather borderline) situations, spending more time optimizing database access and skipping the cache layer entirely is a sounder approach.

## The write-through pattern

With the write-through caching pattern, data updates are first written to the cache and then immediately propagated to the underlying data storage (for example, a database). When an application modifies data, it updates the cache and waits for the cache update to be successfully committed to the storage before acknowledging the write operation as complete. This ensures that the cache and the data storage remain consistent.

Although write-through caching offers data integrity and reduces the risk of data loss, it can introduce higher latency for write operations because it must wait for the data to be written to both the cache and storage.

## Where does caching belong?

In a layered architecture, caching typically sits between the presentation layer and the data storage layer. The application layer is therefore the first place where one can think to install caching—maybe.

Generally, a caching mechanism intercepts data requests from the application before they reach the data storage layer. When a request for data is made, the caching mechanism checks whether the data is already cached. If so, the cached data is returned to the application, avoiding the need to access the original data source through repositories. If not, the caching mechanism retrieves it from the data storage layer, caches it for future use, and then delivers it to the application. Here's some pseudo-code to illustrate this process:

```
public AvailableDocumentsViewModel GetAvailableDocuments(long userId)
{
    // This is likely just one step of a longer workflow

    // Cache-aside pattern being used
    var docs = _cache.Get("Available-Documents");
    if (docs.IsNullOrEmpty())
    {
        docs = DocumentRepository.All();
        _cache.Set("Available-Documents", docs);
    }

    // Proceed using retrieved data
    ...
}
```

This code works, but it's a bit too verbose because the access for each chunk of cached data takes the same few lines every time. As an alternative, consider embedding the caching mechanism in the repositories. Here's how:

```
public AvailableDocumentsViewModel GetAvailableDocuments(long userId)
{
    // This is likely just one step of a longer workflow

    // Cache injected in the data repository (as an instance of IDistributedCache)
    var docs = DocumentRepository.All(_cache);

    // Proceed using retrieved data
    ...
}
```

The resulting code is much more compact. From the perspective of the application layer, there's just one counterpart to ask for data, period.

**Note** For simplicity, this code—while fully functional—doesn't use DI. DI forces you to keep the code clean and more testable but doesn't add programming power. It also clogs constructors and renders them unreadable. As weird as it may sound, DI is a matter of trade-offs, but clean boundaries are essential.

### Organizing data within the cache

A cache is a flat key-value dictionary. When distributed, it's also a remote dictionary. In this case, any cached data is transmitted over the network, at which point it must be serialized. The serialization process involves traversing existing objects, extracting their data, and converting it into serialized data.

The main difficulty with this approach is ensuring that a cached object is serializable, whether to a binary or JSON stream. A common issue is facing circular references within complex object graphs. Circular references may force you to treat data through plain DTOs with the addition of yet another layer of adapters to and from native domain entities.

Related to serialization is how you flatten cached data from the entity-relationship model of a classic SQL database to the key-value space of a dictionary. Possible options are as follows:

- Try to keep cache data one-to-one with database tables and make any data joins and grouping in memory.

- Create ad hoc serializable graphs, use them frequently, and cache them as is.

- Organize data in domain-specific entities that don't have a direct database counterpart but that are used in various use cases.

In the first case, packing cache in repositories is a good option. For the other two scenarios, the recommendation is to create yet another layer of software, called the data-access layer, between the application layer and the infrastructure/persistence layer. If the shape of the cached data looks like domain entities, the data access layer can coincide with the domain services layer covered in Chapter 7, "Domain services."

## Injecting SignalR connection hubs

SignalR is a real-time, open-source library developed by Microsoft to add bidirectional communication capabilities to web applications. Among other things, SignalR enables real-time updates and the sending of notifications from the server to connected browsers. Here, I want to address a scenario that involves setting up a mechanism for the back end to notify clients about the progress of potentially long-running operations, whether end-to-end or fire-and-forget.

### Setting up a monitoring hub

In the `Configure` method of the startup class, the following code sets up a SignalR hub. A *hub* is a high-level programming abstraction that acts as the main communication pipeline between the server and connected clients. It serves as the central point for sending and receiving messages in real time. The hub manages the connection life cycle, including establishing connections, maintaining the connection state, and handling reconnections.

```
App.UseEndpoints(endpoints =>
{
    endpoints.MapControllerRoute(
```

```
        name: "default",
        pattern: "{controller=home}/{action=index}/{id?}");

    // SignalR endpoint for monitoring remote operations
    endpoints.MapHub<DefaultMonitorHub>(DefaultMonitorHub.Endpoint);
});
```

A SignalR hub is essentially a class on the server side that inherits from the Hub class provided by the library. Within this Hub class, developers can define methods that can be called by clients to send data to the server, as well as methods that can be invoked by the server to send data back to connected clients. Most of the time, however, you can just inherit the core services of the base class. So, for the sole purpose of reporting the progress of a server operation, you can use the following.

```
public class DefaultMonitorHub : Hub
{
    public static string Endpoint = "/monitorhub";
}
```

SignalR requires some JavaScript on the client page to trigger the long-running operation and receive feedback about the progress. The controller triggering the task needs to receive just the unique ID of the SignalR connection.

## Propagating the SignalR hub

Here's an example controller that knows how to handle SignalR connections and report the progress of generating a PDF file from a Project Renoir document:

```
private readonly IHubContext<DefaultMonitorHub> _monitorHubContext;

public PdfController( /* other */, IHubContext<DefaultMonitorHub> monitorHubContext)
        : base(/* other */)
{
    _monitorHubContext = monitorHubContext;
}
```

Invoked via POST, the example method GeneratePdf receives the GUID that identifies the SignalR open connection. It packs the connection GUID and the reference to the hub in a container class and passes it to the service methods orchestrating the long-running task.

```
[HttpPost]
[Route("/pdf/export")]
public IActionResult GeneratePdf(long docId, string connId = "")
{
    // Pack together what's needed to respond
    var signalr = new ConnectionDescriptor<DefaultMonitorHub>(connId, _monitorHubContext);

    // Invoke the potentially long-running task to report progress
    var response = _pdfService.Generate(docId, signalr);
    return Json(response);
}
```

The ConnectionDescriptor class is a plain DTO, as illustrated here:

```
public class ConnectionDescriptor<T>
        where T : Microsoft.AspNetCore.SignalR.Hub
{
    public ConnectionDescriptor(string connId, IHubContext<T> hub)
    {
        this.ConnectionId = connId;
        this.Hub = hub;
    }

    public string ConnectionId { get; set; }
    public IHubContext<T> Hub { get; set; }
}
```

What happens next depends on how the long-running task is orchestrated.

## Sending notifications to the client browser

When reporting the progress of a potentially long-running task to the user interface, a message with either the percentage of completion or a description of the current step is sent back to the SignalR listener on the client page. The code that sends messages looks like this:

```
public CommandResponse Generate (long docId,
            ConnectionDescriptor<DefaultMonitorHub> signalr)
{
        // Update status on the client
        signalr.Hub
            .Clients
            .Client(signalr.ConnectionId)
            .SendAsync("updateStatus", new object[] {"STARTING"});

        // Step 1
        ...

        // Update status on the client
        signalr.Hub
            .Clients
            .Client(signalr.ConnectionId)
            .SendAsync("updateStatus", new object[] {"STEP 1"});
        // More steps
        ...
}
```

Essentially, you intersperse update messages with the steps of the operation on which you want to report. But what if the steps are not entirely carried out in the service method? What if, for example, one step involves an operation on some repository with multiple steps within it to report? In that case, you simply inject the connection hub in the repository too.

A final note on the updateStatus tag: That's just the name of the JavaScript function that will receive the message that handles updating the user interface.

# Boundaries and deployment of the application layer

Where the domain layer (covered in Chapter 6, "The domain layer") is the beating heart of the application, the application layer is the nerve center. Any actions requested from the outside, whether through the user interface or an exposed API, are processed by the application layer from start to finish.

## The dependency list

The application layer needs connections to the domain model, the infrastructure layer, and, finally, the persistence layer. If a cached data access layer is implemented, then it needs to access it as well. At the same time, the application layer should have no dependency on the HTTP context or authentication details. Any access control logic should be applied at the controller's gate. If, for some reason, the application layer needs to know details of the logged user (for example, the user ID), cookie items, or request headers, those must be passed as loose values.

## Deployment options

There are many ways to code the application layer, and they are all legitimate—even the often dismissed option of tight coupling with the web application. The following sections discuss three of these approaches, including that one.

### Tightly coupled with the web application

The simplest approach is to code the services in the application layer as classes under the common Application folder in the web application project. (See Figure 5-7.) This approach is by far the most direct and quick to code. It has one drawback, though: Because the code lives in the same ASP.NET web project, it shares the same dependencies as the main web application. So, ensuring that no silent extra dependencies slip in the layer is entirely a matter of self-discipline. In the end, it's the good and bad of tight coupling!

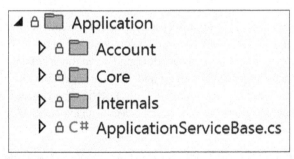

**FIGURE 5-7** In-project implementation of the application layer.

## Separate class library

After a couple of decades of high-level consulting and technical disclosure, I returned to—or maybe just started on—actual core development. In the beginning, we were a small team of five people, and it was relatively easy and inexpensive to keep an eye on every aspect of the code being written. So, for simplicity and directness, our first projects had the application layer tightly coupled to the rest of the web application.

Now the team has grown five times its initial size, and monitoring every aspect of the code is much more problematic. Self-discipline is now really a matter of individual self-control. My perspective has changed, and a tightly coupled application layer is no longer the way to go. Instead, we switched to implementing the application as a separate class library project in the same solution as the main web application. This is also the approach chosen for Project Renoir.

The application layer as a class library forces you to add external dependencies explicitly and to offer reviewers a quick way to check whether something—a NuGet package or an embedded project— is wrongly or unnecessarily referenced.

> **Note** Implemented as a class library, the application layer can be easily wrapped up as an internal NuGet package and reused across projects. Note, though, that the application layer is by design coupled to the presentation layer. This means that although reuse is certainly not prohibited, it shouldn't become your main goal. In other words, duplicating the application layer in different projects, in all or in part, is not a bad thing per se.

## Separate (micro) service

A class library lives in-process with the main web application and doesn't add any extras to the cloud bill. Because it runs in-process, it also provides much better performance than if deployed as an independent, autonomous service. But is deploying the application layer as an independent app service a reasonable approach? As usual, it depends.

Let's first consider a scenario in which you deploy the entire application layer as an independent service. You simply move the class library to a new ASP.NET web application project, add one or more controller classes or minimal API endpoints, connect the necessary dots, and go. In this scenario, any deployed service has its own deployment pipeline, scaling strategy, and resource allocation. This is good because it allows teams to work on different services simultaneously. But this is bad because it increases costs and maintenance operations, and every call to the application layer experiences network latency.

If you want to split the application layer from the rest of the application, then you probably should consider breaking it into even smaller pieces, moving toward a true microservices solution. This is a serious decision, as it involves radical changes to the existing architecture, including the addition of a message queue somewhere and the implementation of an event-driven business logic via sagas or workflow instances. It's not as simple as just creating a new Azure app service and deploying the app to it!

# Summary

The application layer serves as a critical foundation for the development of modern software systems. Through the exploration of task orchestration, cross-cutting concerns, data transfer, exception handling, caching, and deployment scenarios, this chapter equips developers with the knowledge and insights necessary to build robust, scalable, and maintainable applications. By mastering the intricacies of the application layer, developers can unlock new realms of innovation and create software that meets the evolving needs of users and businesses alike.

The application layer is conceptually tightly coupled to the presentation layer and is ideally different depending on the front end used. Historically, types of front ends have included web, mobile, and desktop, but the recent bold advancement of large language models (LLMs), of which GPT is only the most popular, has yielded a fourth type of front end: conversational front ends based on chatbots (which are much more effective than in the recent past).

Deploying the application layer as a separate microservice involves breaking down a monolithic application into smaller, more manageable services. With this approach, the application's core business logic and functionality reside within individual microservices. This promotes better modularity, scalability, and maintainability, but also raises a long list of new problems.

This book is about clean architecture, which is inherently a layered architecture. A layered architecture is not about microservices. That said, the main purpose of this book beyond elucidating clean architecture is to explain and demonstrate separation of boundaries between layers. Using microservices is about enforcing physical separation, while layered architecture is about design and logical separation. You can certainly go from layered architecture to microservices if the business really requires it, but the opposite requires a complete redesign. My best advice is to consider starting with a modular layered (monolithic) architecture and then follow the natural evolution of the business.

The next chapter continues our exploration of the layers of a layered clean architecture, reaching the beating heart: the domain layer.

# CHAPTER 6

# The domain layer

*I'm not a great programmer; I'm just a good programmer with great habits.*

*—Kent Beck*

In DDD, the crucial concept of the domain layer emphasizes the importance of understanding and modeling the core domain of a business to create a shared understanding between technical and non-technical stakeholders. By focusing on the domain layer, DDD aims to capture and implement the business logic in a way that closely aligns with the real-world domain, promoting a richer and more meaningful representation of the problem space. This helps create more maintainable and scalable software systems that reflect the intricacies of the business domain they serve.

The purpose of this chapter is to disambiguate the meanings associated with the term *domain layer* and to provide a practical guide to creating a C# class library that mimics the behavior of entities in the business domain.

## Decomposition of the domain layer

From a purely architectural perspective, the domain layer is the space within the software solution that focuses on the invariant parts of the core business. Unlike the presentation and application layers, though, the domain layer doesn't have just one "soul." Rather, it has two: a business domain model and a family of helper domain services. Not surprisingly, both souls are independent but closely related.

### The business domain model

A *domain model* is a conceptual representation of a business domain in which entities and value objects are connected together to model real-world concepts and to support real-world processes. The business domain model is ultimately the machinery—or, if you prefer, the wizardry—that transforms business requirements into running software.

Abstractly speaking, the model in the domain layer is just that—a model. It's a conceptual representation of the business domain in the software system. Such a definition must be materialized in software form for the application to be built and to work, but it is agnostic of any known programming paradigm such as functional or object-oriented. The domain model, therefore, is just a software model of the business domain. Usually, but not always, it is implemented as an object-oriented model.

Furthermore, following the DDD principles, the object-oriented model is not a plain object model but rather an object model with a bunch of additional constraints.

## The domain layer in perspective

Figure 6-1 provides an overall view of the domain layer in relation to business requirements and the business's ubiquitous language. Understanding the business language helps you identify bounded contexts to split the design. Each bounded context may be, in turn, split into one or more modules, and each module is related to a domain model and a family of domain services.

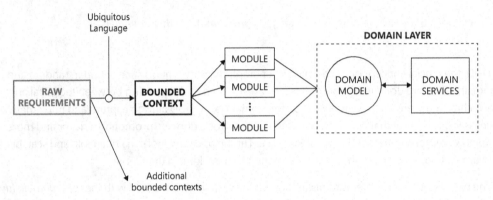

**FIGURE 6-1** From raw requirements to the domain layer, the DDD way via analysis of the ubiquitous language.

How does this correlate to software elements of a layered architecture? A bounded context represents the application as a whole, while modules are close relatives of application services. Chapter 2, "The ultimate gist of DDD," stated that each bounded context is characterized by its own domain model. Well, now that we're closer to the implementation level, that statement can be slightly rephrased to something like, each bounded context is characterized by its own slice of the domain model. In other words, the domain model can be a single artifact shared by multiple bounded contexts (and potentially multiple distinct applications) or just be conveniently partitioned so that each bounded context has its own domain model. Making this architectural decision contributes to your ability to shape a single model that can serve all bounded contexts without making it overly complex, fragile, or unmanageable.

## Internals of a domain model

Within the realm of a domain model, you find software counterparts for concepts such as the following:

- **Entities**   These represent the main actors in the domain and are characterized by unique identities and life cycles. Entities have behaviors and encapsulate business rules related to their state and interactions.

- **Value objects**   These represent characteristics and attributes that are essential to the domain. They have no identity and are immutable. Value objects are used to encapsulate complex data structures and are typically shared by multiple entities.

- **Aggregates**   These are clusters of related entities and value objects that are better treated as a single unit for the purpose of faithfully implementing business processes. They provide transactional consistency and define boundaries within the domain to enforce business rules and invariant conditions.

## Paradigms for a domain model

DDD does not prescribe specific software paradigms or programming languages. Instead, DDD provides a set of principles, patterns, and concepts to guide the design and development of a domain model that accurately represents the business domain. As a result, you can use a variety of software paradigms to build a domain model, depending on the requirements and preferences of the development team. Here are a few common options, roughly in order of popularity:

- **Object-oriented programming (OOP)**   This is probably the most natural approach, as concepts like entities, value objects, and aggregates fit nicely within a class in the OOP paradigm. Likewise, behavior is naturally fit for class methods, and relationships can be represented using inheritance and encapsulation.

- **Functional programming**   With functional programming, domain entities and value objects can be represented as immutable data structures, and domain behaviors can be implemented using pure functions. Note that a pure function always produces the same output for a given set of input parameters and does not depend on any external state or mutable data.

- **Anemic programming**   An anemic model has classes that match the classes in the underlying persistence layer and maps the domain model to the data store. Behavior is usually coded in database-level stored procedures or in dedicated global methods exposed by some standalone class.

Ultimately, your choice of software paradigm depends on factors such as the programming languages and frameworks being used, the team's expertise, the nature of the domain, and the specific requirements of the project.

> **Note**   For the rest of this book, when I say *domain model*, I mean an object-oriented model (unless otherwise specified).

## Persistence of a domain model

Realistically, any domain model must have persistence, but it does not handle its own persistence directly. In fact, the domain model includes no references to loading or saving operations, even though these operations are essential for creating instances of domain entities and implementing business logic.

To handle persistence on behalf of entities, a specific type of component, called a *repository*, comes into play. Repositories are responsible for managing the persistence of entities. They are typically invoked from outside the domain model, such as from the application layer, or from other components within the domain layer, like domain services. The actual implementation of repositories belongs to a separate layer. This layer can be a distinct persistence layer (as in Project Renoir) or just a module within a larger, more general, infrastructure layer.

> **Note** It is correct to state that repositories take care of persisting entities based on what has been discussed so far. However, as you progress through this chapter and gain a broader perspective, you will realize that repositories don't actually persist entities, but rather persist a specific subset of entities called *aggregates* that sometimes coincide with plain entities. If it now sounds a bit obscure, don't worry, I'll shed some light on aggregates and entities in just a few moments.

## Cross-cutting concerns in a domain model

Let's consider four common cross-cutting concerns—validation, logging, caching, and security—and see how they affect the development of a domain model.

The latter two—caching and security—don't really apply to the domain model. As for caching, it's simply not a concern of the domain model. And security should be applied at the gate of the domain model, making it the responsibility of higher layers. Quite simply, no call should reach out to the domain model in unauthorized conditions. Security-at-the-gate means that security restrictions are applied as early as possible in the call stack—often in application services at the beginning of the use case.

As for logging, the decision of what to log and where to log it is entirely up to you. If you determine that logging from within the domain model is essential, you will need a reference to the logging infrastructure directly in the domain model. However, it is important to avoid creating a strong dependency between the domain model and the logger component to maintain flexibility and modularity. To achieve logging from the domain model without tight coupling, you can inject a logger interface into the model classes. This way, the domain model remains unaware of the specific logger implementation. Instead, the actual implementation of the logger is placed in the infrastructure project, where it can be customized and configured as needed.

Finally, validation is a primary concern of the domain model. Classes of the domain model should perform thorough checks and raise specific exceptions whenever they encounter erroneous conditions. The domain model is not intended to be forgiving; rather, it should promptly raise alarms when something deviates from expected behavior. As for error messages, a domain model should define its own set of exceptions and make them accessible to higher layers, such as the application layer. The application layer will then decide how to handle these domain-specific exceptions—whether to propagate them directly to the presentation layer, re-throw them, or handle them internally. However, the actual content of the error messages should be left to the presentation layer. The domain model is focused on the business logic and on ensuring that the application's invariants are upheld, while the presentation layer is better suited for customizing error messages for end users or specific UI requirements.

# Helper domain services

So, classes in a domain model are agnostic of persistence and receive the state to work on from the outside when initialized. Furthermore, domain model classes encapsulate data and expose behavior through methods. Not in all cases, though. The entire behavior expected from a domain can be easily partitioned across the various constituent classes. This is where helper domain services fit in.

## Filling behavioral gaps

Helper domain services are just helper classes whose methods implement the domain logic that doesn't fit within a particular entity or, more likely, spans over multiple entities. Domain services coordinate the activity of entities, aggregates, and repositories with the purpose of implementing a business action. In some cases, domain services may consume additional services from the infrastructure, such as when sending an email or a text message is necessary.

## Bridging domain and infrastructure

All business domains are made of processes, and it's difficult to map these processes to a single behavior on a specific entity. Sometimes, these processes are essential for the domain and involve dedicated calculations, data aggregations, and access to storage.

You start coding the expected behavior using domain entities and aggregate-specific repositories. Whatever doesn't naturally fit in these is a great candidate for a domain service. When you conclude that you need a separate, special container of code that bridges the domain layer and the infrastructure layer, you have a domain service.

Concretely, a domain service can be a class in the domain model—if no persistence is required—or it can be part of the persistence layer if queries and updates are required. Here's a common example of a functionality that is ideal for a domain service. Imagine that an online shop rewards customers for purchases by issuing points. Beyond a certain threshold, the customer changes status, becoming Silver or Gold. Chances are, the `customer` class will have a property that reports the current status and a few Boolean methods, like `IsGold` and `IsSilver`. When the `customer` class is queried from the data store, where does the status value come from? The status is not something that pertains to the demographics of the customer; rather, it is information that descends from the customer's history in the system. It can be handled in either of two ways:

- When an instance of the entity is loaded from the data store, a separate query is run to check the status from the list of purchases and attributed points.

- The customer's status is calculated and saved to the Customers table (or even a separate linked table) every time a purchase is finalized. In this way, the status is guaranteed to be up to date.

In both cases, you need some piece of code that goes through the history of purchases and updates the sum of points. This is the ideal work of a domain service.

**Note** Domain services do not have their own state. They are stateless and maintain no data between invocations. They rely only on the input they receive when performing operations.

## Devising a domain model

A *domain model* is a representation of a domain's concepts and behaviors. The model should reflect the actual problem space and the rules governing it and expressed in the terms of the ubiquitous language. By design, the entities in a domain model are agnostic of the persistence layer, and it is assumed they will be filled with data in some way. Their state is altered by exposed methods that represent business actions rather than by exposing writable properties to be updated from some logic living outside. In a nutshell, DDD shifts the design focus from data to behavior.

**Important** A key point to fully comprehend the turnaround brought by DDD is how entities get their state. Domain entities are definitely stateful objects in the sense that they have properties that determine a state of working. However, such a state must be retrieved from storage and injected in some way into the machinery of the domain entity. In other words, entities expose behavior based on state, but the state itself is an external parameter whose persistence is managed elsewhere. I'll return to this point with examples in a few moments.

## Shifting focus from data to behavior

In a system design driven mostly by the nature of the business domain (like DDD), the focus shifts from mapping data structures directly from the database to building a meaningful, expressive model of the domain. But what's the point of doing this?

Well, there is no point if the domain isn't complex enough. No game-changing benefit will realistically result from DDD for relatively simple domains. Although the principles of DDD are universally valid and ensure that code is more maintainable and flexible, you won't see any concrete benefit or increase in programming expressivity if the model lacks complexity.

Still, adopting a domain-driven approach yields two main benefits: the ability to handle growing levels of complexity and intricacy and to improve communication between technical and non-technical stakeholders. These two benefits are clearly mutually related.

### The evergreen data-centric focus

Since the advent of relational databases, the main approach to building systems has been more or less the following:

1. You gather requirements and analyze them to identify relevant entities and processes involved.

2. Based on this understanding, you design a physical data model, almost always relational, to support the processes.

3. While ensuring relational consistency (primary keys, constraints, normalization, indexing), you build software components against tables in the model that represent critical business entities.

4. Sometimes, you use database-specific features like stored procedures to implement behavior while abstracting the database structure from upper-level code.

5. You choose a suitable data representation model and move data to and from the presentation layer.

This approach to modeling a business domain is not wrong *per se*. It's a mature and consolidated practice. More than that, it just works well. Furthermore, every developer knows about it because it's taught in all programming courses.

So why should you move away from a working and consolidated practice to embrace a different approach that, beyond having an attractive and exotic name like DDD, also represents a sort of leap into the unknown? The answer lies in the subtitle of the highly influential 2003 book by Eric Evans: *Domain-Driven Design: Tackling Complexity in the Heart of Software.*

**Note** The relational model for databases was devised in 1970 by Dr. Edgar F. Codd, a computer scientist working at IBM's San Jose Research Laboratory. Codd introduced the concept of representing data as tables with rows and columns, as well as the principles of data normalization, relationships between tables through primary and foreign keys, and using a query language (Structured Query Language, or SQL) to interact with data. The work laid the foundation for the development of modern relational database management systems (RDBMS) that are widely used in the software industry today.

## Me and DDD

I began studying DDD around 2006. Frankly, my initial interest was mainly fueled by the need to always have cutting-edge topics on hand to write and talk about. However, I found DDD intriguing and decided to try it in some toy projects.

That was my first mistake. One can't realistically experience the power of DDD in toy projects. My first project was a classic to-do list application, and I spent the entire time struggling to figure out what should be considered an entity, an aggregate, or an aggregate root. I also struggled to make sense of persistence—what loaded and saved the state of entities?

At some point, though, I obtained a clear picture of the theory and practice of DDD. This was great for writing insightful books and articles about it, but I was still missing that direct, hands-on, everyday experience that could give me a real sense of DDD. For that, I knew I'd have to wait for the chance to work night and day on a complex project.

The chance came in 2020 when my company started building a new live-scoring platform for a major professional tennis circuit. The platform's ultimate objective was to convert every tap on the chair umpire's tablet into data and transmit it to a central hub that served betting companies—for every match in every tournament. To achieve this, several entities were in play, including tournament calendars, players, umpires, courts, entry lists, draws, schedules, and matches, just to name a few. Plus, there were a variety of other entities to support specific business rules and processes. And every year at the start of a new season—and sometimes in the middle of the season—we needed to update rules and processes.

Ultimately, we articulated the overall business domain in three major bounded contexts, each made by a handful of distinct deployments—mostly Azure app services carrying ASP. NET Core applications. The domain model—an internal NuGet package shared by all related projects and maintained by a single team in conformity with the customer/supplier relationship discussed in Chapter 2—was significant, and the shift to a behavior approach saved us from sinking in a troubled sea of requirements, implementations, and misunderstandings.

## What is a model and why do you need one?

Using the term *model* is dangerous in a software-based conversation. Its meaning depends strictly on the context, so there's a high risk of defining it inaccurately. In DDD, a model is a representation of the business domain. Of these two words, the key one is *business* rather than *domain*. A model built for a domain must faithfully and effectively represent the core business.

Here's an example. Suppose you're working on a logistics application and need to calculate the shortest distance between places in the world. To do this, you would probably use an existing service, like Bing Maps, Google Maps, ESRI, or OpenStreetMap. But how do such services work internally? They use a graphical representation of the world on a map, but it's not the real world!

Major online map providers use Web Mercator—a modified and web-adapted version of the original Mercator projection in use since the 16th century. The Web Mercator projection allows for easy representation of map data on the web, much like how the original Mercator projection proved particularly suitable for nautical purposes. Still, the Mercator projection is a world map model. It does not truly mirror the real world. In fact, it distorts both areas and distances, with the scale increasing toward the poles. This causes some areas to appear larger or smaller than they really are. For instance, Greenland appears to be similar in size to all of South America, when in fact South America is more than eight times larger than Greenland. However, the Mercator projection is invaluable for measuring courses and bearings in nautical cartography due to its constant angles. While not at all suitable as an accurate map of the world, it serves its specific purpose effectively.

Map providers need a model to represent the world and distances and paths between places. They represent the world, but they do not use a universally valid model of the world. Rather, they use a business-specific model that is apt only for the domain.

## Persistence ignorance

Persistence ignorance is a DDD principle that advocates for keeping the domain model classes independent of the persistence layer. Domain model classes should not have direct knowledge of how they are being persisted to or retrieved from a database or storage. Similarly, they should not expose methods that require access to the persistence layer to perform operations like saving or materializing instances.

By adhering to persistence ignorance, the domain model remains focused on representing the business domain and its behavior without being tied to specific persistence mechanisms. This separation of concerns allows for greater flexibility and maintainability in the code base. The responsibility for handling persistence is typically delegated to specialized infrastructure layers or repositories, which interact with the domain model to deal with database operations while keeping the domain classes free from such concerns.

By decoupling the domain model from the persistence layer, the code becomes more reusable and testable, and easier to reason about. It also promotes better separation of concerns and prevents domain logic from being polluted with persistence-related code.

# Life forms in a domain model

The building blocks of a DDD domain model are entities, value objects, and aggregates. *Entities* represent a concept from the business domain, *value objects* represent business-specific primitive types, and *aggregates* are clusters of related entities treated as a single unit for business and persistence convenience. Closely related to these are domain services (which encapsulate domain logic that doesn't naturally belong to entities or value objects) and repositories (which handle the persistence of domain entities).

## Domain entities

All business concepts have attributes, but not all are fully identified by their collection of attributes. When attributes are not enough to guarantee uniqueness, and when uniqueness is important to the specific business concept, then in DDD you have *domain entities*. Put another way, if the business concept needs an ID attribute to track it uniquely throughout the context for the entire life cycle, then the business concept requires an identity and can then be recognized as an entity.

Key characteristics of domain entities include the following:

- **Identity**  An entity has a unique identity that remains constant throughout its life cycle. This identity is typically represented by a unique identifier, such as an ID or a combination of attributes that uniquely identify the entity. Once persisted to a relational database table, the identity often becomes the primary key.

- **Mutability**  Entities are mutable, meaning their state can change over time. They can be modified by applying domain-specific business rules and operations. Such operations take the form of methods, whereas modifiable attributes are ideally implemented as public read-only properties.

- **Life cycle**   Entities have a life cycle, starting with creation and potentially ending with deletion or archiving. They can exist independently and can be related to other entities within the domain. Persistence is managed outside the domain model.

- **Consistency**   Entities enforce invariants and business rules to maintain consistency within the domain. The entity's behavior and attributes are designed to ensure that the domain remains in a valid state. Consistency, however, is just the first constraint you may be forced to sacrifice for the sake of pragmatism.

In terms of implementation, does being recognized as an entity change something? In an object-oriented domain model, an entity is typically a plain class with some optional, but recommended, characteristics, such as a common behavior inherited from a common base class.

## Domain value types

A value type (or value object) represents a simpler business concept that has attributes but no distinct identity. In other words, a value type is defined solely by the value of its attributes.

Key characteristics of value types include the following:

- **Immutability**   Value types are immutable. Their state cannot change after creation. If a value needs to be modified, a new value object with the updated attributes is created.

- **Attribute-based equality**   Value types are considered equal based on their attribute values rather than by their business identity. Two value objects are equal if all their attributes have the same value.

- **No life cycle**   Value types do not have a distinct life cycle. They are created when needed and discarded when they are no longer used. They are often used as part of the state of an entity or within aggregates.

- **Consistency and invariants**   Value types can enforce invariants and business rules related to their attributes. These rules ensure that the value remains in a valid state.

- **Immutable collections**   Value types often contain collections of other value types or primitive data. These collections are typically immutable, meaning their elements cannot be modified directly.

A canonical example of a value type is the concept of a Money value object used to represent an amount of currency. Each Money value object could have attributes like CurrencyCode and Amount, and they can be compared based on their attribute values for equality or used for calculations. Since Money value objects are immutable, operations like addition or subtraction would result in new Money instances with the updated values rather than modifying the original instances.

**Note** Value types are business-specific primitive types. In a generic programming language, you have primitive types like int or string. This is because programming languages are not natively designed to build applications for specific business scenarios. Rather, they are designed with a general-purpose, math-oriented mindset, which makes them flexible enough to be adapted to any business scenario. In a real business domain, you typically have concepts that can be faithfully represented as integers or strings but are not generic numbers or alphanumeric expressions. In a business domain, you might have a temperature, weight, or quantity that is well represented by a language primitive like an integer but, in the business domain, expresses a primitive type of its own. This is where value objects fit.

## Aggregates and roots

The term *aggregate* abstractly refers to a number of domain entities grouped together into a single unit with well-defined boundaries. The primary purpose of an aggregate is to enforce consistency and invariability within a domain, ensuring that the entities within the aggregate remain in a valid and consistent state.

In contrast, the term *aggregate root* refers to a specific entity within the aggregate that acts as the entry point for all access and manipulation of other objects within the aggregate. The aggregate root is the only object that can be accessed from outside the aggregate, and it ensures that all changes to the objects within the aggregate are made in a controlled and consistent manner.

Key characteristics of aggregates include the following:

- **Consistency boundaries**  All domain entities within an aggregate are designed to adhere to the aggregate's invariants and business rules.

- **Transactional boundaries**  All changes to the entities within the aggregate are treated as a single unit of work, and changes are persisted to the database or rolled back as a whole.

- **Isolation**  Entities within an aggregate are isolated from objects outside the aggregate. Access to the objects within the aggregate is possible only through the aggregate root.

- **Relationships**  Aggregates can have relationships with other aggregates, but these relationships are typically represented through references to the aggregate roots rather than direct access to the objects within the aggregate.

As an example of an aggregate, consider an online bookstore with two domain entities: Book and Author. In the domain, each book can have one or more authors. In pseudo-C# code, the aggregate might look like this:

```
class Book : IAggregateRoot
{
    // Book properties
    int BookId { get; private set; }
```

```
string Isbn { get; private set; }
string Title { get; private set; }
    :

// Authors
IReadOnlyCollection<Author> Authors { get; private set; }

// Book methods
Book SetTitle(string title)
{ ... }
Book AddAuthor(Author author)
{ ... }
    :
}
```

The `IAggregateRoot` interface in the pseudo code doesn't need to be a full interface with a defined contract. It can simply be a marker interface used to flag a class in some way. For example:

```
public interface IAggregateRoot
{
    // Marker interface, no members
}
```

Having such a marker interface is only helpful to restrict a generic repository class to accept only aggregate root classes:

```
public class BaseRepository<T> where T : IAggregateRoot
{
    ...
}
```

> **Note** The aggregate should be a different aggregator class (for example, some BookAggregate class), or the aggregation takes place silently within the root entity itself, in which case, an aggregate root contains other child aggregates? In all implementations I have considered, I've never had a separate aggregate class. The option of just designating the root to be a root is also much closer to the real world in which you may use Entity Framework for persistence. In this case, the aggregate results from the database level of table relationships and constraints.

## Loading state into domain entities

Due to their ignorance of persistence, domain entities should not be designed to allow access to storage either directly or via references packages. That's great, but where does an instance of, say, the Book entity grab any state that makes it qualify as an instance representing the author, ISBN, and title of a given manuscript? As shown in Figure 6-2, state must be loaded into a domain entity.

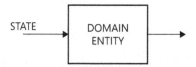

STATE → DOMAIN ENTITY →

**FIGURE 6-2** Because entities are persistence ignorant, any state must be explicitly injected.

One option is to incorporate a public constructor in the entity class that allows you to set all the data—something like this:

```
public Book( /* all properties forming a valid state for the book */ )
{ ... }
```

To be used directly, such a constructor must be public. To avoid misuse, you should clearly document it, specifying that it's intended solely for data construction and should not be used elsewhere. Alternatively, you can consider using a factory.

In a realistic implementation of an object-oriented domain model, you might want to leverage an object-database mapper library like Entity Framework Core, which handles the data population process automatically. Within your infrastructure layer, you can directly query the domain entity from the database. To facilitate this, add private setters for each property and include a private default constructor. The Entity Framework will then instantiate your object using the default constructor and populate its properties using reflection. (You'll see this demonstrated later in this chapter.)

## The domain model in Project Renoir

Project Renoir has the domain model implemented as a C# class library in the main solution. Should it be shareable with other projects in the context of a larger bounded context, you can configure the build pipeline to produce and deploy it as a private NuGet package within your Azure DevOps. (Sharing the class library as an assembly or a public NuGet package is an option too.)

### The dependency list

The domain model class library has no project dependencies. For convenience, it references a house-made NuGet package for utilities—the Youbiquitous.Martlet.Core package—which supplies a variety of extension methods for working with primitive types like numbers, strings, and dates. If resource strings are required, you can place them in a resource embedded in the project or, for larger projects, link to a specific resource project.

As for the target of the project, you must decide whether to go with .NET Standard or a specific version of the .NET Core framework. In general, .NET Standard is designed for cross-platform compatibility and facilitates code sharing between different .NET platforms. If your model is intended to be used across .NET Framework, .NET Core, MAUI, Xamarin, and others, well, go for it. On the other hand, if your library is designed exclusively for a particular .NET implementation, such as .NET Core 8, you might consider directly targeting the specific framework version. This approach may provide additional optimization opportunities or enable you to take advantage of platform-specific features.

## Life forms in the library

The Project Renoir domain model is centered around a few entities and counts a couple of aggregates. All entities descend from a base class that provides a bunch of predefined attributes and overridable methods:

- **Product**   This refers to the software products for which release and roadmap documents are created. A product is not part of any larger aggregation; it is a plain simple entity characterized by its own identity and life cycle.

- **ReleaseNote**   This represents a release notes document and is composed of a list of `ReleaseNoteItem` entities In this regard, it is an aggregate root. It also references a `Product`.

- **Roadmap**   This represents a roadmap document and is composed of a list of `RoadmapItem` entities. In this regard, it is an aggregate root. It also references a `Product`.

Two more sections form the domain model of Renoir: classes related to membership (user accounts, roles, and permissions) and classes related to bindings between entities necessary for the persistence of the authorization layer (user-to-product, user-to-release note, and user-to-roadmap).

## Persistence-driven definition of aggregates

A domain model library should be designed to be independent of any specific object-relational mapping (O/RM) dependencies. Ideally, you have a domain model and a persistence layer devised in total freedom with some intermediate layer to make necessary transformations to and from storage. (See the left side of Figure 6-3.) With this approach, you don't just code a domain model, you also code a mapper and any wrapper around the data store (for example, stored procedures). The model can be designed in full observance of DDD principles, using some other code to understand it and map it to storage. To save to storage, you can still use an O/RM.

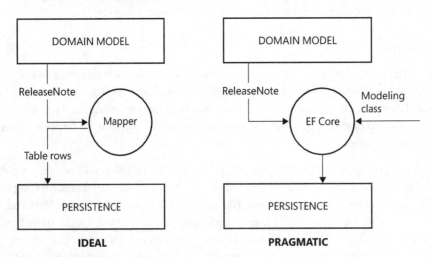

**FIGURE 6-3** A mapper takes care of turning domain classes into storage items.

A more pragmatic approach is to use a rich O/RM like Entity Framework Core to simplify things, at the cost of dirtying the model a bit. The right side of Figure 6-3 shows that with EF Core, you can use just one model and a modeling class that declaratively sets a correspondence between entities and database objects. When this occurs—for mere convenience—it is not uncommon to make some minor concessions in the O/RM to facilitate model serialization. For instance, you might need to include a hidden constructor or introduce an additional property and some scaffolding to enable the serialization of arrays or enumerated types. Property setters also must be defined, although they can be private.

The ultimate objective is a domain model with as few infrastructure dependencies as possible—ideally zero. While achieving complete independence might not always be feasible due to specific serialization requirements or other practical considerations, a realistic goal is to keep the domain model's dependency on infrastructure to an absolute minimum. In Project Renoir, we opted for a pragmatic approach, so the same model presented as the domain model is used as the model that lets Entity Framework Core persist data to the database.

## The hitchhiker's guide to the domain

Having a domain model instead of a plain list of anemic classes—essentially DTOs—guarantees neither faster development nor bug-free code. It's a habit with a couple of plusses—readability and subsequently the ability to handle complexity. Figure 6-4 summarizes the decision tree.

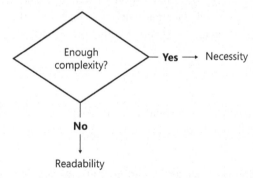

**FIGURE 6-4** A basic decision tree for choosing a domain model versus a more anemic model.

Do you have enough complexity? If so, a domain model is nearly a necessity to avoid sinking in the troubled waters of requirements and features. Is it simple enough that you can just produce functional code successfully? Even then, learning to use a domain model is not an excessive investment. If you use an O/RM like Entity Framework, you already have a bunch of classes ready; you just need to put a bit more attention and vision into their code and design. It's not a matter of being a great developer or visionary architect; it's simply a matter of having "good habits."

> **Note** In modern business, complexity is a monotonic increasing function, its graph moving ever upward as you jump from one project to another or as the same project evolves and expands.

## Treating software anemia

Software anemia is typically assessed by the amount of behavior present in classes. In a model that is merely inferred from a database, there is usually very little behavior, making the model anemic. Is software anemia a serious disease, however?

### Technical threat

In humans, anemia—caused by a deficiency of red blood cells, which are responsible for delivering oxygen to body tissues for vitality and energy—leads to weariness. In a software context, anemia signifies a lack of energy to cope with changes, but it is not considered a disease. An anemic model can still function effectively if the development team can manage the complexity of the domain and its evolution.

Ultimately, an anemic model is not a mistake *per se*. But like the sword of Damocles, it poses a threat to your code. According to Greek myth, Damocles sat on a throne with a massive sword hanging over him, supported only by a single hair. This serves as a fitting metaphor: everything is fine as long as the sword remains suspended. So, an anemic model is not certified technical debt; rather, it is a sort of technical threat that could one day (in near time) become technical debt. For this reason, DDD pundits argue that models should not be anemic.

### Methods over properties

DDD's emphasis on behavior serves two main purposes: to create objects with a public interface that closely resemble entities observable in the real world, and to facilitate easier modeling that aligns with the names and rules of the ubiquitous language.

When modeling, a kind of backward thinking drives us to focus on attributes first, perhaps because the relational data model often drives our learning path. We then mark attributes with properties that have public getters and setters. At that point, having methods to alter the state of properties seems a useless extra effort. This is precisely where the change must happen.

Here's a quick example. Suppose you have a `UserAccount` class that models the concept of a signed-up user to some software system. The user forgets their password, and the system manages to reset it. The state of the persisted user should change to host a password-reset token and the time it was requested. The user is then sent an email with a link that incorporates the token. When the user follows the link, the system uses the token to confirm the identity, checks the expiration of the link, and sets the new password.

How would you code the change of state due to the initial request? You would probably use code like this:

```
user.PasswordResetToken = Guid.NewGuid();
user.PasswordResetRequested = DateTime.UtcNow;
```

But what about using this, instead?

```
User.RequestPasswordReset();
```

Internally, the method includes just the two lines shown here to set properties. What's the difference? You simply shifted from a data-centric vision to a behavior-centric perspective. Where is readability? In the name of the action. Where is maintainability? In your ability to change how the password reset is implemented by simply rewriting the method in one place only.

# Common traits of an entity class

A domain entity is a straightforward C# class designed to encompass both data (properties) and behavior (methods). While an entity may have functional public properties, it should not be intended as a mere data container.

## General guidelines

Following are some general guidelines that any C# class should adhere to when becoming a part of a domain model:

- Behavior is expressed through methods, both public and private.

- State is exposed through read-only properties.

- There is very limited use of primitive types; value objects are used instead.

- Factory methods are preferred over multiple constructors.

Let's make it clear up front: these are just guidelines. Using, say, primitive types instead of value objects and constructors instead of factory methods won't make any project fail. Still, guidelines exist for a purpose. To borrow from the dictionary, a guideline is a comprehensive set of recommended instructions that offer guidance and direction for performing tasks or making decisions effectively and appropriately. It serves as a reference to achieve desired outcomes or standards.

## Top-level base class

Project Renoir has a top-level base class for entities that provide support for auditing, state validation, and soft deletion to all derived classes. Here is the code:

```
public partial class BaseEntity
{
    public BaseEntity()
    {
        Deleted = false;
```

```
        Created = new TimeStamp();
        LastUpdated = new TimeStamp();
    }

    protected bool Deleted { get; private set; }
    public TimeStamp Created { get; private set; }
    public TimeStamp LastUpdated { get; private set; }
}
```

The TimeStamp class in the example is a helper class that tracks who made the change—creation or update—and when: Here's the list of methods saved to a separate partial file:

```
public partial class BaseEntity
{
    public virtual bool IsValid()
    {
        return true;
    }

    public bool IsDeleted()
    {
        return Deleted;
    }

    public void SoftDelete()
    {
        Deleted = true;
    }

    public void SoftUndelete()
    {
        Deleted = false;
    }
}
```

In particular, the method IsValid can be overridden by derived classes to add any invariant logic necessary for the specific entity.

## The need for identity information

Each entity within the domain is typically expected to have a distinct identity that sets it apart from other entities, even if they share similar attributes. For example, consider a Person class in a domain model. Each individual person would have a unique identity, often represented by an ID or a combination of attributes that collectively serve as a unique identifier. The identity of an entity allows the system to track and manage individual instances, supporting operations such as retrieval, update, and deletion.

The definition of an identity is entity-specific. Most of the time, it takes the form of a GUID, a progressive number, an alphanumeric string, or some combination of these.

## Application-specific base class

What can an application-specific entity base class add on top of the core base entity class? Not much, except that you keep the base class in a separate library or package, and for a particular application you need something more or something less. As long as all the source code is in the domain model class library, another application-specific base class may add something significant, especially with multi-tenant applications. In these cases, the identity of the tenant can be packaged in the application's domain base class to be shared by all other entities, along with a few helper methods. Here's an example:

```csharp
public class RenoirEntity : BaseEntity
{
    public RenoirEntity()
        : this(new Tenant())
    {
    }

    public RenoirEntity(Tenant owner)
    {
        Owner = owner;
    }

    [Required]
    [MaxLength(30)]
    public string OrganizationId
    {
        get => Owner.OrganizationId;
        set => Owner.OrganizationId = value;
    }

    [Required]
    [MaxLength(30)]
    public string DeptId
    {
        get => Owner.DeptId;
        set => Owner.DeptId = value;
    }

    public int Year
    {
        get => Owner.Year;
        set => Owner.Year = value;
    }

    public Tenant Owner { get; protected set; }

    public string ToName()
    {
        return $"{Owner}";
    }
}
```

The tenant identity is defined as a triple containing the organization, department, and year. All classes that inherit from RenoirEntity get the Owner tenant property and a few helper methods.

## Use of data annotations

In the preceding code snippets, you may have noticed sparse attributes decorating some properties—Required and MaxLength in particular. These attributes are part of the .NET Core framework. Specifically, they belong to the Data Annotations namespace. To use them, you won't need to add any external dependencies to the domain model class library.

So, why use them? Being decorations, they won't add any special capabilities to your code. However, such decorations do help the Entity Framework code that maps domain classes to the database structure to figure out which column attributes to use. In particular, MaxLength saves you from having nvarchar table columns set to MAX. Faced with string properties, in fact, Entity Framework would generate table columns of type nvarchar(MAX) unless MaxLength is specified.

Note, though, that the same effect on the database structure achieved through Required and MaxLength attributes can also be obtained using fluent code in the class in the infrastructure layer that does the object-to-relational mapping. (More on this in Chapter 8, "The infrastructure layer.")

> **Important** Having string table columns with a maximum possible length (2 GB) simplifies data handling because you don't have to worry about the actual size of the string being stored. At the same time, you must employ nvarchar(MAX) fields with care. Indeed, their use should be considered a mistake unless proven otherwise. Storing large amounts of data in fields can reduce performance compared to using fixed-length fields when querying or indexing the table. In addition, it can dramatically increase the size of the database, affecting backup, restore, and storage operations. Finally, large nvarchar(MAX) fields may lead to page fragmentation, affecting data-retrieval performance.

## Rules of etiquette

Although the exact definition of clean code may not be precise, its outcomes are clear. Clean code tells a story, much like a well-written novel. Easy-to-read code facilitates understanding and subsequently cost-effective maintenance and extension. Code never belongs to a single individual; at some point, other people will need to get hold of that code. Beyond the functional effectiveness of the code, readability falls somewhere between a courtesy and a duty. It's a matter of etiquette.

This section contains 10 essential coding recommendations that warrant meticulous consideration. These suggestions encompass reducing nesting, minimizing loops, simplifying convoluted logic, avoiding magic numbers, and prioritizing conciseness and clarity in your code. Following these rules ensures that you don't violate coding etiquette.

## The early return principle

The early return (ER) principle calls for code to return from a method as soon as a certain condition is met or a specific result is obtained. Instead of using nested if...else statements, you use early returns to handle each case separately. Here's an example:

```
public string BuildReport(int year)
{
    if (year < 2021)
        return null;
    // Proceed
    ...
}
```

Related to ER are a method's preconditions. At the beginning of each method, it's a good practice to quickly exclude all known situations that are not acceptable or supported and just return a default value or throw an exception.

## Reducing `if` pollution

As a conditional construct, the if statement, along with loops and assignments, is a pillar of programming. But in modern code, which is so rich in nuances and complexity, the classic if...then...else statement—while crucial to control the flow of code—is too verbose and consumes too much space. To reduce so-called if pollution, you have three, non-mutually exclusive options:

- **Invert the condition** If the then branch is much larger than the else, invert the Boolean guard to apply ER and save one level of nesting. That is, treat the else branch as a precondition and then proceed with the direct coding of the then branch.

- **Use `switch` instead of `if`** Both if and switch are conditional statements. The if handles multiple conditions sequentially and executes the first true branch. For a large set of conditions, though, the switch syntax is shorter and less polluted. switch is ideal for discrete value-based decisions, while if offers more flexibility. Human reasoning tends to be if-centric, but with three conditions to handle, moving to switch is an option.

- **Merge multiple `if` statements** When turning business rules into code, we typically reason step by step, and sometimes each step is an if statement. In our learning path, it may not be obvious when two or even more if conditions could be merged without affecting the outcome. However, merging if statements reduces the number of conditions and branches and keeps your code cleaner.

## Pattern matching

In recent versions of C#, pattern matching has become an extremely flexible feature that enables conditional checks on data by matching its shape, structure, or properties. Pattern matching goes well beyond traditional equality checks to handle different types and structures effectively.

With pattern matching, you combine the `is` and **when** operators with familiar conditional constructs such as `switch` and `if` to compose concise, human-readable conditions that would be much more convoluted to express and hard to make sense of otherwise. Here's an example:

```
if (doc is ReleaseNote { RelatedProduct.Code: "PUBAPI" } rn)
{
    // Use the rn variable here
}
```

Pattern matching does a couple of things. It first checks whether the doc variable is of type `ReleaseNote` and then if the expression `RelatedProduct.Code` equals PUBAPI. If both checks are successful, it returns a new variable named `rn` to work on the release note document for product PUBAPI.

However, pattern matching offers even more flexibility than this. Suppose you need to apply the following business condition to a search operation: all documents released between 2015 and 2022, but not those released in 2020. The following classic-style code works.

```
if (doc != null &&
    doc.YearOfRelease >= 2015 &&
    doc.YearOfRelease < 2023 &&
    doc.YearOfRelease != 2020)
{
    // Do some work
}
```

Here's how it could be rewritten with pattern-matching operators:

```
if (doc is
    { YearOfRelease: >=  2015 and
                     <   2023 and
                     not 2020 })
{
    // Do some work
}
```

This code looks a lot like the sentence in the preceding paragraph that describes the business condition to check.

Overall, I believe the issue with pattern matching is that its extremely flexible syntax may be harder to grasp than a plain `if`...`then`...`else` syntax, even for seasoned developers. However, code assistant tools do a great job of silently suggesting similar changes. (More on this in a moment.)

## Using LINQ to avoid emissions of loops

The Language Integrated Query (LINQ) syntax resembles natural language and makes it easier to express the intent of a query. Furthermore, LINQ allows you to chain multiple operations together, creating a pipeline of operations. This enables developers to break down complex tasks into smaller and more manageable steps. More importantly, with LINQ you have no explicit loops. Like `if` statements, loops are the pillars of programming but tend to pollute code with nested blocks and consume too many lines of the code editor.

With LINQ, you don't need to write explicit loops (such as `for` or `foreach`) to perform operations on collections. The query operators encapsulate the iteration logic, reducing the need for boilerplate code and enhancing clarity.

Here's a demonstration of how to generate a list of even numbers without using LINQ:

```
var numbers = new List<int> { 1, 2, 3, 4, 5 };
var squares = new List<int>();
foreach (int n in numbers)
{
  if (n % 2 == 0)
  {
    var squared = n * n;
    squares.Add(squared);
  }
}
```

One easy way to improve readability is to invert the `if` statement within the loop. But using LINQ, you can do even more, with less:

```
var numbers = new List<int> { 1, 2, 3, 4, 5 };
var squares = numbers.Where(n => n % 2 == 0).Select(n => n * n);
```

LINQ is primarily focused on working with collections, so not all loops can be turned into LINQ calls. For example, general-purpose `while` or `do-while` loops based on a condition cannot be directly converted to LINQ calls. The same goes for `for` iterations except when they just iterate a collection (and could be replaced with `foreach`). Finally, loops with complex nested structures, especially if they interact with multiple variables and conditions, cannot be easily expressed using a single LINQ pipeline. In general, LINQ is more suitable for single-pass transformations and for filtering operations. All loops that fall into this range may be effectively replaced, making the code much more concise.

## The Extract Method refactoring pattern

The Extract Method refactoring pattern is a technique to improve code structure and readability. It involves moving a group of statements within a method into a new, separate method with a meaningful name that reflects its purpose.

Imagine a scenario in which you import content serialized in a comma-separated string into a RoadmapItem entity. At some point, you need to have the code that instantiates a RoadmapItem and copies in it any serialized content:

```
public IList<RoadmapItem> ImportFrom(IList<string> csvLines)
{
    var list = new List<RoadmapItem>();
    foreach(var line in csvLines
    {
        var tokens = line.Split(',');
        var rmi = new RoadmapItem();
        rmi.ProductCode = tokens[0];
        rmi.Text = tokens[1];
```

```
        rmi.Eta = tokens[2];
        list.Add(rmi);
    }

    return list;
}
```

It's just 15 lines of code—not even the most cryptic code you could write—but it can still be refactored for clarity and conciseness by using the Extract Method pattern with LINQ. First, move the code involved with the creation of the RoadmapItem to a factory method on the entity class, like so:

```
public static RoadmapItem FromCsv(string line)
{
    var tokens = line.Split(',');
    var rmi = new RoadmapItem();
    rmi.ProductCode = tokens[0];
    rmi.Text = tokens[1];
    rmi.Eta = tokens[2];
    return rmi;
}
```

Next, make the loop disappear using LINQ. The entire code is now four lines long—two more if you opt to break long instructions into multiple lines for further clarity:

```
public IList<RoadmapItem> ImportFrom(IList<string> csvLines)
{
    return csvLines
            .Select(RoadmapItem.ImportCsv)
            .ToList();
}
```

Here, the details of the creation of the roadmap item are hidden from the main view but are accessible if you drill down. Moreover, you added a factory to the entity, accepting the fact that the entity in the domain can be created—on business demand—from, say, a CSV file. So, you didn't just compact the code, but you also made it more business focused (moving business and implementation details one level downward) and immediately comprehensible.

## Extension methods

The term *syntactic sugar* in programming refers to language features that don't add new functionality but offer a more convenient syntax for existing operations. Extension methods fit this definition as they allow developers to add new functionality to existing types without modifying their original code. For example, here's how to add a new Reverse method to the type string:

```
public static class StringExtensions
{
    // Extension method for type String that adds the non-native
    // functionality of reversing content
    public static string Reverse(this string theString)
    {
        var charArray = theString.ToCharArray();
        Array.Reverse(charArray);
```

```
        return new string(charArray);
    }
}
```

Technically, extension methods are static methods that can be called as if they were instance methods of the extended type. The trick is to use the `this` keyword as the first parameter; this allows the compiler to identify the target type and successfully resolve dependencies.

Extension methods enhance code readability, reusability, and maintainability, enabling developers to create custom methods that seamlessly integrate with built-in or third-party types. To experience the power of extension methods, look at the following code snippet based on the free Youbiquitous. Martlet.Excel NuGet package (which, in turn, depends on the DocumentFormat.OpenXml package):

```
// Get a SpreadsheetDocument using the OpenXml package
var document = SpreadsheetDocument.Open(file, isEditable: false);

// The Read extension method does all the work of preparing a worksheet object
// The injected transformer will turn into a custom class
var data = document.Read(new YourExcelTransformer(), sheetName);
```

Using the OpenXml library, going from a file or stream to manageable data takes several lines of code and involves several Excel objects. But at the end of the day, all you want is to specify an Excel reference and some code that accesses content and copies it into an app-specific data structure:

```
public static T Read<T>(this SpreadsheetDocument document,
        IExcelTransformer<T> transformer, string sheetName = null)
        where T : class, new()
{
    if (transformer == null)
        return new T();

    // Extract stream of content for the sheet
    // (Uses another extension method on SpreadsheetDocument)
    var (wsPart, stringTable) = document.GetWorksheetPart(sheetName);
    return transformer.Read(wsPart, stringTable);
}
```

Even more nicely, in the `transformer` class, you can use the following code to read the content of cell C23 as a DateTime object:

```
var day = wsp.Cell("C23").GetDate();
```

In essence, extension methods are useful for adding utility methods to classes that are not directly under the developer's control, such as framework types or external libraries.

## Boolean methods

Earlier in this chapter, I presented the following code as a significant improvement because of the use of LINQ to remove the inherent loop:

```
var squares = numbers.Where(n => n % 2 == 0).Select(n => n * n);
```

To be honest, though, this snippet has a readability problem: the Boolean expression. At a glance, can you say what filter is being applied to the `numbers` collection? Here's how to rewrite it for readability:

```
var squares = numbers.Where(n => n.IsEven()).Select(n => n * n);
```

Especially if named following conventions such as `IsXxx`, `HasXxx`, `SupportsXxx`, `ShouldXxx`, or perhaps `CanXxx`, a Boolean method is incomparably clearer than any explicit Boolean expression.

Where does the example method `IsEven` come from? It could, for example, be an extension method:

```
public static bool IsEven(this int number)
{
    return number % 2 == 0;
}
```

This approach is pretty good for primitive .NET Core types, but it's even more powerful if you scale it up to the level of domain entities. The "behavior" to add to domain entities definitely includes Boolean methods for whatever conditions you want to check.

## Naturalizing enums

You can apply extension methods and the Boolean method rule to values of enumerated types. In programming, an enum type defines a distinct set of named numeric values, making it easier to work with a predefined set of related constants and improving code readability:

```
public enum RevisionStatus
{
    Unsaved = 0,
    Draft = 1,
    Published = 2,
    Archived = 3
}
```

How would you verify whether a specific document has been published? Based on what's been stated so far, you would likely go with a method on the entity:

```
public class ReleaseNote : RenoirEntity
{
    public bool IsPublished()
    {
        return Status == RevisionStatus.Published;
    }

    // More code
    ...
}
```

Great, but now imagine that the enum value is passed as an argument to some method. Consider the following:

```
public enum BulkInsertMode
{
    SkipExisting = 0,
    Replace = 1
}
public void DocumentBulkCopy(IList<ReleaseNote> docs, BulkInsertMode mode)
{
    // Classic approach
    if (mode == BulkInsertionMode.SkipExisting)
    { ... }

    // More readable approach
    if (mode.ShouldSkipExisting())
    { ... }

    // More code
    ...
}
```

Needless to say, ShouldSkipExisting is another extension method defined to work on individual enum values:

```
public static bool ShouldSkipExisting(this BulkInsertMode mode)
{
    return mode == BulkInsertMode.SkipExisting;
}
```

Surprised? Well, that's exactly how I felt when I found out that extension methods could also work with enum values.

## Using constant values

Hard-coded values without meaningful context or explanation should never appear in code. That doesn't mean your million-dollar project will fail if you use a constant somewhere, nor does it mean that you should toss an entire code base if you find a few hard-coded values here and there. Instead, you need to take a pragmatic stance.

As long as explicit constants remain confined to a method, a class, or even an entire library, then they are basically harmless. It's more a matter of technical threat than technical debt. It's a different story, however, if those constants are interspersed throughout the entire code base without a clear map of where, how, and why. So, as a rule, don't use magic numbers and magic strings. Constants are part of a business domain and belong to a domain model; as such, they should be treated as value types.

In a business domain, quite often you encounter small groups of related numbers or strings. For numbers, you can use enum types. But for strings? Very few programming languages natively support string enums (Kotlin, Rust, TypeScript), and C# is not in the list. In C#, string enums can be implemented through a proper class, as shown here:

```
// Valid surfaces for tennis matches
public class Surface
{
    private static readonly Surface[] _all = { Clay, Grass, Hard };
    private Surface(string name)
    {
        Name = name;
    }

    // Public readable name
    public string Name { get; private set; }

    // Enum values
    public static readonly Surface Clay = new Surface("Clay");
    public static readonly Surface Grass = new Surface("Grass");
    public static readonly Surface Hard = new Surface("Hard");

    // Behavior
    public static Surface Parse(string name)
    { ... }

    public IEnumerable<Surface> All()
    {
        return _all;
    }
}
```

As the string enum is ultimately a class, you may not need extension methods to extend its functionality as long as you have access to the source code.

## Avoiding the Data Clump anti-pattern

The *Data Clump anti-pattern* describes a situation in which a group of data items or variables frequently appear together in multiple parts of the code. These data items are tightly coupled and are often passed around together as loose parameters to various methods.

Data clumps are problematic primarily because the resulting code is harder to read and understand due to the scattered and repeated data. In addition, the same group of data is duplicated in different parts of the code, leading to redundancy. Finally, code with data clumps is fragile. That is, if the data structure changes, you must update it in multiple places, increasing your odds of introducing bugs.

Here's an example data clump:

```
public IEnumerable<ReleaseNote> Fetch(string tenant,
        int year, string productCode, string author, int count)
{
    // Expected to filter the list of documents based on parameters
}
```

This method applies a dynamically built WHERE clause to the basic query that fetches release note documents. There are up to five possible parameters: tenant code, year, product code, document author, and maximum number of documents to return.

In a web application, all these data items travel together from the HTML front end to the presentation layer, and from there through the application layer down into a domain service or repository. This is a relatively safe scenario, as the data clump moves unidirectionally and through application layers. Writing the necessary code is ugly and boring but hardly error-prone. But what if, at some point, you need to add one more item to the clump—say, release date? At the very minimum, you need to put your hands in various places.

In general, data clumps may indicate that there is a missing abstraction or the need to create a separate data structure. Fortunately, addressing the data clump anti-pattern is easy. Just encapsulate related data into a single class—for example, `QueryFilter`. This promotes better organization, improves code readability, and reduces code duplication. Additionally, using data structures with a clear purpose makes it easier to understand the intent of the code and makes future changes less error-prone.

# Style conventions

In addition to coding design practices, it also helps to adhere to common style practices. The resulting code is prettier to read and inspect. It also promotes positive emulation among developers, as no one wants to push code that looks ugly and untidy.

## Common-sense coding guidelines

For the most part, the following coding style practices—which nobody should ignore—are just common sense. Each developer should follow them whenever writing code, and enforcing them across a team is critical. The guidelines are as follows:

- **Consistent indentation and bracing**   Use consistent indentation (preferably with tabs) to visually align code blocks and improve readability. Be consistent with braces too. In C#, the convention is Allman style, where the brace associated with a control statement goes on the next line, indented to the same level as the control statement, and statements within braces are indented to the next level.

- **Meaningful naming**   Use descriptive and meaningful names for variables, methods, and classes that reflect their purpose. Files and directories within a project should also be named and organized in a logical and consistent manner, following project-level conventions. (Typically, you want to have one class per file.)

- **Consistent naming convention**   Follow the naming convention of the programming language. For C#, it is camelCase for variables and fields and PascalCase for classes and their properties. Exceptions (for example, snake_case) are acceptable but in a very limited realm such as a single class or method.

- **Proper spacing** Use proper spacing around operators, commas, and other elements to enhance code readability. Also, add one blank line between related groups of method calls to mark key steps of the workflow you're implementing.

## Partial classes

In C#, partial classes are used to split the definition of a single class across multiple source files. In this way, a large class can be divided into more manageable parts, each in its own file, while still being treated as a single cohesive unit at compile time. Partial classes are compiled as a single class during the build process; the separation is only a developer-time feature. Note that partial classes cannot be used to split non-class types (for example, structs or interfaces) or methods across multiple files.

With partial classes, related code members (for example, properties and methods) can be grouped together, enhancing code navigation and organization within the integrated development environment (IDE). The overall code base becomes more organized and easier to work with. To some extent, partial classes also assist with team collaboration, as multiple developers can work on different parts of a class simultaneously without having to merge their changes into a single file.

**Note** In general, partial classes are just a tool to better organize code; how you choose to split a class is entirely up to you.

Partial classes are widely used in Project Renoir, and most entity classes are coded over two or more partials. (See Figure 6-5.) The core classes of Project Renoir, `BaseEntity` and `RenoirEntity`, are split into two partial classes: the primary class with constructors and properties, and a child class with methods with a `Methods` suffix. Most repository classes in the infrastructure layer (see Chapter 8) have distinct partial classes for query and update methods.

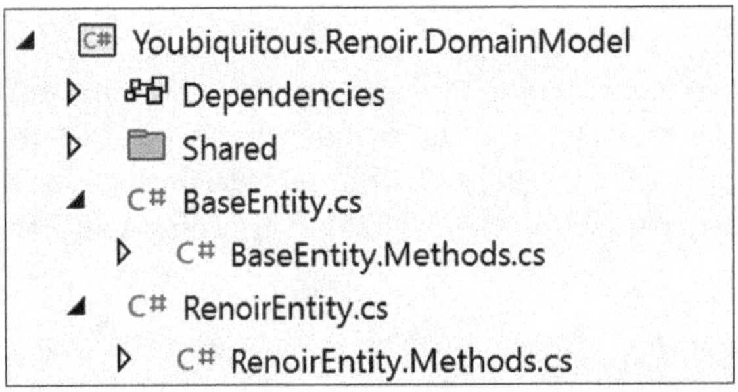

FIGURE 6-5 Partial classes in the Project Renoir domain model.

**Note** With the File Nesting mode of the Visual Studio Solution Explorer set to Web, partial classes with a common prefix in the name (for example, BaseEntity and BaseEntity.Methods) are rooted in the same tree view node and can be expanded and collapsed, as in Figure 6-6.

## Visual Studio regions

Visual Studio regions are another developer-time tool for working with large classes more effectively. A *region* is a code-folding feature that allows developers to organize and group sections of code within a file. It is used to create collapsible code blocks, providing a way to hide or show sections of code as needed.

Regions are commonly used to group related code, such as methods, properties, or specific functional sections. They can also be used for documentation purposes by adding comments explaining the purpose of the region.

Both partial classes (a C# feature) and regions (a Visual Studio feature) are helpful for organizing code, but both should be used judiciously. In particular, overusing regions can give a false sense of readability when in fact the class (or method) is bloated or polluted and in desperate need of refactoring. Similarly, misuse of partial classes may distribute complexity over multiple files, again giving a false sense of readability and organization when, in the end, all you have is a giant god-style class.

> **Note** Regions are not a tool for magically making the code modular. Their use case is to logically group code and improve code organization, not to hide excessive complexity and code smells. So, you should make thrifty use of regions, but do use them.

## Line and method length

Too often, we face blurry recommendations, such as, "Keep each method short and focused." But what kind of guidance do we really get out of it? Beyond the general recommendation of conciseness and focus, we need to be much more specific about numbers and measures. For example, what is the recommended length for a single line of code? The C# compiler doesn't pose limits, but most coding style guidelines rightly recommend keeping the maximum length to around 100, maybe 120, characters. (See Figure 6-6.)

```
89      /// <summary>
90      /// Works out the appropriate title of the view
91      /// </summary>
92      /// <returns></returns>
93      public string GetTitle()
94      {
95          return Title.IsNullOrWhitespace()
96              ? $"{Settings?.General.ApplicationName} {Settings?.Secrets.GetBackendModeForDisplay()}"
97              : Title;
98      }
99  }
```

**FIGURE 6-6** Visual measurement of line lengths.

The longest line of code in Figure 6-6 would exceed 150 characters if it were not broken. As shown in the figure, instead, the longest line spans 93 characters, leaving approximately 6 cm of whitespace to the right on a hi-res laptop screen and using the Cascadia Mono font with a default size of 12 points. So, in addition to improving code readability, limiting line length helps prevent horizontal scrolling and ensures code is more accessible on different screen sizes or when viewed side by side during version control.

As for the length of methods, giving a specific number is more problematic, but the same general principles apply. Methods that are too long can be harder to comprehend and maintain. Therefore, it is considered good practice to keep methods relatively short and focused on a single task. So, what is the recommended number of statements for a class method? My reference number is 300 lines, but the shorter the better.

To keep methods short, there are various approaches. One is to keep in mind that less logic requires fewer lines and to therefore focus the method on just one key task. Another is to use the most concise syntax reasonably possible. (Note that concise doesn't mean cryptic!) Finally, you can break code into smaller components and use abstractions so that each piece of code describes only its main task, leaving separate, dedicated classes or methods elsewhere to deal with the details.

As an example, consider the following code to extract the content of an Excel file into a custom data structure using the extension methods of the Youbiquitous.Martlet.Excel package:

```
public partial class YourExcelImporter : IExcelImporter<List<YourDataStructure>>
{
    public List<YourDataStructure> Load(Stream stream, string sheetName = null)
    {
        var document = SpreadsheetDocument.Open(stream, false);
        var obj = document.Read(new YourDataStructureTransformer(), sheetName);

        document.Close();
        return obj;
    }
}
```

The Read extension method eliminates at least 20 lines of code, and the injected transformer—another file—does the work. For a fairly sophisticated Excel file, such a transformer would consume more than 200 lines.

## Comments

Opinions on comments in code vary among developers, and there is no one-size-fits-all approach. Different developers and teams may have different perspectives on the value and use of comments in code. But nearly everyone agrees that well-written comments enhance code comprehension and provide insights into the code's intent and purpose. Unfortunately, there are quite a few varying definitions of what qualifies as a "well-written" comment.

Some developers believe that code should be self-explanatory and that comments are a sign of poorly written code. They prefer to write clean and expressive code that doesn't require comments to understand its functionality. Other developers just write random comments, depending on their mood and the task at hand. Yet other developers try to be as precise and verbose as they can—at least at first. Their effort inevitably diminishes with the pace of pushes to the repository.

When it comes to comments, here are some general considerations to keep in mind:

- Although comments are valuable, too many comments can clutter code and hinder readability.

- Relying only on inherent code readability is not ideal, but it's probably better than dealing with outdated or incorrect comments.

- Comments can sometimes be an indicator of code smells, such as excessive complexity, lack of modularity, or unclear variable/function names.

- In general, over-commenting is never a great statement about the code.

Here are my directives to the teams I work with:

- Always enter XML comments to describe the purpose of methods and public elements of a class. (I find it acceptable to skip over method parameters.)

- Whether you comment or not, ensure that the purpose and implementation of each group of methods is clear to other developers (including yourself, when you get back to the code weeks later).

- When you comment, be precise and concise, not chatty, silly, or long-winded.

Who's the primary beneficiary of comments in code? Your peers, for sure. So, comments are not directed at newbies—meaning you should reasonably expect that whoever reads your comments has the requisite programming skills and knowledge of the domain context.

# Writing truly readable code

A common sentiment among developers is, "Write (and test) it first, and make it pretty later." Unfortunately, one thing I've learned during three decades in the software industry is that nobody ever has the time (or the will) to make their own code prettier once it's been pushed. The quote at the beginning of the chapter says it all. It's not a matter of being a great developer; it's simply a matter of being a good developer with great habits—and writing readable code is one of the greatest.

Fortunately, modern IDEs (such as Visual Studio, Visual Studio Code, Rider, and so on) and code assistant plugins can considerably accelerate your efforts to absorb the techniques discussed in this chapter and turn them into everyday habits. So, too, can principles like those in the SOLID framework. Both are discussed in this section.

## Me and readable code

I started my career in the early 1990s as a regular product developer. A few years later, I became a freelance writer, consultant, and trainer. For several years, I focused on technology and demo code. When writing books, articles, and courseware, I simply put myself in the imaginary role of a professional developer coming to grips with any given technology and patterns. It mostly worked.

A decade later, I began taking on occasional professional development gigs and faced the first ins and outs of maintainable code. Even though these projects were intermittent, I had enough of them that I became even more comfortable in the shoes of a professional developer and was able to write even better and more realistic books, articles, and courses.

Then, in late 2020, I switched completely to product building. My attitude and sensitivity toward readable code have grown exponentially since then. When I look back, I realize it took me more than a decade to write readable code as my default mode. Had I focused more on development during my career, I would have achieved this more quickly, but it still would have been a matter of years.

## The role of code assistants

So, how do I write readable and maintainable code? I focus on the task at hand and make a mental model of the necessary software artifacts. In my mental model, conditions are `if` statements and loops are `while` or at most `foreach`; I don't even think about pattern-matching. Then I get going.

As I write, I rely on code assistants, particularly ReSharper. My code is constantly under review for conciseness and readability. I take nearly any suggestion a plugin may have with respect to style and patterns, and I avidly seek out any squiggles or tips I silently receive.

Code assistants suggest when and how to break complex expressions into multiple lines, when to invert or merge `if` statements, when a `switch` is preferable, and especially when your code can be rewritten using LINQ or pattern matching expressions. Visual Studio and other tools also offer refactoring capabilities to extract methods and, more importantly in a DDD scenario, rename classes and members. It all takes a few clicks and a few seconds. No excuses.

A new generation of code-assistant tools is surfacing following the incredible progress of AI technologies. GitHub Copilot employs sophisticated machine-learning models trained on publicly accessible code from GitHub repositories. As you input code in Visual Studio, the underlying AI examines the context and offers pertinent suggestions in real time. Additionally, you can type comments about the code you will write and have the AI use your notes as a prompt to generate code on the fly.

**Note** Using Visual Studio and ReSharper together can be problematic in terms of memory consumption and overall stability, but nothing that a middle developer-class PC with a good amount of RAM can't handle.

## SOLID like personal hygiene

When it comes to software principles, I believe that it's important to strike a balance and not rigidly enforce the principles in every situation. For this reason, I look skeptically at posts and articles that enthusiastically illustrate the benefits of SOLID, as if deviating from these principles would inevitably lead to project failure. SOLID is an acronym for the following five principles:

- **Single responsibility principle (SRP)**  This principle suggests that a class (or method) should encapsulate a single functionality and should not take on multiple responsibilities. In essence, it says, "Focus on just one task." But the boundary of the task is up to you, based on your expertise and sensitivity. What's the right granularity of the task? Nobody knows, and anyway, it might change on a case-by-case basis. I don't see any strict and concrete guidance in it, such as inverting an `if` or using Boolean methods.

- **Open/closed principle (OCP)** This principle states that software entities, such as classes, should be open for extension but closed for modification. This means that you should be able to add new functionality through inheritance or interface implementation without altering the existing code.

- **Liskov's substitution principle (LSP)** This has to do with when you inherit one class from another—specifically, the derived class should never restrict the public interface of the parent class. Clients using the base class should not need to know the specific subclass being used; they should rely only on the common interface or contract provided by the base class.

> **Note** LSP was introduced by Barbara Liskov in 1987 and was popularized as one of the SOLID principles by Robert C. Martin over two decades ago. Today, the C# compiler emits a warning if you break LSP, and the new keyword has been added to enable developers to work around poor inheritance design and avoid exceptions. In the end, LSP remains a valid point in design, but only if you extensively use object orientation. Surprisingly, this is not so common these days. Now, we use flat collections of classes, and when we inherit, we mostly override virtual members or add new ones. In all these common cases, LSP doesn't apply.

- **Interface segregation principle (ISP)** This one's obvious: Don't make classes depend on more interfaces than they need to. Sometimes I think it's included just to obtain a nicer acronym than SOLD.

- **Dependency inversion principle (DIP)** This principle suggests that high-level modules, such as application services, should not depend on low-level modules, like database access or specific implementations. Instead, both should depend on abstractions, allowing for flexibility and ease of modification in the system.

Personally, I would reduce both OCP and DIP to one core principle of software design: program to an interface, not to implementation. However, this principle is helpful when it's helpful. If used blindly, however, it only results in the over-engineering of projects.

Overall, SOLID principles aim to make software development more modular and maintainable. The problem is that they are relatively easy to understand but not so easy to turn into code—as evidenced by the counterarguments noted in some of the preceding bullets. These counterarguments do not dismiss the value of SOLID principles entirely; they simply raise a caution in terms of making sure you know how to translate them into effective actions in a project. Like personal hygiene, you must know about and practice SOLID. But it won't save you from any serious disease.

# Summary

Dedicated to the unchanging aspects of the core business logic, the domain layer consists of two distinct but interconnected components: a domain model and an optional set of domain-specific services.

This chapter focused on the key aspects of an object-oriented domain model. The domain model embodies the underlying conceptual framework and essential business rules of a software application. It serves as an abstract portrayal of the problem the software intends to solve, encompassing elements such as entities, relationships, events, and business logic.

By depicting the significance and interactions among domain entities, the domain model aids development teams in giving life and substance to business processes within the context of a cohesive and flexible solution. When well-crafted, the domain model enhances communication between technical and non-technical teams and fosters the creation of robust and requirements-focused software.

This chapter also delved into the process of constructing a domain model as a C# class library composed of highly readable and aesthetically pleasing code. It also explored the benefits of utilizing IDE plugins to aid in this endeavor.

The next chapter is about domain services. As you'll see, in simple cases, domain services are interspersed as plain helper classes in the application and infrastructure layers. Yet, they play a role in the DDD vision, and that's where we'll start.

# CHAPTER 7

# Domain services

*Before I came here, I was confused about this subject. Having listened to your lecture,*
*I am still confused. But on a higher level.*

*—Enrico Fermi*

The primary focus of the domain model is to accurately model the real-world concepts and processes of the domain it represents. In the model, domain entities are objects that possess a unique identity and encapsulate state and behavior related to the domain. Entities contain the business logic and invariants that ensure the consistency and integrity of the data they hold. Where needed, aggregates group together entities and value objects, serving as a transactional boundary and ensuring consistency within the domain.

Unfortunately, the domain model is often insufficient to cover the entire set of necessary operations and behaviors. There might be specific processes to implement that do not naturally belong to a single entity or aggregate. These are typically operations that encapsulate multifaceted logic that involves interactions between multiple entities or requires coordination across various components of the system.

Enter domain services.

Domain services encompass operations that are essential for the functionality of the domain but are not inherently tied to any specific entity. Unlike domain entities, domain services do not have their own state; they are stateless machines that simply retrieve and process data.

Let's state this up front: Although domain services have a distinct place in the DDD framework, they aren't absolutely essential in a practical real-world application. The tasks that domain services are intended to take on can always be assigned to application services. Furthermore, some of these tasks can also be assigned to repositories if it is acceptable to raise the abstraction level of repositories from the granularity of a traditional CRUD library. (More on repositories in the next chapter.)

So, why even talk about domain services? Well, domain services offer more than pure programming power. They also offer precision and clarity in the software rendering of the domain. By housing multifaceted domain logic within dedicated services, domain entities can focus on their core responsibilities, remaining cohesive and maintaining a clean separation of concerns. At the same time, the application layer remains responsible solely for the orchestration of use cases, and the infrastructure layer focuses only on persistence and external services.

# What is a domain service, anyway?

In his book *Domain-Driven Design: Tackling Complexity in the Heart of Software*, Eric Evans identifies three distinct attributes of a well-crafted domain service:

- A domain service handles any operation that pertains to a domain concept that is not inherently part of any domain entity.

- In contrast to application services that employ DTOs for communication, a domain service operates directly with domain entities.

- Any performed operation is stateless; some data flows in, and some other data flows out.

## The stateless nature of domain services

Domain services are usually designed to be stateless for a few reasons. The primary reason is to prevent unintended side effects and unwanted interactions with other parts of the system. Because they are stateless, domain services are not tied to any specific context. So, their behavior remains consistent regardless of where or when they are called. The overall behavior of a domain service is not affected by mutable internal states, so it is predictable and deterministic. Predictability makes it easy to reason how the service will respond to different inputs, making it simpler to understand, test, and maintain.

The lack of a shared state brings other benefits too. For example, multiple requests can be processed simultaneously without risking data corruption or unexpected interactions. Additionally, services can be used across different parts of the system without carrying along any contextual baggage. Implementation and testing become easier, minimizing the chances of bugs related to state inconsistency.

> **Note** Overall, designing domain services to be stateless aligns well with the principles of DDD, emphasizing clear boundaries, separation of concerns, and focused responsibilities.

## Marking domain service classes

Because they're intended to work only with domain entities, domain service classes remain out of direct reach of the presentation layer. They are just one of the tools that application services may use to orchestrate use cases. (See Figure 7-1.)

Although not strictly necessary, you can adhere to convention and mark each domain service class with some `IDomainService` interface and, in case of common functionality (for example, logging, localization, or application settings) a `DomainService` base class. The `IDomainService` interface can simply be a marker interface, as shown here:

```
// A plain marker interface
public interface IDomainService
{
}
```

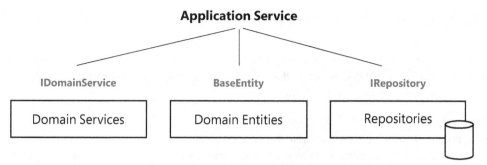

**FIGURE 7-1** Application services orchestrate use cases coordinating the activity of domain services, entities, and repositories.

You can leverage a common root—whether in the form of an interface or base class—to automatically register domain services as transient instances in the .NET Core dependency injection (DI) system. Nevertheless, even without inheritance, the service can still be injected as necessary.

In a DDD implementation that relies on several different classes of services (application, domain, and external), communicating the clear intent of each class with an unambiguous name is a great practice. So, it is advisable to give domain services clear and descriptive names that accurately convey their purpose. This intentional naming approach—respectful of the ubiquitous language—also promotes efficient communication among the team.

## Domain services and ubiquitous language

Because domain services are responsible for carrying out tasks that involve coordination between multiple entities, they are tightly bound to the names and concepts crystalized in the ubiquitous language vocabulary. By design, a domain service is a piece of business logic; as such it must be aptly named, strictly following business conventions. Choosing the appropriate business name is particularly important in the event of a logical or implementation bug because it streamlines communication between domain experts (usually non-technical stakeholders who understand the business requirements) and developers.

Consider an e-commerce system in which calculating the total price of an order typically involves discounts, taxes, and currency conversion. It's likely an array of entities and value objects, none of which naturally bear the full responsibility of the task. What should you name the domain service, then? Would something like `OrderPricingService` be good? Well, it depends on the language used by stakeholders. If the business terminology commonly used is, say, "finalize the order" then the right name is (a variation of) `OrderFinalizerService`. Not following this rule leaves a crack in the system's wall and will likely create a logical bug.

# Data access in domain services

The behavior of a stateless component such as a domain service is solely determined by provided inputs. The domain service doesn't store any data about past interactions and treats each request as an independent interaction. If data is required for a particular operation, it must be provided as input to that operation, and such external data is not stored.

Statelessness doesn't mean that a component can't have any data at all. Rather, it means that any data a component requires must be explicitly provided when needed through method parameters or injected dependencies. Statelessness emphasizes autonomy, predictability, and separation of concerns, not a total absence of stateful data. So, to function effectively, domain services typically rely on externally persisted data stored in a durable storage medium.

This brings us to a fundamental question: Should a domain service directly engage in retrieving the data it operates on that may also be modified as part of its core business task? There's no one-size-fits-all answer. Certainly, domain services should not have any direct exposure to database details or connection strings and should rely on separate repositories for any such needs. Beyond that, the decision of whether domain services should directly access data or receive it from the outside depends only on the application. The more a specific domain operation requires coordination between multiple entities and involves complex data retrieval logic, the more it might orchestrate these interactions internally and use repositories to fetch any necessary data.

# Data injection in domain services

In a design where domain services are seen as pristine logic entities, deliberately isolated from repositories, who assumes the responsibility of retrieving necessary data? As it happens, it is up to the application layer to coordinate the interaction between domain services and repositories.

Within an application service, you would use the appropriate repositories to retrieve required data. This data could be transformed, if necessary, into domain entities or value objects. The application service is also responsible for preparing the necessary data before passing it to the domain service. Once the data is retrieved and prepared, the application service invokes the domain service, passing the transformed data as parameters. The domain service then carries out its domain-specific logic without having to worry about data retrieval.

By structuring your application in this way, you fully adhere to the principle of separation of concerns. Each component has a clear responsibility: Domain services focus on domain logic, repositories handle data access, and application services coordinate the interactions. Furthermore, components can be developed, tested, and maintained independently. In particular, domain services can be unit-tested with controlled inputs, and application services can be tested for their interaction and orchestration.

# Common scenarios for domain services

Usually, domain services are employed when a specific business operation involves complex rules and calculations over multiple domain entities or aggregates to mediate these interactions while maintaining aggregate boundaries. This section explores a few examples from a functional viewpoint before reviewing a few concrete implementation facts.

## Determining the loyalty status of a customer

Suppose that within an e-commerce system, every time a customer finalizes an order, the system needs to add points to that customer's loyalty card. To achieve this, the application service can simply delegate the task to some `LoyaltyStatusService` domain service. Here's a possible programming interface:

```
public class LoyaltyStatusService : IDomainService
{
    public int AccruePoints(Order order)
    {
       // Return new total of points
    }
    ...
}
```

This interface is too simplistic. Realistically, the domain service method can't operate without also fetching the customer's purchase history. Moreover, the number of points to add is not necessarily a linear function based on the purchased amount. There might be extra points or other benefits (for example, a change of customer status to silver or gold) depending on the duration of the customer's fidelity. Furthermore, fetching data is only one step; you also likely need to write back some updated information. If you leave the application layer in control of everything, the system will access the database multiple times, which may (or may not) be an additional issue.

A more realistic interface could be as follows:

```
public int AccruePoints(Order currentOrder, IEnumerable<Order> history)
{
    // Return new total of points and/or other
    // information such as the new customer status
}
```

Yet another interface could pass an `IOrderRepository` reference to the service to enable it to fetch and save data autonomously. All these interfaces could be good or bad; the ultimate decision of which one to use belongs to the architect. This decision is typically made by looking at the dynamics of the business domain and nonfunctional constraints—for example, how often campaigns change, the presence of legacy code, team skills, and organizational preferences.

# Blinking at domain events

Domain services can also play a role in publishing or subscribing to domain events. They can broadcast events related to specific domain actions or subscribe to events from other parts of the system. Broadly speaking, a *domain event* is an event that could be triggered within the domain model's scope.

An alternative implementation for the loyalty status scenario might involve the application layer triggering an event within the domain that requires one or more handlers. A domain event can take the form of a straightforward C# event within an aggregate class, or it might use a publish/subscribe infrastructure. Information is placed on a bus, and designated handlers receive and process it as required. Handlers belong to domain service classes.

> **Important** Domain events are a powerful aspect of DDD, but mainly if the application is designed around events and its overall architecture qualifies as an event-driven architecture. Domain events implement business logic in a more extensible and adaptable way than hard-coded workflows. It's a new architectural resource for addressing the same problem and smoothing the work required to keep the system aligned to the business needs in the long run.

# Sending business emails

Could an action like sending an email (such as a confirmation email or a legal reminder) be thought of as behavior intrinsic to the domain logic? Yes and no. Whether it is or not depends on the specific context and requirements of the application.

In many cases, sending an email is not considered a core domain concern, but rather a technical detail associated with communication and notifications. However, there are scenarios for which sending emails might be closely related to the domain and should be treated as such. In a recent project, we treated the task of sending a particular email as a core domain behavior. The email was an unofficial legal reminder about an upcoming deadline, and we determined that it was directly tied to a core business process.

In general, to determine whether sending an email should be part of the domain logic, you should look at the domain relevance of the action and how tightly it relates to some business rule or task. If the timing, content, recipients, or other attributes of the email are dictated by specific business requirements, this indicates that sending the email is more than just a technical concern.

Still, not all emails an application may send involve a core domain behavior. If sending even a legal reminder is purely a technical detail and doesn't directly relate to the inherent behavior of your application's domain, it might be better suited as part of the application or infrastructure layer. In such cases, an application service or a dedicated service responsible for communication might handle this responsibility.

```csharp
public class LegalReminderService : IDomainService
{
```

```
    public NotificationResponse NotifyDeadline(string recipient, DateTime deadline)
    {
        // Return success or failure of sending the reminder
    }
    ...
}
```

**Note** An important signal about the domain relevance of an email action is if nothing in the names of the methods and classes involved refers explicitly to the act of sending an email. What ultimately turns out to be an automatic email is referred to as a legal reminder in the ubiquitous language.

Whenever interacting with an external system, API, or email service is part of the business logic, the domain service responsible must receive a reference to some service that knows how to do it. The email service is often an external component built around a third-party email provider such as SendGrid or Mailgun.

```
public class LegalReminderService : IDomainService
{
    private readonly IEmailService _email;
    public LegalReminderService(IEmailService emailService)
    {
        _email = emailService;
    }

    public NotificationResponse NotifyDeadline(string recipient, DateTime deadline)
    {
        // Use _email reference to send actual emails
        // Return success or failure of sending the reminder
    }
    ...
}
```

The logic of the service must abstract away the technical details and provide a clean interface for the domain to receive.

**Note** The definition of the interface (for example, `IEmailService`) belongs to the domain model, whereas the actual implementation (that uses, say, Sendgrid) lives in the infrastructure layer.

## Service to hash passwords

In a typical domain model, there is often a `UserAccount` entity, and its associated password might find storage within the application's database. However, retaining passwords in their clear state within this database inevitably introduces a substantial security vulnerability. So, the business logic firmly dictates the need to transform passwords into hash values before storage. The question is, where does the password-hashing functionality belong? Is it a domain service?

Password hashing is generally considered a technical concern and not a part of the domain logic. It's quite unlikely that the ubiquitous language contains business wording that relates explicitly to password storage. At most, you might find a requirement that clarifies the level of hash security to target. So, password hashing is more closely related to security and infrastructure, and it's commonly implemented as an infrastructure security service invoked from the application layer. Although there might be some rare situations for which you could argue that password hashing is tightly integrated with some specific domain security processes, DDD generally recommends treating it as a technical detail separated from the core domain logic.

Imagine code that handles a login attempt. The application layer receives the input from a visual form and retrieves the user that matches the identity. The job of checking hashed passwords occurs within a dedicated hashing service injected in the application layer, like so:

```
public class AccountService
{
    private readonly IHashingService _hash;
    public AccountService(IHashingService hashing)
    {
        _hash = hashing;
    }

    public bool ValidateCredential(string email, string clearPassword)
    {
        var user = _userRepository.Find(email);
        return _hash.Validate(user.Password, clearPassword);
    }
}
```

It's plain, simple, and well-isolated—and kept outside the domain logic.

## Implementation facts

The first commandment of domain services is to perform operations strictly related to the business domain working on domain entities and value objects. The first warning that you might not be on track comes from the names chosen for classes and methods. Whenever you find it natural and seamless to use terms that are too technical (for example, email, hashing, caching, tables, or auditing) to code the body of a service, you should carefully reconsider what you're doing. It might even be that you're treating as a domain service something that's better handled as an external, non-domain concern. When this happens, the primary risk is not introducing bugs, but rather spoiling the overall design, which may ultimately result in convoluted code and tight coupling—in short, technical debt.

### Building a sample domain service

Project Renoir deals with documents—release notes and roadmaps—created and managed by authorized users. One of the tasks accomplished through the application is therefore assigning users to a given document. The nature of this task can vary based on the desired business logic, encompassing anything from adding a record in a binding table to a more intricate endeavor entailing the validation of policies and constraints. The former case requires nothing more than a plain repository invoked from the application layer. The latter case, however, involves some business logic that might ideally be placed in a domain service.

## Dependencies on other functions

In Project Renoir, the domain service layer is a separate class library project referenced by the application layer. The library maintains a dependency on the domain model and the persistence layer where repositories live.

Checking policies to validate the assignment of a user to a document might require you to check the latest actions performed by the user within the system as well as any documents they've worked on in the past. Past actions can be fetched by the application layer and passed as an argument. However, in Project Renoir, we have opted to keep the domain service entirely focused on the task of validating document policies with full autonomy.

## Creating the interface

The behavior of the domain service is summarized by the interface in the following code. It's called IDocumentPolicyValidator—a name that implies that the service simply evaluates whether outstanding policies are reflected in any document assignment to a given user.

```
public interface IDocumentPolicyValidator: IDomainService
{
    bool CanAssign(UserAccount user, ReleaseNote doc);
    bool CanAssign(UserAccount user, Roadmap doc);

    AssignmentResponse Assign(UserAccount user, ReleaseNote doc, AssignmentMode mode);
    AssignmentResponse Assign(UserAccount user, Roadmap doc, AssignmentMode mode);
}
```

The interface is made by two pairs of methods—one per type of document supported. One method checks whether the document assignment violates any outstanding policy and returns a Boolean flag. The other method attempts to make assignments based on the value of the AssignmentMode enumeration.

```
public enum AssignmentMode
{
    AssignAndReportViolation: 0,
    FailAndReportViolation: 1
}
```

In the default case, the assignment is performed, and any detected violations are reported. In the other case, no assignment is performed, and violation is reported.

## Implementing the *DocumentManagerService* class

The domain service class DocumentManagerService is solely responsible for ensuring that users are assigned documents based on established policies (if any). Here's the skeleton of the class:

```
public class DocumentManagerService
        : BaseDomainService, IDocumentPolicyValidator
{
    public const int MaxActiveDocsForUser = 3;

    private readonly IDocumentAssignmentRepository _assignmentRepository;
    public DocumentManagerService(IDocumentAssignmentRepository repository)
    {
        _assignmentRepository = repository;
    }

    // More
    ...
}
```

The class receives a reference to the repository that deals with records in the document/user binding table. Both methods in the domain service interface—Assign and CanAssign—deal with specific business policies. An example policy might be that each user can't be assigned more than, say, three documents at the same time. Another might require checking the calendar of each user and skipping over users who are expected to be on leave before the next document deadline.

```
public AssignmentResponse Assign(UserAccount user, ReleaseNote doc, AssignmentMode mode)
{
    // Check whether already assigned
    var binding = assignmentRepository.Get(user.Id, doc.Id);
    if (binding != null)
        return AssignmentResponse.AlreadyAssigned();

    // Check whether document is ready for public assignment
    if (!doc.IsReadyForAssignment())
        return AssignmentResponse.NotReady();

    // Evaluate specific policies
    var response = EvaluatePolicies(user, doc);
    if (mode.IsFailAndReport() && !response.Success)
        return response;

    // All good, just assign
    var assignment = new DocumentUserAssignment(doc, user);
    return _assignmentRepository.Add(assignment);
}
```

Here's a snippet from EvaluatePolicies:

```
public AssignmentResponse EvaluatePolicies(UserAccount user, ReleaseNote doc)
{
    if (HasMaxNumberOfAssignments(user))
        return AssignmentResponse.MaxAssignments();

    if (HasIncomingLeave(user))
        return AssignmentResponse.MaxAssignments();

    return AssignmentResponse.Ok();
}
```

The HasMaxNumberOfAssignments and HasIncomingLeave methods are protected (or even private) methods of the domain service class. They have access to any necessary repositories and perform data access to arrange a response.

> **Note** If you face a scenario like the one depicted in HasIncomingLeave, then the domain service needs an additional repository reference to access the calendar of each user to determine whether they will take leave at some point in the near future.

## Useful and related patterns

You may have noticed that the earlier code snippets used tailor-made methods from some AssignmentResponse class to describe the outcome of a domain service method call. Why not just throw an exception?

### The *If...Then...Throw* **pattern**

The decision to raise an exception within a domain service or to maintain control over potential issues is a matter of individual preference. From my perspective, exceptions should primarily address extraordinary circumstances. If there's an opportunity to anticipate a specific code malfunction, a more elegant approach would involve managing the situation properly, providing relevant feedback to upper layers, and leaving them free to handle the response. Also, it should take into account that any try/catch block used to handle a thrown exception is costly compared to dealing with a regular method response.

Here's a glimpse of a method defined on a response class that describes a specific failure in the business logic:

```
public class AssignmentResponse
{
    public bool Success { get; private set; }
    public string Message { get; private set; }
    public int FailedPolicy { get; private set; }

    public AssignmentResponse MaxAssignments()
    {
        return new AssignmentResponse
        {
            Success = false,
            Message = "Maximum number of assignments",
            FailedPolicy = MaxAssignments
        };
    }
}
```

The FailedPolicy property is optional and may represent application-specific code to quickly communicate to the caller the reason for the failure. MaxAssignments can be a constant or maybe a value of a new enumerated type.

**Note** Although I generally avoid throwing exceptions from domain services and repositories, I lean toward implementing this practice within the domain model instead. The reason is that the domain model is a self-contained library intended for external use, particularly within various modules of the same application. Considering the pivotal role the domain model plays in the application, I believe that its code should be forthright in signaling any instances of invalid input or potential failures. I deem it acceptable to throw exceptions from domain services or repositories in the case of glaringly invalid input.

## The REPR pattern adapted

The request-endpoint-response (REPR) pattern is typically associated with a microservices architecture. However, it also clearly describes the flow of communication between any caller (typically an application service) and any responder (for example, a domain service or repository). As indicated by its name, this pattern consists of the following:

- **Request** This contains input data to process. In an API scenario (more on this in Chapter 9, "Microservices versus modular monoliths"), it may also include HTTP information and express data as JSON or XML payloads. In this application context, it often consists of a handful of loose values, possibly grouped in a data clump.

- **Endpoint** In an API scenario, this represents a specific URL to receive incoming requests. More generally, it defines the location and context of the requested operation.

- **Response** This comprehends the responses generated after processing the request. It typically includes the Boolean result of the operation, plus additional data such as an error message and other metadata the client may need (for example, IDs or redirect URLs).

Outside the native realm of microservices architecture, the REPR pattern provides a structured approach for clients and services to communicate. It also acts as a safeguard against resorting to exceptions for application flow control—a practice that stands as an anti-pattern.

## Dependency injection

Among the relevant patterns for a domain service implementation, dependency injection (DI) furnishes the domain service with essential resources like repositories, factories, and other services. Meanwhile, interfaces play a pivotal role in delineating the agreements between the domain service and its dependencies.

In the ASP.NET Core stack, you typically inject services via the native DI subsystem. In particular, domain services being stateless operations, you can configure them as singletons. Notice, though, that in ASP.NET Core, registered services can be injected into controllers, middleware, filters, SignalR hubs, Razor pages, Razor views, and background services. You can't have a plain class, such as a domain service class, instantiated and all its declared dependencies resolved automatically.

This brings up the point of a small pragmatic optimization known as *poor man's DI*. Consider the following class:

```
public class SampleDomainService : BaseDomainService
{
    private readonly ISampleRepository _repository;

    public SampleDomainService() : this(new DefaultSampleRepository())
    {
    }
    public SampleDomainService(ISampleRepository repo)
    {
        _repository = repo;
    }

    ...
}
```

This class shows off a couple of constructors—the default parameter-less constructor and another one that allows the injection of an implementation of the needed ISampleRepository interface. Interestingly, the default constructor silently invokes the passage by the other constructor of a fixed implementation of the interface. Is this a poor form of tight coupling? Well, pragmatically, you'd use just one implementation in the various use cases. In this regard, there's no reason to use a DI container and all its extra machinery. All you want to do is to get a new instance of the domain service class with a valid reference to a particular implementation of the repository. It's you, not the DI container, who resolves the dependency on ISampleRepository. The code obtained couldn't be simpler or more direct.

What are some possible disadvantages? One could be that code becomes tightly coupled and therefore potentially less maintainable. We're simply silently using the same concrete class we're supposed to use. Tightly coupled? Yes, but at the level of an individual class, doing otherwise would smell of overengineering.

Another disadvantage could be that you might (I repeat, *might*) experience difficulties in changing or swapping dependencies. Again, it's overengineering. Realistically, you have just one repository doing the job for the entire application. If you need to change it, you just replace the class and recompile. If something weird happens, like having to replace the underlying database, well, that would be a huge change—well beyond the granularity of one repository interface.

The only sensible objection to the poor man's DI, however, is that testing might become more challenging and ultimately lead to hidden dependencies. The second constructor—silently used also in case the default one is invoked—simply explicitly accepts an interface. You can still unit-test the domain service in full isolation without the risk of overengineering.

Overall, injection right in the constructor of the class is considered a best practice in modern software design. It provides a more robust and maintainable architecture than the poor man's DI approach. Although the poor man's DI might seem easier in the short term, it can lead to problems as your application grows in complexity. DI containers in frameworks like ASP.NET Core make it convenient to manage the creation and injection of dependencies, resulting in more modular and testable code.

> **Note** Did the ASP.NET Core team make a mistake by setting up a dedicated DI container? Although the ASP.NET DI container does a great job letting you access system services, it is not as powerful for general use as other products and requires developers to blindly use it without making sense of what they need. It just makes doing a good enough thing easy enough. Note, though, that you can still plug in your favorite DI library and a more powerful DI container comes with .NET 8. In contrast, the poor man's DI requires discipline and understanding. It's not worse; moreover, it's more direct, faster, and equally testable and declarative.

## Handling business rules with the strategy pattern

In a realistic application, the domain service layer typically handles most business rules due to the fundamental fact that, in most instances, the process of applying rules entails retrieving data from one or more tables. It's worth restating that the domain model, instead, should remain entirely detached from the details of persistence and data storage.

Processing business rules is dynamic, especially in B2C contexts. Business rules and policies of diverse kinds might undergo frequent changes. You should feel free to hard-code business-rule validation if those rules remain consistent or only shift over longer spans—say, every few years. However, the landscape changes significantly when business rule updates happen more frequently, such as on a weekly basis. In this case, you should avoid even the slightest chance of encountering hidden dependencies or tangled code.

This is where the strategy pattern may be beneficial. The strategy pattern is a design principle that allows you to dynamically swap algorithms or behaviors within a class. Encapsulating these behaviors as interchangeable strategies promotes flexibility, reusability, and easier maintenance. This pattern enables the selection of a specific strategy at runtime, aiding in adapting to changing requirements without altering the core code structure.

Here's an example in which the strategy pattern is used to abstract the payment method. The `IPaymentStrategy` interface defines the expected course of action:

```
public interface IPaymentStrategy
{
    void ProcessPayment(double amount);
}
```

Here's a possible implementation for the preceding strategy:

```
public class CreditCardPayment : IPaymentStrategy
{
    public void ProcessPayment(double amount)
    {
        ...
    }
}
```

Finally, the strategy will be used by some domain service, as shown here:

```
public class PaymentProcessorService
{
    private IPaymentStrategy _paymentStrategy;

    public PaymentProcessorService(IPaymentStrategy paymentStrategy)
    {
        _paymentStrategy = paymentStrategy;
    }

    public void MakePayment(double amount)
    {
        _paymentStrategy.ProcessPayment(amount);
    }
}
```

From the application layer, it all works like this:

```
var processor = new PaymentProcessorService(new CreditCardPayment());
processor.MakePayment(amount);
```

In summary, the IPaymentStrategy interface defines the common method for processing payments. Concrete payment methods implement this interface. The PaymentProcessor class uses the selected payment strategy to process payments dynamically at runtime. This pattern allows for easy addition of new payment methods without modifying existing code. Back to our initial policies evaluation example, you can use a strategy pattern to encapsulate the logic that evaluates document-user policies.

## The special case pattern

The special case pattern tackles a fundamental question: what is the recommended behavior when a code segment intends to return, say, a Document object, but there's no appropriate object available? Should the code just return null? Should the code opt for some unconventional return values? Or should you introduce intricacies to discern the presence or absence of some result?

Look at the following code snippet, which attempts to retrieve a document from storage:

```
public Document Find(int id)
{
    var doc = _documentRepository.Get(id)
    return doc;
}
```

If the search failed, what's returned? In a similar situation, most methods would commonly return a valid Document instance or null. Therefore, the idea behind the pattern is to return a special document that represents a null document but, in terms of code, is still a valid instance of the Document class. Applying the special case pattern leads to the following:

```
public class NullDocument : Document
{
    ...
}
```

`NullDocument` is a derived class that initializes all properties to their default or empty values. This allows any code designed for `Document` to also handle `NullDocument` instances. Type checking then aids in identifying any potential errors.

```
if(order is NullDocument)
{
    ...
}
```

This is the essence of the special case pattern. In addition to this fundamental implementation, you have the freedom to incorporate numerous extra functionalities, such as introducing a singleton instance or even integrating an optional status message to circumvent the need for type checking.

# Open points

At this point, we have established that domain services excel at handling cross-entity operations and domain-specific functionalities based on the history of past operations. Domain services are not database agnostic. Quite the reverse. They often need access to stored or cached data through repositories. In summary, the nature of domain services is to facilitate complex interactions and orchestrations across the domain model.

Considering that domain services are usually called from the application layer (refer to Figure 7-1), it's understandable to question why the application service doesn't encompass all the logic that is typically found within the domain service. The purpose of this section is to address this question.

## Are domain services really necessary?

At the design level, one open point is this: Why not just use application services to arrange the business flow otherwise delegated to domain services? More generally, if all tasks specific to domain services can be performed by application services or some richer repository classes, are domain services really necessary? Let's find out more.

### Domain services versus application services

Application services and domain services may have conceptual similarities, but they are distinct entities. Although both entail stateless classes capable of interacting with domain entities, this is where their resemblance ends. The key differentiation arises from the fact that only domain services are meant to embody domain logic. (See Figure 7-2.)

Application logic and domain logic are different segments of the application. Whereas application logic deals with the orchestration of use cases, domain logic deals with business decisions. Unfortunately, the boundary between use cases and business decisions is thin and blurred. There's no quick and safe answer to the question of which is which. To some extent, any answer is questionable. It depends on how much you know about the business domain and its future evolution. It also depends on the quality of the guidance you receive from stakeholders and domain experts. What seems to fit perfectly in the boundaries of a use case today may qualify as domain logic tomorrow, and vice versa.

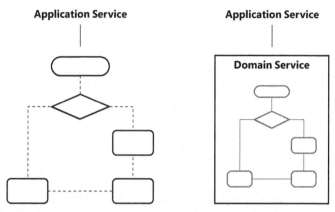

**FIGURE 7-2** Keeping domain logic isolated from application logic.

Always using application services is far from a perfect solution—although it causes minimal (though non-zero) damage. When you take this approach, instead of spending time on granular decisions, you can simply assume that every step is part of a use case. A guiding principle for determining whether to extract a domain service from an application use case is if you identify a business decision that necessitates supplementary information from the external world (for example, the database) and cannot be made solely by entities and value objects.

> **Note** When it comes to implementation aspects of domain-driven design, the belief that you can attain one ultimate truth is simply unrealistic. There will always be someone who questions any choice. As long as the code works, is relatively fluent, and, more importantly, matches your current understanding of the domain, you should feel confident about its quality and relative maintainability.

## Pure and impure domain services

Let's return to the widely accepted definition of a domain service. The purpose of a domain service is to span voids in the domain model to address behaviors that cannot be sufficiently encapsulated within a single entity. They're about plain logic, but also about business decisions that may require access to external sources—typically a database.

A pure domain service is a domain service that algorithmically deals with crucial business decisions. A pure domain service is plain logic that doesn't need external input. It would be like the plain behavior assigned to a domain entity if a single domain entity could logically host it. Conversely, an impure domain service is a domain service that performs data-related business operations in reading and writing. For example, determining whether a customer deserves the status of gold requires checking their payment and purchase history.

## Expanding the scope of repositories

Imagine the following scenario: You are registering a purchase, and there's an added discount accessible to customers with gold status. How would you handle that? Here's some sample code you may use in the application layer:

```
// Use the Fidelity domain service to know about the customer status
if (_fidelityService.IsStatus(customer, CustomerStatus.Gold))
    purchase.Discount += 0.05;  // extra 5% discount

// Plain update operation on the database
_purchaseRepository.Save(purchase);
```

Once you've found out about the status of the customer, you can add the extra discount to the purchase and save it permanently. With a domain service in the middle, the use case would reduce to the following:

```
_fidelityService.RegisterPurchase(purchase)
```

Internally, the `RegisterPurchase` method retrieves the customer, checks their status, and adjusts the discount rate.

What if you used the following instead?

```
_purchaseRepository.RegisterPurchase(purchase);
```

In this case, the repository is not simply a CRUD proxy for aggregate roots, but also holds some business logic. What kind of practice is this? Good? Bad? Neutral?

As you'll see in more detail in the next chapter, repository methods must refrain from encompassing business or application logic. Their scope should solely encompass data-related or ORM-specific tasks. Furthermore, the number of dependencies on other services should be zero or kept to a bare minimum.

From a pure DDD perspective, expanding the scope of repositories beyond pure persistence is not a best practice. That's mostly because in DDD, databases tend to be just a detail, and according to many purists, the same model should be persisted regardless of the physical storage.

The real world is different, and no application is designed without the actual database in mind. Furthermore, relational databases allow you to save business logic in stored procedures—which is within the database server—and that's still the fastest way to run it. From a persistence perspective, therefore, merging domain services and repositories—custom made and richer than just CRUD proxies—is as acceptable as having everything done from within the application layer or having domain services with unclear boundaries.

## Additional scenarios for domain services

The situations for which you might want to employ domain services depend on the nuances and subtleties of the domain. The objective is to maintain a pristine, targeted, and articulate domain model, employing domain services to encapsulate business logic that doesn't seamlessly integrate into any of the identified entities.

Domain services are a mere tool for augmenting the isolation of the domain model from the more operational parts of the whole application. Beyond implementing cross-entities logic, domain services may apply in several additional scenarios.

- **Domain validation**   When certain validations involve complex rules that span multiple entities or value objects, a domain service can centralize the validation logic, ensuring consistent validation across the domain.

- **Data normalization**   In cases where data needs to be transformed or normalized before being used by domain logic, a domain service can handle the transformations to ensure that the data is suitable for the operations. Similarly, if the domain needs to process data in a format that's not native to the domain model, a domain service can convert and adapt external data into a compatible format.

- **Security and authorization**   Even though authorization is better handled at the gate of the presentation layer, you might want to enforce security and authorization checks within the flow of operations, especially when those checks involve complex domain-specific rules. In this case, the ideal place to implement security checks is in domain services.

- **Integration with legacy systems**   A domain service can effectively serve as an adapter when integrating with legacy systems that don't align with the existing domain model. They can, for instance, be used to translate between the legacy system's structure and your domain's structure.

## Summary

DDD has emerged as a potent methodology for (giving teams a better chance of) crafting robust and maintainable systems. At the heart of DDD is the domain model, covered in the previous chapter. This chapter was devoted to domain services, which, along with the domain model, form the application's domain layer.

Although the domain model establishes the fundamental elements of the domain, outlining its entities, connections, and principles, domain services assume the role of orchestrators for more complex business logic that extends beyond individual domain entities. In synergy, the domain model and domain services constitute a potent amalgamation within the DDD methodology for closely mirroring the slice of the real world behind the application. Overall, domain services may still be considered optional, but their use promotes precision and clarity in the domain-driven design of a business application.

The next chapter, which covers repositories and the infrastructure layer, concludes the exploration of the DDD-inspired layered and clean architecture.

# CHAPTER 8

# The infrastructure layer

*What goes up must come down.*

*—Isaac Newton*

The infrastructure layer provides the technical foundations that support the core domain and application layers. Its primary objective is to handle concerns that are not directly related to the core business logic but are necessary for the system's operation. These concerns include data storage, communication with external services, dedicated services for the user interface, and various technical integrations, such as with legacy platforms.

> **Note** From a mere functional perspective, all these tasks can be loosely accomplished by various components in the application layer or maybe domain services. However, segregating these technical details from the domain layer promotes an even cleaner and more maintainable architecture.

One of the key components of the infrastructure layer is the repository pattern. Repositories are responsible for managing the persistence and retrieval of domain objects. The idea is to abstract the data access logic from the domain layer, enabling a separation of concerns to facilitate changes to the underlying data storage technology without affecting the core domain logic. More realistically, however, although a mere physical separation of concerns between the domain model and persistence— distinct class libraries and contracted interfaces—is achievable, a hidden thread will still link the domain model and the database structure. The ideal of a mapping layer that can persist "any" domain model to "any" storage remains just that—an aspirational goal or maybe a benchmark to attain.

This chapter focuses mainly on the implementation of persistence in a realistic application. It discusses domain models and persistence models and how to merge both concerns in a single, slightly impure library. In addition, one section is devoted to data access frameworks (O/RM and micro-O/RM) and data storage architecture. However, keep in mind that although persistence is a pivotal responsibility of the infrastructure, it's not the only responsibility. Let's start with a quick refresher of the various concerns of the layer.

# Responsibilities of the infrastructure layer

The infrastructure layer is not just about persistence. It also relates to any dependencies on external services that are not clearly constituent blocks of the business domain—from emails to printing, and from external web services to internal clock and time zone management.

Whether you keep the infrastructure layer coded as a single project with multiple features or split it into two or more feature-based projects, the logical set of responsibilities is fairly large. Appropriately separating it from the rest of the application is necessary whether or not you adhere to DDD. This section lists core responsibilities of the infrastructure layer.

## Data persistence and storage

The primary responsibility of the infrastructure layer is to handle data persistence and storage. This involves interacting with databases, caching mechanisms, and any external storage systems that the application may require. The term *primary responsibility* relates more to the fact that few business applications can thrive without storage than to the relative relevance of storage compared to other infrastructural responsibilities.

Persistence is about having an API that knows how to deal, in reading and writing, with the data storage. The DDD domain model is ideally 100% persistence ignorant; yet its objects, at some point, must be saved to storage and rehydrated from there. This requires an extra software component. In DDD, these components are repository classes.

The domain model does not need to know how its classes are saved. That's the sole responsibility of repositories. A repository class is a plain utility class that serves the superior purpose of saving the domain model while encapsulating persistence logic and all necessary details.

Regardless of the thousands of articles that advertise the best homemade recipe for the perfect repository class, no dictates exist on how the repository class should be designed internally. There are some common practices, though. The most relevant of these is to have one repository class for each aggregate recognized in the domain model. The repository is therefore responsible for several CRUD tasks on the root object of the aggregate.

Apart from this, whether you persist the domain model directly through stored procedures or map it to another persistence model managed by an O/RM tool, well, that's up to you! It's your design and your choice. In both cases, however, you will adhere to DDD—assuming strict adherence to DDD principles is a plus for the production application.

## Communication with external services

Nearly every modern application needs to communicate with one or more external services, whether publicly accessible web services, messaging systems, or legacy applications. The infrastructure layer manages these interactions, including handling network requests, authentication, and data serialization. These infrastructure services encapsulate the communication complexities and ensure that the domain layer remains decoupled from the specifics of external interactions.

The link between the infrastructure layer and external services is realistically established in one of the following ways:

- **Web API**   With this approach, and with some authentication on top, the application connects via HTTPS and downloads JSON payloads. The JSON classes should remain confined to the library that downloaded them. At the same time, they should be exposed to the rest of the application using an intermediate layer of classes that remain constant to the application. In terms of DDD, this is an instance of the anti-corruption layer (ACL) pattern mentioned in Chapter 2, "The ultimate gist of DDD." Should the JSON format of the web API change, you must simply fix the JSON-to-C# mapper, with no need to intervene in more than just one place.

- **WCF reference classes**   Legacy applications usually expose their connection points as old-fashioned Windows Communication Foundation (WCF) services. Visual Studio and Rider allow you to import WCF endpoints as reference classes. In other words, your code just deals with methods in these classes, which internally manage the details of the protocols required to establish the connection and exchange data.

- **Shared files or databases**   When no HTTPS or WCF endpoints exist, communication may occur via FTP or, more likely, through access to shared folders to read/write files or via ad hoc logins to some relational database server.

 **Note**  Sending emails or creating PDF printouts is a recognized example of a web API being incorporated in the infrastructure layer.

## Communication with internal services

The phrase *internal services* is relatively uncommon in software architecture. But in this case, having used *external services* to refer to remote web services and legacy applications, I find it acceptable to employ a form of name symmetry to refer to another family of services typically implemented in the infrastructure layer: frameworks for the user interface, logging, dependency injection (DI), authentication/authorization, localization, configuration, and more.

Configuration and environment management is another internal concern that may be delegated to the infrastructure layer. It deals with different running environments (development, staging, production, and so on) that may require varying configurations.

An often-disregarded internal service that is extremely helpful within the boundaries of a contracted service is the clock service. The clock service is the application API responsible for returning the current application time. Within a web platform, the question "What time is now?" is difficult to answer. Of course, you can easily obtain the UTC time, but that's it. Keeping track of the time zone of the logged-in user (assuming the User entity tracks a fixed time zone) helps convert UTC time to a more usable local time. Still, the time you get—local or universal—is always the current time. You have no way to test your application as if it were assigned a random date and time. For this reason, for applications for which the current time is an issue, you should code a workaround to take control of the system current time. Here's an example of a class to achieve this, which would live in the infrastructure layer:

```
public static class ClockService
{
    public static DateTime UtcNow()
    {
        return Now();
    }

    public static DateTime Now(int timeZoneOffsetInMins = 0)
    {
        var now = _systemDate.HasValue ? _systemDate : DateTime.UtcNow;
        return now.AddMinutes(timeZoneOffsetInMins);
    }
}
```

This code snippet defines a couple of global static methods that override the .NET UTC time with the value of a variable read from some setting storage (such as a file or database). All you need to do is use `ClockService.Now` or `ClockService.UtcNow` wherever you would use `DateTime` counterparts.

**Note** As weird as it may sound, no form of time abstraction existed for years in .NET Core or in the .NET Framework. .NET 8 finally brings support for this feature through the `TimeProvider` base class.

# Implementing the persistence layer

The persistence layer forms the bedrock upon which the seamless interaction between application and data storage is built, ensuring the durability and integrity of vital information. The constituent blocks of the persistence layer don't have an obvious and common configuration. Persistence could come in many ways, and no single approach is right or wrong as long as it maintains separation with other layers.

In general, you will have a data access layer made of classes that know how to access the database. You can craft these classes in many ways, with a domain-centric or database-centric view. No approach is right or wrong per se. It all boils down to looking at a few possible ways (and related technologies) to code such a data access layer. In DDD, the classes that form a general-purpose bridging layer across the domain model and any durable store of choice have a particular name: repositories.

**Note** There's no right or wrong way to implement repositories that could qualify the whole application as well or poorly written. Repositories are just an architectural element whose implementation is completely opaque as long as it works as a bridge from storage to the rest of the application.

# Repository classes

A repository class acts as an intermediary between the application code and the underlying data storage. It typically provides methods to perform CRUD operations while abstracting the complexities of data interaction and manipulation.

While a repository class typically handles CRUD operations, its actual role can extend beyond basic data manipulation. It can encapsulate more complex data access logic, including querying, filtering, and data aggregation. This allows the repository to abstract various data-related tasks, promoting a cleaner separation between application code and data storage concerns.

## Domain services or rich repositories?

Richer repositories may extend to intersect the space of domain services. The borderline between them is blurry—hence my statements that there's no right or wrong way to write repositories.

If a line must be drawn—and one does—between domain services and rich repositories, it is on the domain specificity of data manipulated by repositories. The more specific it is to the business domain, the more it is a domain service. And the more it involves plain query or (bulk) updates, the more it is rich repositories.

## The repository pattern

When building a repository class (or just a plain data access class), it may be advisable to look at the repository pattern. This is a popular software-design pattern that provides the logical backbone for repository classes. The repository pattern centralizes data access logic by encapsulating CRUD operations and other data-related tasks for specific domain entities within repository classes.

Using the pattern brings a few clear benefits:

- It decouples the application code from data-storage details, increasing maintainability.

- Repositories can be easily mocked or replaced with test implementations during unit testing, allowing for thorough testing of application logic without involving the actual data store.

- By centralizing data access logic, the repository pattern can facilitate scalability, as the resulting data access layer can be optimized or adjusted as needed without affecting the rest of the application.

Most recognized implementations of the repository pattern begin with the list of operations to be supported on the target entity. Here's an example:

```
public interface IReleaseNoteRepository
{
    ReleaseNote GetById(Guid documentId);
    IEnumerable<ReleaseNote> All();
    void Add(ReleaseNote document);
    void Update(ReleaseNote document);
    void Delete(Guid documentId);
}
```

An actual repository class simply implements the interface:

```
public class ReleaseNoteRepository: IReleaseNoteRepository
{
    public ReleaseNoteRepository(/* connection details */)
    {
        ...
    }

    public IEnumerable<ReleaseNote> All()
    {
        ...
    }

    // More code
    ...
}
```

Gaining access to the database, whether through a direct connection string or a more complex object such as an Entity Framework DbContext object, is one of the responsibilities of the repository. The repository's implementor must decide what data access API to use. In the .NET space, common options are as follows:

- **ADO.NET**  This is a low-level API to access databases centered around connections, commands, and data readers. For a long time, it was the only data access API in .NET. While still fully functional, it is now largely considered obsolete. Many developers opt instead for Entity Framework Core (discussed next) due to its higher level of abstraction, modern features, and alignment with the architectural goals of .NET Core applications.

- **Entity Framework (EF) Core**  A modern object-relational mapping (O/RM) framework for .NET applications, EF Core simplifies data access by allowing developers to work with database entities as plain .NET objects, abstracting the complexities of SQL queries and data manipulation. With features like LINQ support and migrations, EF Core streamlines database-related tasks and facilitates a more object-oriented approach to data access.

- **Micro O/RM**  A micro-O/RM is a lightweight O/RM framework for mapping database records to objects in software applications. It focuses on simplicity and minimalism, offering basic CRUD operations and limited features compared to full-fledged O/RM solutions such as EF Core. The most popular micro-O/RM framework is Dapper. Micro O/RMs are suitable for scenarios in which a lightweight data access layer, made only of relatively simple queries and plain CRUD operations, is sufficient to fulfill the needs of the application.

Consider that, unless blatant mistakes are made in the arrangement of a query, no .NET data access framework can perform better than ADO.NET data readers. This is because both EF and any .NET micro-O/RMs are built on top of ADO.NET. So, why not just use ADO.NET? Developed more than 25 years ago, when the O/RM model was little more than an academic concept, ADO.NET doesn't know how to map plain table records to typed C# objects. ADO.NET allows cursor-based navigation over the stream of data provided by the database server and can load the whole result set in memory untyped dictionaries. In a nutshell, ADO.NET is not suitable for modern data access coding strategies and doesn't meet the expectations of today's developers.

Faithfully mapping database objects to C# objects is the mission of full O/RM frameworks. Micro O/RMs represent some middle ground, offering basic (and faster) object-to-database mapping but lacking more advanced features such as change tracking, lazy loading, LINQ, and migrations.

Here are my two cents when it comes to coding the internals of a repository class: Start with EF but be ready to switch to Dapper (or other micro-O/RMs) when you need to optimize specific queries. And when you need to optimize update commands, consider switching to plain SQL commands or stored procedures.

## Is the repository pattern really valuable?

I am not particularly inclined toward design patterns in general. It's not that I disregard the idea of common solutions for common problems—quite the reverse. Rather, I don't see any value in using design patterns just for the sake of it.

I am fully aligned with the DDD vision of using repository classes to decouple the whole application from the data storage details. I also agree with the directive of having one repository class per aggregate in the domain model. But I question the use of explicit interfaces and even more generic repository interfaces, like so:

```
public interface IRepository<T> where T : class
{
    T GetById(object id);
    IEnumerable<T> GetAll();
    void Add(T entity);
    void Update(T entity);
    void Delete(T entity);
}
```

Each real-world aggregate (outside the realm of toy example applications) has its own set of business characteristics that hardly fit with the schema of a generic CRUD-oriented repository. Yet, using a generic repository brings value only if it solves a precise design problem. There's no value in using it just because it exists.

Using an interface for every repository allows you to switch implementations without affecting any code that depends on it. This modularity makes it easier to mock the repository during testing, enabling unit testing of application layer and domain services without involving a real database. If you test extensively, this is important.

On the other hand, resorting to repository interfaces because at some point you might decide to change the underlying data access technology isn't realistic. Choosing the data access technology is a key project decision. In general, starting with meticulous interfaces for every repository sounds like overengineering.

In the end, although the repository pattern is a valuable tool, it might not be necessary for every application. It's beneficial in larger applications where data access complexity is high and maintaining a clear separation of concerns is a priority. Smaller applications might call for simpler data access strategies, however.

**Important** The higher the degree of code reusability, the lower its actual usability tends to be. The appeal of the generic repository pattern approach lies in the notion that you can create a single, universal repository and employ it to construct various sub-repositories to reduce the amount of code required. In practice, though, this approach is effective only at the beginning. As complexity increases, necessitating the addition of progressively more code to each specific repository, it becomes inadequate.

## The unit-of-work pattern

In discussions about repository patterns, another frequently referenced design pattern is the unit-of-work (UoW) pattern. The purpose of this pattern is to manage and track multiple database operations within a single cohesive transactional context. The main idea is to encapsulate database-related operations—like inserts, updates, and deletes—within a transaction boundary. This boundary is defined by the lifespan of the UoW controller, which represents the unit of work—namely, a session of interactions with the database. By grouping these operations, the pattern prevents data inconsistencies that could arise from partially completed transactions.

The UoW pattern typically involves the domain entities subject to changes and updates and the repository classes that would perform database operations on those entities. All operations take place under the supervision of the UoW controller, an object responsible for tracking changes to entities and coordinating their persistence to the database. The UoW controller manages the transaction life cycle, ensuring all operations are either committed or rolled back together. Ultimately, the UoW pattern is a software abstraction for the use of the canonical SQL transactional commands (BEGIN TRAN, ROLLBACK, and COMMIT).

By using the UoW pattern, applications gain the ability to work with multiple repositories in a consistent transactional manner at an abstraction level higher than the actual SQL commands. This is invaluable. However, the UoW pattern might not be necessary for all projects, especially smaller applications in which the complexity and overhead might outweigh the benefits.

**Note** If you use EF (Core or .NET Framework) as the data access technology, then you can blissfully ignore the UoW pattern, as it is already implemented within the framework. In fact, the root object you need to use to execute any database access—the DbContext object— acts as a perfect UoW controller.

## Using Entity Framework Core

EF Core is a feature-rich O/RM framework developed by Microsoft. It is designed to work with a wide variety of databases and supports automatic generation of SQL statements for queries and updates, which results in rapid application development. EF Core also includes features such as change tracking, automatic relationship handling, migrations, lazy loading, and LINQ.

EF Core brings substantial advantages but does have a performance trade-off: The essential abstraction layer that facilitates these sophisticated functionalities introduces some performance overhead. Furthermore, EF Core provides you with no control over the actual SQL code being generated. This is both good and bad news, however. It's good because it enables developers to plan data access code reasoning at a higher level of abstraction; it's bad because it prevents developers from producing more optimized commands if really necessary.

The following sections reflect on a few facts related to using EF Core in the repository classes.

> **Note** Overall, EF Core is the best default option for any data access task. If for certain operations (queries or updates) you need more performance, however, then consider a micro-O/RM like Dapper. Dapper offers excellent performance and is suitable for scenarios in which raw SQL control, performance, and simplicity are priorities. For updates, the best option is still raw SQL commands via EF Core utilities. This said, I am reluctant to use a micro-O/RM for any data access need in a large enterprise application, although exceptions do apply.

## Connecting to the database

When you use EF Core, any data access operation passes through an instance of the DbContext class. As mentioned, the DbContext class represents a collection of tables (and/or views) in your database and behaves as a UoW transactional controller. You don't use DbContext directly; instead, you create your own database-specific context class, as shown here:

```
public class RenoirDatabase : DbContext
{
    // List of table mappings
    public DbSet<ReleaseNote> ReleaseNotes { get; set; }
    public DbSet<Product> Products { get; set; }
    ...

    // Configure the database provider and connection string
    protected override void OnConfiguring(DbContextOptionsBuilder optionsBuilder)
    {
        optionsBuilder.UseSqlServer("connection-string-here");
    }

    // More methods if needed: model creation, initial data, mappings to stored-procs
    ...
}
```

The UoW controller must be configured to use a particular data access engine (for example, SQL Server) and must receive identity information to connect. Of course, you can have multiple DbContext instances in the same application to access different databases or even different views of the same physical database.

The following code snippet ensures that the configured database exists. If not, the code automatically creates the database, either locally or in the cloud, depending on the connection string.

```
var db = new RenoirDatabase();
db.Database.EnsureCreated();
```

If created in a cloud, the new database may be subject to default settings based on your service tier, and its maximum size may be different from your expectations and budget. So, don't let the code blindly create new databases without immediately checking what's been created.

A DbContext is a lightweight and non-thread safe object whose creation and disposal do not entail any database operations. As a result, most applications can create a new instance of it in the constructor of the repository class without discernible performance implications. An alternative to direct instantiation is using dependency injection (DI), as shown here:

```
public class ReleaseNoteRepository: IReleaseNoteRepository
{
    private RenoirDatabase _db;
    public ReleaseNoteRepository(RenoirDatabase db)
    {
        _db = db;
    }

    public IEnumerable<ReleaseNote> All()
    {
        return _db.ReleaseNotes.ToList();
    }

    // More code
    ...
}
```

In this case, the DbContext instance is set up in the ASP.NET DI system at application startup:

```
var connString = /* Determine based on application static or runtime settings */
services.AddDbContext<CorintoDatabase>(opt => opt.UseSqlServer(connString));
```

The code snippet also shows how to set a connection string determined dynamically based on runtime settings. Any application or domain service that needs to access repositories will receive a new instance through the constructor. By default, the DbContext instance has a scoped lifetime.

 **Note** Is there any relevant difference between having a repository-wide DbContext instance and creating a new instance in every method? Yes, a global instance shares the same context across multiple methods possibly called on the same repository. This is usually a plus, but in some cases, it could become a problem with regard to change tracking. The best approach is to make any decisions based on the facts of the specific scenario.

## Building an EF Core-specific persistence model

EF Core needs an object model to bridge the conceptual gap between the relational nature of databases and the object-oriented nature of modern application development. This object model is often referred to as the *persistence model*.

The classes within a persistence model need not have behavioral functionality. They essentially function as straightforward DTOs, maintaining a one-to-one relationship with the tables in the intended database and reflecting foreign-key relationships and other constraints. The persistence model is created by all the classes declared as DbSet<T> datasets in the DbContext body.

EF Core maps any referenced class to a database following a set of default rules. Here are a few of them:

- The name of the table is the name of the DbSet<T> property.

- For each public property on the T type, a table column is expected with a matching type.

- If the class has a collection property, by convention or by configuration, a foreign-key relationship is expected.

- If the T type has value type properties, they result in table columns with a specific naming convention of the type ValueTypeName_Property.

- String properties are always mapped as nvarchar(MAX) columns.

As a developer, though, you have full power to modify mappings as well as to create indexes, identity values, constraints, and relationships. You do this by overriding the OnModelCreating method on the DbContext custom class.

The following code snippet indicates that the Product class from the persistence model has an index on the ProductId column and its Name column has a max length of 100 characters and cannot be null:

```
// Configure the model and define the mappings between your entities and DB tables
protected override void OnModelCreating(ModelBuilder modelBuilder)
{
    modelBuilder.Entity<Product>()
            .HasKey(p => p.ProductId);
    modelBuilder.Entity<Product>()
            .Property(p => p.Name)
            .IsRequired()
            .HasMaxLength(100);

    // Additional configurations...
    ...
}
```

The next snippet instead maps the `ReleaseNote` entity to the `ReleaseNotes` table:

```
public class ReleaseNote
{
    // Public properties
    // ...

    // Reference to the related product
    public int ProductId { get; set; }
    public Product RelatedProduct { get; set; }

    // ...
}
```

The class contains an integer property for the product ID and an object property for the full object to be internally resolved via an `INNER JOIN`. Following is an example mapping that also checks for a one-to-many relationship between the product and all its release notes and a cascading delete rule that automatically drops release notes if the parent product is deleted:

```
modelBuilder.Entity<ReleaseNote>()
            .HasOne(rn => rn.RelatedProduct)
            .WithMany(rn => rn.ReleaseNotes)
            .HasForeignKey(rn => rn.ProductId)
            .OnDelete(DeleteBehavior.Cascade);
```

One more example relates to owned types. In the EF Core jargon, an *owned type* is a custom value type encapsulating a group of related properties that can be reused within multiple entities. When an entity is queried or saved, EF Core automatically handles the persistence and retrieval of these owned properties. In the following snippet, `Timestamp` is an owned type in an EF Core persistence model:

```
public class ReleaseNote
{
    public Timestamp Timestamp { get; set; }

    // More public properties
    // ...
}

public record Timestamp
{
    public DateTime? LastUpdate { get; set; }
    public string Author { get; set; }
}
```

Mapping the `ReleaseNote` entity with a `Timestamp` property requires the following:

```
modelBuilder
    .Entity<ReleaseNote>()
    .OwnsOne(rn => rn.TimeStamp);
```

Owned types can also be nested. In addition, an owned type such as `Timestamp` can have properties of another custom value type. In this case, you chain multiple `OwnsOne` statements.

**Note** EF Core 8 reintroduced the Complex type, which has been absent since EF6—the last non-.NET Core version. The Complex type bears a striking resemblance to an owned entity, with a key difference: Unlike an Owned type, the same Complex type instance can be reused multiple times within the same or different entity.

**Important** You can express the mappings between the classes in the persistence model and the actual database tables using the EF Core fluent API (as in the preceding examples) or through data annotations. You can also combine these two techniques. The fluent API is the recommended choice, however. First, it's more expressive. And second, if the implementation of domain and persistence model coincides (more on this in a moment), it enables you to keep the domain model free from dependencies on the database. In fact, some data annotations—such as Key and Index—could decorate domain model classes but require a dependency on some EF Core NuGet package.

### Comparing domain models and persistence models

If you do DDD, you end up with a domain model. If you choose to persist the state of your application expressed by domain entities through EF Core, you need a persistence model. So, what is the relationship between domain models and persistence models?

Chapter 5, "The application layer," briefly hinted at the conceptual difference between the business domain model and the persistence model required by O/RM tools such as Entity Framework. It is useful to recall and expand the points here in a broader perspective.

A basic principle of DDD is that the domain model should be made of plain old class object (POCO) classes that are ignorant of any database concerns, and that storage is the responsibility of data access classes, period. (See Figure 8-1.)

If data is stored and reloaded without the help of an O/RM framework (for example, via stored procedures or ADO.NET), then you end up with a separated layer of code responsible for mere persistence. This persistence layer belongs to the infrastructure of the application, and neither its technology nor its implementation has any impact on domain aggregates.

Should you instead opt for an O/RM solution like EF Core, the scenario would vary. An O/RM tool necessitates the unique representation of data, which it employs to align with database structures like tables and fields. In essence, it's another object model with different characteristics from the domain model discussed in Chapter 6, "The domain layer." This additional model is the persistence model.

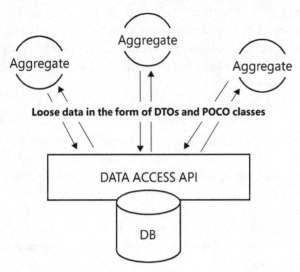

**FIGURE 8-1** Using a non-object-based API to serialize and deserialize domain model aggregates.

From a conceptual point of view, therefore, a domain model and a persistence model are radically different things. One focuses on business views, and the other focuses on database views. From a pure and ideal design perspective, you should have both domain and persistence models, well separated from each other. An additional layer of mapper classes would perform the task of building a domain aggregate from persistence classes and saving domain aggregates to persistence classes. (See Figure 8-2.)

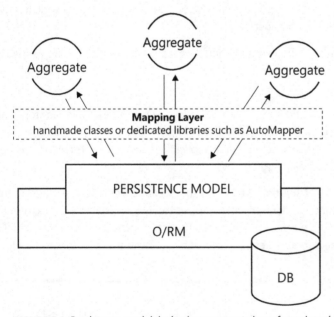

**FIGURE 8-2** Persistence model devised as a separate layer from domain.

Of course, managing two distinct object models involves significant extra effort when not a straight pain in the neck. So, is using a single data model for domain and persistence acceptable? As usual, it depends. But I tend to use a single model as much as possible.

## Impure but persistent domain models

The infrastructure layer is meant to shield the domain layer from the complexities of data storage and retrieval, thus maintaining the separation of concerns advocated by DDD. However, the entities in the domain model must be populated from some existing persisted state. Therefore, although the domain model must be isolated from the physical implementation of data storage, it cannot be logically disconnected from it.

A domain model in which some logical constraints are released to allow that same model to work as the persistence model for the O/RM of choice is probably not as pure as might be ideal. However, this compromise between code, design, and performance is worth exploring. I'd even go as far as to say you should consider it as your first option.

Suppose you adopt a single model for both domain logic and data storage. The application operates smoothly in production, but as time passes and changes accumulate, performance concerns arise. Despite having meticulously planned tables, views, and indexes, the tables grow at an alarming pace, necessitating some denormalization to maintain performance. So, a new database design emerges to accommodate performance demands. Unfortunately, though, the redesign dramatically alters the table structure. As a result, domain entities span multiple tables instead of adhering to the original one-table-per-entity approach. Under these circumstances, separating the domain and persistence models becomes a logical move, regardless of the associated costs. However, this extra cost surfaces only when you really need to tackle specific challenges.

As long as the organization of the database tables is close enough to the domain model hierarchy of classes, you don't need to do much to make a domain model persistent through EF Core. The list of required changes for each entity class is very limited and, better yet, does not affect the public interface:

- **Add a private parameter-less constructor** This would only be used by EF Core for object materialization. Any other public constructors and factories you may have will remain available to callers as originally planned.

- **Mark all property setters as private** The state of a domain entity is rarely altered by assigning values to public setters but rather by calling methods that internally change the state as needed. Adding private setters helps EF Core to programmatically assign values corresponding to a fetched state and doesn't alter the class's public programming interface. When EF Core retrieves data from the database, in fact, it uses reflection to access the private setters and initialize the properties. This allows you to maintain control over the internal state of the entity while still enabling EF Core to populate the entity with data.

Applying these tricks and using the fluent API to mark mappings to database tables represents an acceptable compromise: a sufficiently elegant and independent domain model that also works well as a persistence model.

## Unavoidable EF Core practices

There are certain practices in EF Core programming that, while not mandatory, are often necessary to work effectively within the EF Core framework. In most cases, there is no valid reason (except unawareness) to ignore them.

■ **Eager loading**   Lazy loading (the opposite of eager loading) frequently seems to be an advantageous approach to database logic. When lazy loading is enabled, related entities are automatically retrieved from the database when accessed in the code. This minimizes the loading of unnecessary related data (unlike explicit loading) and seemingly relieves developers from managing related entities. However, lazy loading can result in redundant roundtrips, which impedes application performance. With lazy loading, you also don't know when data is actually queried, so the potential for the SELECT N+1 problem is high. Finally, lazy loading works only within the same DbContext instance, so it is not suitable for use within repositories. For this reason, you should use eager loading whenever possible. To use eager loading, you simply specify Include clauses in the LINQ queries for any related data to be loaded as early as possible.

■ **Disable object tracking**   This technique instructs EF Core not to track retrieved entities. This can improve performance and reduce memory usage when you are querying data but do not intend to modify or update it. If you are fetching a record in the context of an update operation, then all is well. But if you are simply fetching one or more records to return as a list of objects, it is advisable to chain AsNoTracking in the LINQ expression for better performance.

■ **Use DbContext object pooling**   As mentioned, DbContext is a lightweight object whose frequent instantiation and disposal is not usually an issue. However, for applications that require extensive DbContext management, it can become a problem. In EF Core, object pooling improves resource utilization and subsequently overall performance. DbContext pooling involves reusing existing instances from a pool instead of creating new ones, reducing the overhead of object creation and disposal. If you use DI to enable DbContext instances to reach out to the repositories, then all you need to do is replace AddDbContext with AddDbContextPool at startup. To use context pooling independently of DI, you initiate a PooledDbContextFactory and create context instances from it.

```
var options = new DbContextOptionsBuilder<RenoirDatabase>()
    .UseSqlServer("connection-string-here")
    .Options;
var factory = new PooledDbContextFactory<RenoirDatabase>(options);
using (var context = factory.CreateDbContext())
{
    // ...
}
```

■ **Compiled queries**   With compiled queries, you optimize performance by precompiling LINQ queries into reusable query execution plans. Compiled queries can then be stored and reused. Using compiled queries instead of dynamically generating and executing queries each time they are needed improves query execution times and reduces overhead.

From a developer's perspective, they are just public methods on the DbContext class called in lieu of an EF Core LINQ expression.

```
public class RenoirDatabase : DbContext
{
    public static Func< RenoirDatabase, int, IEnumerable<ReleaseNote>> ByYear =
        EF.CompileQuery((RenoirDatabase context, int year) =>
                        context.ReleaseNotes.Where(rn => rn.Year == year));
}
```

Essentially, you provide EF with a lambda that accepts a DbContext instance and a parameter of your choice to feed into the query. You can then trigger that delegate at your convenience whenever you want to run the query. In the code snippet, you can call ByYear, passing a database context and a year value.

**Note** Compiled queries represent a minor performance improvement—roughly 10% better than the same noncompiled query. While compiled queries are valuable, they aren't the remedy for every query-performance issue.

- **Pagination** When managing large datasets, paging through an otherwise very long list of records is advisable. For this, EF Core provides Take and Skip methods to slice just the segment of records you want. However, in this context, it is key to note that DbContext instances are not thread safe. This means that employing multiple threads to concurrently query tables via the same shared DbContext instance is decidedly a bad idea.

- **Batch operations** This technique enables you to execute multiple database operations as a single batch rather than issuing individual SQL commands for each operation. This can lead to significant performance improvements when dealing with numerous database updates, inserts, or deletes. It's not a native feature of EF Core and requires you to install a dedicated Microsoft NuGet package: Microsoft.Entity-FrameworkCore.Relational.

```
// Enable batch operations
optionsBuilder.UseSqlServer("connection-string-here", options =>
    {
        options.UseRelationalNulls();
        options.UseBatching(true);
    });
```

Once installed, the package operates silently, forcing EF Core to automatically group similar database operations together and execute them in a single batch when you call methods like SaveChanges.

## Using Dapper

Dapper is a lightweight, open-source mini-O/RM library for .NET developed by Stack Overflow. It was originally created to cater to the specific data-access needs of StackOverflow, the huge and high-performing Q&A website for programmers. Dapper was designed to mimic the appealing object-based experience with databases of full O/RM while minimizing the overhead of such complex libraries.

## How Dapper works internally

Unlike EF Core, Dapper does not aim to abstract away the database entirely. Instead, it seeks to provide a simpler and convenient mapping mechanism between database results and object properties. Dapper does not automatically generate SQL statements; rather, it requires developers to craft SQL statements manually. This allows developers to gain full control over the actual query and leverage their SQL skills.

Dapper works by mapping the results of database queries to .NET objects. It uses reflection to match database columns to object properties. Dapper doesn't generate SQL statements for you by translating some proprietary query syntax. Instead, you write your own (parameterized) SQL queries and let Dapper work on them. Dapper then uses the ADO.NET's `IDataReader` interface to read data from the executed query. It iterates through the rows returned by the query, uses reflection to create instances of the object type, and sets the property values based on the column data. Dapper also supports batching, which allows you to execute multiple queries in a single roundtrip to the database, and multi-mapping, which facilitates mapping data from multiple tables or queries into complex object structures.

## Dapper in action

The pattern of a Dapper call is the same as a classic database access: You connect to the database, prepare a (parameterized) command, and execute it. If the command is a query, Dapper returns a collection of objects. Here's a first query example:

```
public IList<ReleaseNote> All()
{
    using var connection = new SqlConnection("connection-string-here");
    var query = "SELECT * FROM ReleaseNotes";
    var docs = connection.Query(sql);
    return docs;
}
```

Here's an example that illustrates updates (note that parameters are resolved by name):

```
public int Update(ReleaseNote doc)
{
    using var connection = new SqlConnection("connection-string-here");
    var sql = "UPDATE ReleaseNotes SET Description = @doc.Description WHERE Id = @doc.Id";
    var rowCount = connection.Execute(sql);
    return rowCount;
}
```

Dapper was created over a decade ago by the Stack Overflow team to be used in lieu of the old-fashioned Entity Framework. Starting with EF 6, however, the performance of EF improved significantly—and even more when it was completely rewritten for .NET Core. Today, every new version of EF Core brings better performance, whereas Dapper is close to its physical limit with the performance of ADO.NET data readers. A significant performance gap will remain. A combined use of EF Core and Dapper is definitely a viable option.

# Hosting business logic in the database

Hosting business logic in the database involves placing application-specific logic and processing within the database itself, typically in the form of stored procedures, functions, or triggers. This approach contrasts with traditional application design, where business logic is split between the application and domain layers.

## Pros and cons of stored procedures

Stored procedures are as old as relational databases. For decades, they were the most common (and recommended) way to code business logic strictly related to data. Legacy applications commonly have large chunks of crucial business logic coded as stored procedures. In this case, any new development on top must reuse the database hard-coded logic.

What if your project is a greenfield project, instead?

In general, you should carefully consider whether to host business logic in the database based on factors like your application's architecture, performance requirements, data integrity needs, and team expertise. This said, it's a mere matter of trade-offs between design and development comfort and raw speed.

The use of stored procedures is often contrasted with the use of O/RM frameworks, as if one choice would exclude the other. An O/RM framework aims to streamline development tasks, albeit with a trade-off in performance. For a project, the bulk of database operations typically involve basic CRUD operations. Allocating efforts toward these aspects might not be productive. Instead, delegating these routine responsibilities to the O/RM framework may be advisable. For intricate tasks or those demanding superior performance, stored procedures would indeed be a more suitable choice.

My personal take is to go with O/RMs by default and then adopt a hybrid approach—switching to stored procedures when particularly critical database-related operations surface. At any rate, using O/RM is OK, and using stored procedures is OK too. Not using one or the other doesn't necessarily result in poor choices or poor code.

## Using stored procedures in EF Core

Using stored procedures from within repository classes is definitely possible, whether you use EF Core or Dapper. Here's an example in EF Core:

```
using var db = new RenoirDatabase();
var list = db.Set<SampleProcData>()
            .FromSqlRaw(db.SampleProcSqlBuilder(p1, p2, p3))
            .ToList();
```

Connecting to a stored procedure may require a bit of preliminary work. In both Entity Framework and Dapper, you need to compose the SQL command that will run the stored procedure as if within the database console. For SQL Server, it would be the following:

```
EXEC dbo.sp_SampleProc 'string param', 2
```

In this snippet, the procedure takes two parameters of type string and integer, respectively. It is assumed that the underlying database holds a stored procedure named sp_SampleProc. In EF Core, the stored procedure is run through the FromSqlRaw method. You can pass the command text as a plain string or have its definition abstracted in a method in the DbContext class.

```
Public string SampleProcSqlBuilder (string p1, int p2)
{
    return $"EXEC dbo.sp_SampleProc '{p1}', {p2}";
}
```

Each returned row must be abstracted as a C# DTO class, named SampleProcData in the snippet.

```
Public class SampleProcData
{
    public string Column1 { get; set; }
        :
    public string ColumnN { get; set; }
}
```

The caller then receives a list of SampleProcData or scalar values, if that is what the stored procedure returns.

# Data storage architecture

So far, we've considered a monolithic data architecture in which data flows in and out of the application using the same tracks. A single stack of code and a shared data storage layer are used to handle both read and write operations.

A single stack data storage has the advantage of being consistent and easier to maintain in terms of data models, business rules, and user interfaces. On the other hand, it faces challenges when read-heavy and write-heavy workloads compete for resources. Furthermore, a single stack data architecture might limit your ability to use different data access technologies for different parts of the application. Let's explore alternatives to a single read/write stack.

## Introducing command/query separation

All actions carried out within a software system can be classified into one of two distinct categories: queries or commands. In this context, a *query* constitutes an operation that leaves the system's state untouched and exclusively retrieves data. Conversely, a *command* is an operation that actively modifies the system's state and doesn't typically yield data, except for status acknowledgments.

## An architectural perspective of CQRS

The inherent separation between queries and commands becomes less apparent when both sets of actions use the same domain model. Consequently, a new architectural approach has arisen in recent years: command/query responsibility segregation (CQRS). Figure 8-3 illustrates the architectural imprint of CQRS.

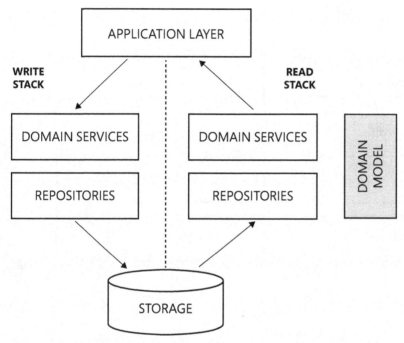

**FIGURE 8-3** CQRS at a glance.

A CQRS solution has two distinct projects for domain services and repositories taking care of command-only and query-only operations. The cardinality of the application layer and domain model is questionable, and no approach is right or wrong on paper. It can be a unique application layer serving both families (command/query) of use cases, or it can be two distinct application layers. The same goes for the domain model.

However, splitting the domain model in two stack-specific parts has a stronger connotation. The command domain model is essentially a simplified version of the single-stack domain model. The query domain model is essentially a *read model*—nothing more than a collection of DTOs tailor-made for the needs of the user interface and external callers and devoid of most business rules. (See Figure 8-4.)

**Note** When the architecture adopts the structure shown in Figure 8-4, the necessity for a comprehensive domain model becomes less rigid. Queries, meant solely for data display, don't require the intricate relationships of classic domain models. For the query side of a CQRS system, a simplified domain layer can consist only of tailored DTOs. This may lead to domain services functioning as implementers of business logic atop a much simpler model, even anemic for the query part.

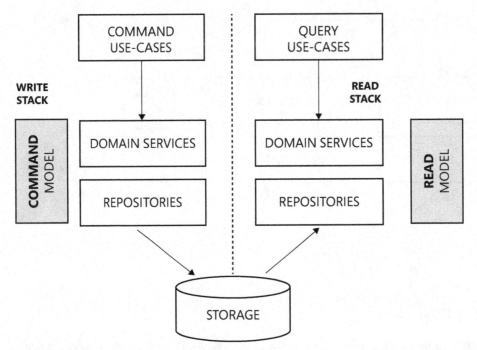

**FIGURE 8-4** More in-depth split of command/query stacks.

## A business perspective of CQRS

Decoupling queries and commands enables you to independently address scalability for each part. Furthermore, the clean segregation ensures that modifications to one stack won't inadvertently affect the other, preventing regressions. This approach also encourages a task-based user interface, enhancing the user experience. Honestly, I see minimal drawbacks in using CQRS. A more relevant point is whether you really obtain concrete benefits from (learning and) adopting CQRS.

CQRS emerged from the need to handle complex collaborative systems where multiple users and software clients concurrently interact with data under intricate and frequently changing business rules.

These systems involve ongoing data changes due to the actions of various users and components, resulting in potential data staleness. To address this situation, architects have two options:

- Lock the entire aggregate during every operation, leading to poor throughput.

- Permit ongoing aggregate modifications, risking potentially inconsistent data that eventually converges to coherence.

The first option quickly becomes unfeasible for collaborative systems. The second option, though plausible, can deliver inaccurate outcomes if the system lacks proper tuning, and may require excessive time to synchronize. This backdrop set the stage for the formalization of CQRS around 2010.

In summary, beyond the domain of collaborative systems, the effectiveness of CQRS wanes considerably. This underscores the importance of approaching CQRS as a viable architecture but with a lot of caution, and certainly not as a trend of the moment.

## CQRS with shared databases

The architecture in Figure 8-4 is articulated in two parallel branches that converge in the same shared database. Admittedly, this results in a nicer picture, but it does not necessarily improve the architecture.

Using CQRS with a shared database is definitely possible, but the rationale behind CQRS also suggests it might not always be the most optimal choice. CQRS is employed to separate an application's read and write concerns, allowing each to be optimized independently. However, if you use a shared database, some of these benefits might be diminished.

Introducing CQRS, even with a shared database, adds complexity to the architecture. You'll need to manage two different models and potentially handle data synchronization and consistency issues. Even with a shared database, however, CQRS can lead to performance improvements if read and write operations have vastly different demands.

What does the trade-off look like? In a nutshell, CQRS mainly makes sense when read and write operations generate significantly different workloads. In this case, to maximize throughput, you might also want to use separate storage mechanisms for reads and writes so you can optimize each side for its specific use case and employ the most appropriate data storage and data access technology for the intended purpose.

## CQRS with distinct databases

Figure 8-5 goes one step further, illustrating a CQRS architecture in which both the read stack and the command stack have their own data stores.

No matter what, CQRS starts as a small thing and ends up forcing radical changes to the entire architecture. For this reason, no one should blissfully embark on using it without compelling business reasons.

Suppose you opt for distinct read and write data stores, as in Figure 8-5. The good news is that you can use different database technologies in each stack. For example, you can use a relational DBMS in the command and a NoSQL store in the read stack. But whichever database technologies you use, an extra layer synchronizing the two stores is vital. For example, if a command saves the status of a document on the command store, then at some point a sync operation must update the status of the same information on the read store. Data synchronization can take place as soon as the command task ends as a synchronous or asynchronous operation or occurs as a scheduled job. The longer this takes to happen, though, the more data written and presented will be out of sync. Not all applications can afford this.

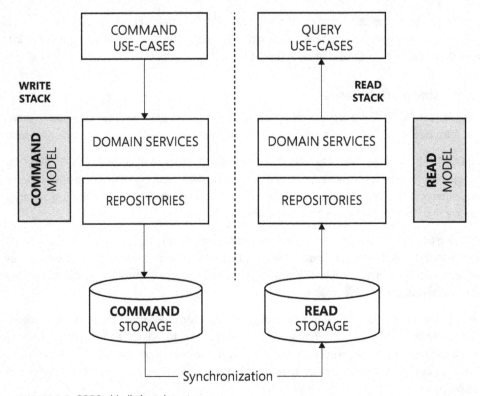

**FIGURE 8-5** CQRS with distinct data stores.

There's an even deeper point, though. The separation between commands and queries introduces an alternative approach for the design of the application layer, potentially paving the way for even higher levels of scalability. Instead of performing any requested tasks internally, the application layer simply passes a command request to a dedicated processor. The processor then assumes the responsibility of command execution, by directly executing the command, dynamically assigning the command to a dedicated handler, or simply posting a message on a bus where registered listeners will react. (See Figure 8-6.)

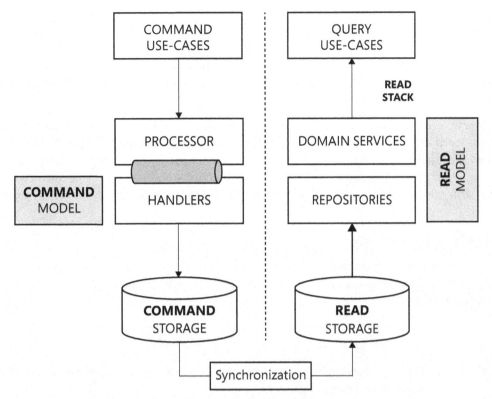

FIGURE 8-6 A message-based implementation of the business logic.

## An executive summary of event sourcing

The ultimate destination of an architectural journey that starts with the separation of commands and queries is event sourcing. In the real world, we initiate actions and observe corresponding reactions, either instant or delayed. At times, reactions trigger subsequent actions, setting off a chain of responses. This mirrors the natural course of events. Over the years, however, conventional software design hasn't consistently mirrored this pattern. Event sourcing is a software-development approach that grants primary importance to discernible business events, treating them as fundamental entities.

> **Note** Event sourcing is a big topic—even more impactful than plain CQRS—and rightly deserves a book of its own. The purpose of this section is merely to provide an executive summary.

### Characterizing traits

Event sourcing (herefter ES) departs from the traditional model of storing only the current state of an application's data. Instead, it captures and stores a chronological series of business events that lead to changes in data state. Each event represents a discrete action that is deemed relevant in the context of the application's domain. These events collectively form a comprehensive and unalterable audit trail, enabling a holistic view of an application's history and evolution.

Instead of storing only the current state of the system after each update, ES allows you to store only the various changes (events) that occur over time and to recalculate the current state from it any time you need it, in any form you need it.

To grasp event sourcing, think of your bank account balance. It is a number that changes after each transaction. It is not stored, though, as a plain number overwritten every now and then. Instead, it reflects the result of all the discrete actions (expenses, withdrawals, payouts) performed on the account. The reported transactions constitute a list of events that occurred and are saved in the command data store, while the balance is one possible rendering of the state of the account in the form of a read model.

ES offers several advantages:

- By recording every business event, it enables the precise reconstruction of an application's state at any point in time. This audit trail proves invaluable for debugging, analysis, and regulatory compliance.

- The event log provides the ability to query the data state at various historical moments—a capability that traditional databases often lack or don't offer by default.

- The audit trail mitigates data loss by enabling you to reconstruct states based on events. This enhances system reliability and disaster recovery.

ES presents challenges too. For example:

- ES requires a fundamental shift in design thinking, which may introduce complexity in development, testing, and maintenance.

- Evolving event structures while maintaining backward compatibility can be challenging and requires careful planning.

- Careful synchronization strategies are often a necessity to guarantee consistency.

- Storing events might consume more space compared to traditional state-based approaches.

## Architectural implications

As mentioned, ES aligns well with the CQRS pattern and indeed represents its ultimate variation. Any ES solution is implicitly a CQRS solution because of the neat and structural separation between the write and read stacks. ES, though, makes mandatory a couple of architectural choices that are optional in CQRS.

At the core of ES is the event store—a specialized data repository responsible for persisting events. Unlike traditional databases, an event store captures every event as an immutable record, ensuring a complete and accurate historical record of application actions. Architects must carefully select an event store that aligns with the application's requirements for performance, scalability, and fault tolerance. NoSQL databases (for example, Cosmos DB, Mongo DB) are a frequent choice.

ES naturally encourages asynchronous processing of events. Events are captured and stored first, and then processed by event handlers. An architecture that implements message-based business logic is therefore the natural choice. Furthermore, ES can replay events to re-create past states. Architects should consider incorporating tools and mechanisms to facilitate event replay for debugging, testing, and analytical purposes.

## Summary

The infrastructure layer plays a pivotal role in ensuring the efficient and reliable functioning of the entire system. Often referred to as the "plumbing" of the application, the infrastructure assumes responsibilities that are crucial for the success of an application.

The infrastructure layer primarily contains code that deals with persistence and facades to access external services. This chapter covered repositories and various data access technologies, including EF Core and Dapper.

Even though the term *infrastructure layer* may evoke DDD, the technical concerns addressed by the layer are universal and common to any applications, whether or not they follow the dictates of DDD.

This chapter concludes the analysis of layered architecture. At this point, you should have enough vision to plan a monolithic but highly modular application. In the following chapters, you will complete your journey learning about clean architecture, including the difference between (modular) monoliths and microservices.

# Common dilemmas

# CHAPTER 9

# Microservices versus modular monoliths

*All things are subject to interpretation; whichever interpretation prevails at a given time is a function of power and not truth.*

—*Friedrich Nietzsche*

In the past decade or so, the microservices architecture has become an increasingly popular approach to designing and managing distributed applications. The microservices architectural style revolves around the development of independent, modular services, referred to as *microservices*, each focused on performing a distinct function.

Put this way, microservices can be seen as a clever idea—an important harbinger of great changes in how we think about and build applications. For a moment, let's compare the advent of microservices to the advent of the wheel. At first, both look like groundbreaking inventions capable of increased efficiency and greater results. However, it didn't take long for humans to recognize that the wheel alone was not sufficient to support the progress it enabled; as the challenge of transporting heavier and heavier loads on dirt paths arose, so too did road construction.

With microservices, we face nearly the same pattern. Transitioning to a microservices architecture raises the challenge of altering the communication model between the logical parts of the application. Simply converting in-memory method calls to remote procedure calls (RPCs) over some protocol inevitably results in excessive communication and a negative performance hit. Hence, it is essential to switch from a *chatty* communication model to a *chunky* model that, instead of exchanging numerous small messages, exchanges fewer but more comprehensive messages. This is a radical change that affects the whole application stack and, deeper still, the way we devise applications.

Although the microservices architecture is largely understood (mostly by top-level management) as a plain alternative to rewriting monolithic applications, using it changes the face of the resulting application and its underlying network architecture. With microservices, you have the wheel, but until you construct some roads, things may be even worse than before. For this reason, the microservices architecture is far from being universally applicable.

# Moving away from legacy monoliths

To grasp the essence of the microservices architecture, let's start by discussing its architectural antagonist: the traditional monolithic style. *Monoliths* are software applications built as single, self-contained units. All functionalities are incorporated in the unit, potentially making it large and problematic to manage and update. Much like the Agile methodology was developed in response to the sequential—and much more rigid—waterfall approach, the microservices architecture initially emerged to address challenges in scalability, maintainability, deployment, and even technology diversity, due to the innate nature of monolithic applications.

> **Note** According to this definition, Project Renoir is a monolith. Is that a problem? Does it mean this is the worst book ever about clean architecture and good software practices? The answer to both these questions, as you'll soon see, is no.

## Not all monoliths are equal

In software, not all monoliths are terrible in terms of maintainability, scalability, deployment, and the like. The reality is that monoliths aren't the enemy of microservices. Instead, applications written as tightly coupled, monolithic tangles of code are. These applications are often referred to as *legacy applications*.

### Origin of legacy applications

Legacy applications are line-of-business applications that have been in use for quite some time, often well over a decade. These applications often play a critical role in an organization's operations even though they have been written with old programming languages, use outdated technologies, or lack modern features. A legacy and aged application is not a big problem per se, but it becomes a huge problem when it needs to be enhanced or integrated with newer systems. Legacy applications, in fact, are typically difficult to maintain and update.

Why are legacy applications monolithic?

The monolithic software architecture has existed since the early days of computer programming. In those days, programs were often written as single, large, and self-contained pieces of code due to the limitations of the hardware and software systems of the time. So, the structure of legacy applications is simply the natural outcome of decades of cumulative programming efforts. That is, their monolithic structure is merely a sign of their times.

### Dealing with legacy applications

For all companies and organizations involved, legacy applications are therefore a problem to solve or, at the very least, mitigate. At the same time, migrating from a legacy application to a newer one can be expensive and risky, leading some organizations to continue using the existing system despite its limitations.

For management, a legacy application means being faced with a devil's alternative. On the one hand, if they keep using the old application, they take a risk on the business side because the issues that prompt consideration of a rewrite won't resolve on their own over time. On the other hand, if they choose to build a new application, they will invest significant funds without a guarantee of success. Although whether to rewrite a legacy application may be a tough decision on the management side, it's one that must be made.

In a similar stalemate, every piece of good news that arrives sounds celestial. So, several early success stories, and quite a bit of tech hype, contributed to labeling (legacy) monoliths as evil and microservices as the savior. The gracious and positive storytelling about a new architectural style provides non-technical management executives with the impetus needed to make the technical decision of spending money on a big rewrite of the legacy application using a microservices architecture.

The truth is somewhere in the middle. Not all monoliths are bad, and not just any microservices architecture is successful. The rest of this chapter sorts through the facts of monoliths and microservices and outlines a reasonable decision workflow.

**Note** In some very special cases, such as when the old application is a desktop Windows Forms or WPF application, you can try some dedicated commercial frameworks that can bring desktop Windows applications to new life in the cloud in the form of pure ASP.NET Core, Blazor-style applications. When applicable, this represents a pleasant exception to the rule that obsolete applications, at some point and in some way, should be renewed.

## Potential downsides of monoliths

Like it or not, the natural approach to any software application is inherently monolithic. You see the whole thing built as a single unit. All the processing logic runs in a single process; it's the basic features of the programming language and your framework of choice that enable you to split the whole thing into libraries, classes, and namespaces.

This approach to software development is not bad per se; it just requires a lot of self-discipline and team discipline to ensure modularity. And deployment pipelines should exist to guarantee that changes are properly deployed to production. As for scalability, horizontal scale may be an option as long as you run the instances behind a load balancer with no overlapping of state.

In a nutshell, a monolithic application can be successful, but without strict self-discipline to preserve a modular structure over time, it can soon turn into a tightly coupled beast that is nearly impossible to maintain or scale. This section discusses these and other problematic aspects of a monolithic application architecture.

### Code development and maintenance

Initially, a monolithic architecture offers some clear plusses, such as simplicity of coding in the early stages of development and one-shot, immediate deployment. The problems with monoliths usually come later, as more use cases are added, and lines of code grow.

As new functions accumulate in monolithic applications, their complexity tends to grow. Moreover, this complexity occurs in the single, monolithic unit rather than being distributed—and therefore mitigated—across smaller units. Furthermore, if the code is not structured in watershed modules, then the application's complexity can increase in a more than linear fashion. This makes it significantly harder for anyone on the team to understand and debug the code.

Testing may also become problematic due to limited isolation of software components. So, it may happen that changes in one part of the code base have unintended consequences in other parts. And the whole development cycle (coding, testing, and committing) takes time, making it challenging to respond quickly to functional requirements.

## Merge conflicts

In larger teams, multiple developers may need to work on the same code base simultaneously. Git helps with branches and pulls, but conflicts are always lurking. Conflicts typically occur when two developers change the same lines within a file or when one developer deletes a file while another developer is modifying it. In such scenarios, Git cannot automatically ascertain the correct course of action, making manual intervention the sole (time-consuming) option.

To speed up the development cycle and reduce merge conflicts, discipline is the only remedy—but self-discipline more than team discipline. All developers should split extensive modifications into smaller increments and keep files and classes distinct to the extent that it is possible. If merge conflicts still occur (and they will), then developers should spend more time thoroughly reviewing the changes before merging. The only definitive way out is refactoring the code base into smaller, relatively independent chunks, both logical (behavior) and physical (files).

## Scalability challenges

Monolithic applications lend to scale vertically but are challenging to scale horizontally. Vertical scaling (also known as *scaling up*) entails making the single server that runs the application more powerful by adding resources. It's not just the server, though. Sometimes the underlying database also needs to be fine-tuned when traffic increases. Vertical scaling may not have a huge impact on the budget, but it does have the potential to turn into a fairly inefficient and costly option. Ultimately, it all depends on the amount of increased load.

In general, horizontal scaling (also known as *scaling out*) is a more effective technique, although it might not work for all applications. Horizontal scaling involves increasing the application's capacity by running it on multiple servers instead of increasing the capability of a single server. (See Figure 9-1.)

With horizontal scaling, multiple instances of the same application run at the same time, usually under the control of a load balancer. This means that two successive requests may be handled by different instances, making statelessness a crucial application characteristic. This is why not all applications—especially those grown with little control in the wild—are a good fit for horizontal scaling.

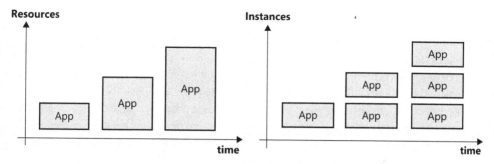

**FIGURE 9-1** Vertical versus horizontal scaling.

## Deployment challenges

Because monolithic applications exist as a single unit, they must be deployed in their entirety. So, even if all you change is a localized string, the entire application must be redeployed to any environments.

This is a fact. But is it really a problem?

In a massively distributed architecture, you typically deploy one piece at a time, meaning that only that piece will potentially be down during the update or offline if something goes wrong. The rest of the application will be up and running. In contrast, a monolithic application doesn't let you deploy parts of an application. Still, using zero-downtime deployment techniques, you can release updates frequently and reliably.

These days, in fact, thanks to DevOps and cloud services, it's easy to achieve zero downtime during deployment. In Azure, for example, you simply use app services with deployment slots enabled, deploy to preview, and swap to production only if all is good.

## Technology diversity

Technology diversity refers to the presence and integration of a variety of technologies within a given software system. It emphasizes the coexistence and use of different software stacks to address diverse needs, challenges, or functionalities. This approach aims to leverage the strengths of various technologies while fostering innovation, adaptability, and resilience in the face of evolving requirements.

Technology diversity doesn't structurally belong to monoliths.

Monoliths typically rely on a single technology stack. An ASP.NET web application, for example, can have parts written in C# and parts written in another language (for example, F# or Visual Basic), but remains locked to the .NET Core framework of choice. That same application, though, may be linked to external web services controlled by the same team, which may leverage other stacks such as Python and Java. This is another fact. Again, is it a problem? Personally, I don't think so, but it's a matter of perspective rather than absolute truth.

# Facts about microservices

The practice of building software as a collection of small, loosely coupled, and independently deployable services gradually evolved from the principles of service-oriented architecture (SOA) that have been around since the early 2000s. SOA is a broader architectural approach that focuses on organizing software components (known as services) to support business processes. Services in SOA are larger, encompass modules, and are often subject to some centralized governance model so that changes to one service might have cascading effects on others. In other words, SOA services are aware of each other and are fairly coupled, though formally independent.

SOA laid the groundwork, and the microservice architectural style evolved over time as a response to the challenges posed by monolithic architectures and the changing landscape of software development. Compared to an SOA, a microservices architecture is made of more numerous and more granular and independent components.

However, there's no specific time when microservices, as an architectural style and approach to software development, was born. Rather, the microservices style emerged organically in response to the evolving needs of the software industry.

## Early adopters

Companies like Amazon and Netflix are often cited as early adopters—in some way, inventors—of microservices. In reality, they have simply been labeled as such. To be honest, it is even questionable whether their disclosed architectural diagrams really represent a microservices architecture or a distributed application articulated on multiple cohesive services.

The fact is that nobody initiates a project with the sole intention of inventing a new architectural style. Amazon, Netflix, and many other companies simply set out to develop their own method for building highly scalable and distributed systems to serve their business needs in the best possible way. They only cared about the results; others just played with putting labels on visible outcomes.

The resulting set of practices and principles attracted the attention of many individuals and organizations, eager to learn how a big company uses software to support its business. Over time, the practices and principles employed by early adopters have been refined and popularized, with contributions from various thought leaders, authors, and practitioners leading to their wider adoption. Some input also came from the Agile methodology and later from DevOps. Their emphasis on the importance of smaller, more frequent releases and closer collaboration between development and operations teams naturally drove developers to design and build new applications using a microservices approach.

## Tenets of a microservices architecture and SOA

The microservices architecture calls for the development of applications as a collection of services. Each service:

- Is structured around a specific business functionality
- Operates in its dedicated process

- Communicates through lightweight mechanisms such as HTTPS endpoints

- Can be deployed individually

As mentioned, microservices are an evolution of SOA. Out of curiosity, let's review the fundamental tenets of SOA. Although there isn't an established official standard for the SOA, consensus within the community indicates the following four fundamental principles of an SOA. In an SOA, each constituent service:

- Has a clear definition of service boundaries

- Operates in full autonomy

- Shares contracts, not code, with its clients

- Establishes compatibility through policies

The sense of *déjà-vu* is strong, isn't it? In SOA, systems are decomposed into distinct services, each encapsulating a specific piece of functionality or business capability. These services have well-defined boundaries and are designed to be modular, autonomous, and independently deployable. Contracts delineate the business functionalities accessible through a service boundary, whereas policies encompass various constraints, including communication protocols, security prerequisites, and reliability specifications. Considering this, I dare say that a microservices architecture is essentially an SOA with a couple of unique traits. First, it's not as strict or rigorous as an SOA. And second, there are no policies (or anything like them) to mediate—and therefore complicate—communication between components.

# How big or small is "micro"?

In the industry, the term "microservice" is often used interchangeably to describe both a tiny, highly specialized, and self-contained deployable service, and a comprehensive web service still focused on a single task but defined at a significantly higher level of abstraction and resembling an application in its logical scope. In fact, the term "microservice" does have a clear definition, but one so broad that it spills over into the territory of ambiguity: each microservice is designed to handle a specific business capability or function. It has a well-defined purpose and does one thing well.

Note that the term "micro" is relative and should not be interpreted as a strict size constraint. The size of a microservice can vary based on the specific requirements of the application and the organization's goals. What's essential is that each service is focused, independent, and aligns with the principles of microservices architecture.

## Logical decomposition of the system

In the early 2000s, within the Windows environment, Windows Communication Foundation (WCF) was the framework specifically designed to facilitate the implementation of SOA principles. It was a huge subject that inspired tons of books, articles, and conference talks. At some point, a somewhat bold idea surfaced: turning every application class into a service.

From a WCF standpoint, services represented a means to separate the business logic from the essential infrastructure needed to support it, such as security, transactions, error handling, and deployment. Devoid entirely of every plumbing aspect, managed by the WCF infrastructure, services were isolated business components, completely autonomous in behavior, and exposing clear contracts to the outside world.

The question arose, how big should each service be? People soon began attempting to maximize the benefits of services by decomposing them to their most fundamental level, transforming even primitive elements into microscopic services. In other words, microscopic services represented the natural result of a carefully deconstructed system.

What began merely as an intellectual challenge within the realms of SOA and WCF has since evolved into a predominant characteristic of the microservices architectural approach. Indeed, this is the debatable point around which rotates both the good and the bad aspects of the microservices architecture: that the analysis should go as deep as possible to fully decompose any system into primitive and microscopic service units.

## Physical deployment of microscopic services

Still, microscopic services are logical services. But the size of a deployable service (one we commonly refer to as a microservice) might not match the size of any logical microscopic services we may identify during the system analysis. (See Figure 9-2.)

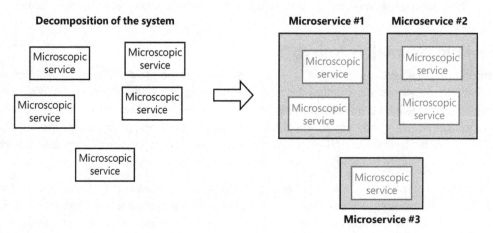

**FIGURE 9-2** Decomposing a system into microservices.

Missing the point of logical and physical microservices may jeopardize the whole design of the system and skyrocket costs and latency. A one-to-one relationship between logical and physical microservices is at one extreme. At the other extreme is a (modular) monolith. (See Figure 9-3.) I'll return to microservices and modular monoliths later in the chapter. For now, let's just find out more about the good and not-so-good parts of the microservices architectural style.

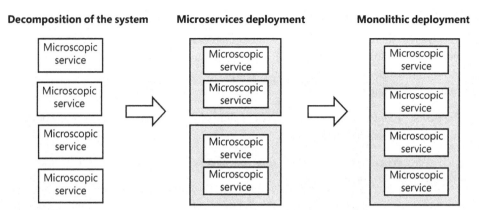

FIGURE 9-3 Logical decomposition may lead to microservices as well as to monoliths.

**Note** "Smart endpoints and dumb pipes" is a guiding principle in microservices architecture. It emphasizes placing intelligence and functionality within the microservices themselves while keeping communication channels simple and generic. The key idea is that microservices should be self-sufficient and self-contained, capable of processing data and making decisions independently.

## An archipelago of services

In geography, the term *archipelago* describes a group of islands that are scattered close to each other in a large body of water, whether an ocean, enclosed sea, or lake. These islands can vary in size, and they are typically separated from each other by bodies of water like small seas or straits. Archipelagos can consist of just a few islands or extend to include tens of islands within the same chain.

I like the metaphor of the archipelago to describe a microservices architecture over the plain concept of suites or a collection of services because ultimately, services are scattered across a large body (the cloud), can vary in size, and are separated (and connected) by protocols like HTTPS, gRPC, TCP, and message buses.

# The benefits of microservices

Just because the microservices style emerged as a way to settle the troubled waters of distributed applications, it offers a considerable list of benefits that are objectively difficult to deny. After all, any architectural style in which an application is composed of independently deployable, small, and modular services clearly promotes flexibility, scalability, and the ability to develop, deploy, and maintain services separately. The following sections constitute a more structured list of the good parts of microservices.

## More Agile development cycles

Decomposing the system into a reasonable number of interacting components lays the groundwork for unprecedented flexibility and parallelization of development. Each microservice can be developed, tested, and released independently, allowing developers to focus on one task at a time and make changes without affecting the entire system. This brings several benefits:

- The development of separate microservices allows for more efficient division of work among development teams and members.

- Each microservice is typically owned by a specific team (or developer), which promotes clear accountability and responsibility.

- Each microservice can be managed and updated independently, reducing the risk of system-wide disruptions during maintenance.

- Each microservice can exhibit technological diversity (programming stack, language, data storage), resulting in augmentation of developers' skills.

- Isolated (and ideally smaller) services are more manageable when it comes to unit testing, integration testing, and end-to-end testing.

Furthermore, more Agile development cycles encourage a culture of continuous deployment and DevOps practices, fostering rapid iteration and continuous improvement of the application. In this way, organizations can respond quickly to changing business requirements and market conditions. For example, the fact that microservices can be easily integrated into a larger ecosystem of systems facilitates collaboration with external partners and third-party services.

## Increased potential for scalability

Microservices' great potential for scalability stems directly from its architectural principles and represents one of their most significant advantages. The chief enabling factor is the granularity of services.

Because services are decoupled and independent, they can be individually scaled to meet varying levels of demand. This means you can allocate more resources to critical services (for example, CPU, memory, network bandwidth) while keeping less-used services lean to optimize resource use. This contrasts with monolithic architectures, where scaling typically involves ramping up the entire monolith, including components that may not require additional resources.

You can automatically manage and orchestrate this horizontal scalability using real-time metrics to accommodate traffic spikes and fluctuations. Note, though, that automated resource optimization isn't exclusive to microservices but is a feature provided by the hosting cloud platform. Nevertheless, the level of granularity offered by microservices significantly enhances this capability. Likewise, you can fine-tune load balancing—which is also not unique to microservices—at the service level rather than at the application level, thus ensuring that no single service instance becomes a bottleneck.

## Fault tolerance

The separation of microservices reduces the likelihood that an error in one service will compromise the entire application. There are two possible types of errors: a failure in the code (bug, incoherent status) or a network failure. In the latter case, only one service is down or unreachable; the rest of the application is up and running, and all functions that do not involve the failed service operate as usual. In contrast, if a monolithic application experiences a network failure, no one can use it.

In a scenario in which the failure is caused by a code exception, I see no relevant differences between microservices and a monolithic application. Any call that addresses the troubled service fails in much the same way as in a monolithic application, which throws an exception after any attempt to call a certain function. In both cases, to give users a friendly response, callers must catch exceptions and recover nicely. And with both microservices and monoliths, functions that do not relate to the troubled code work as usual.

# The gray areas

While microservices offer numerous benefits, they also introduce considerable complexity in terms of service coordination, data management, and operational overhead. The interesting thing about the microservices architecture is that the same characteristic, in different contexts, can be seen as either good or bad. An illustrious example is the granularity of services. This is a great characteristic of microservices in that it improves the development cycle and increases fault tolerance. But it's a bad characteristic because it adds a lot of complexity and communication overhead. This section covers the downsides of the architecture.

> **Note** My two cents are that microservices surfaced as an approach with clear benefits in the implementation of some (large) early adopters. Among everyone else, this generated the idea that microservices could be the long-awaited Holy Grail of software. In practice, though, the microservices architecture—like nearly everything else in life—has pros and cons. I'd even dare say that for most applications, it has more cons than pros. I'll return to this later in this chapter.

## Service coordination

Let's face it: The first point in the preceding list of good characteristics—more agile and accelerated development cycles—is frequently (over)emphasized to make the microservices approach more appealing to decision makers. In reality, no application is an island, let alone an archipelago. So, you don't just need digital bridges and tunnels to connect islands (for example, protocols); you also need some centralized service management and coordination. This results in additional—and to some extent, accidental—complexity.

Centralized service management refers to standard ways of handling various aspects of the development cycle such as deployment, configuration settings, authentication, authorization, discovery of available microservices, versioning, monitoring, logging, documentation, and so on. The general guideline is to keep centralized management of microservices operations to a minimum and favor independence of individual modules. It's a delicate trade-off, though: Addressing cross-cutting services within an archipelago (or just an island) is much more problematic than on the mainland.

Coordination, in contrast, refers to the mechanisms used to ensure that the various microservices within an application work together harmoniously to achieve the intended functionality. This is normally achieved via *orchestration* or *choreography*. In the former case, a central workflow engine coordinates the execution of multiple microservices in a specific sequence driven by business logic. In contrast, the latter case relies on microservices collectively collaborating to achieve a desired outcome. Each service performs its part of the process autonomously based on the events and messages it receives, usually via a bus. A message bus, though, represents another level of complexity.

## Cross-cutting concerns

A *cross-cutting concern* is an aspect of a software application that affects multiple constituent parts. All applications deal with concerns such as security, monitoring, logging, error handling, and caching, but handling these within a monolithic application is much easier than with microservices because everything takes place within the same process. In contrast, in the realm of microservices, cross-cutting concerns may affect multiple processes—let me repeat: multiple processes. They may also require global collection and centralized handling of distributed results captured by each running service.

You can use an identity provider for security, distributed memory caches for caching, centralized loggers for tracing and health checks, and standardized error responses for error handling. Note, though, that the list of cross-cutting concerns is also longer in a microservices architecture than it is within a monolithic one. Microservices' cross-cutting concerns include managing service registries, load balancing, dynamic routing, and auto-scaling. In addition, defining consistent communication protocols, API standards, and data formats is crucial for enabling microservices to interact seamlessly. Hence, cross-cutting concerns should also include API versioning, contract testing, and documentation.

## Centralized logging service

Tracing the activity and monitoring the health of individual microservices poses challenges because the logs for each microservice are typically stored on its respective machine. Implementing a centralized logging service that aggregates logs from all microservices, such as an Application Insights agent, is highly advisable.

Within a microservices architecture, it's common to encounter never-before-seen errors. But you don't want to have to navigate numerous log files to gain insights into the root causes of these errors. If one or more microservices fail, you must be able to answer questions such as which services were invoked and in what order. Understanding the flow of requests across microservices is also essential for diagnosing performance bottlenecks and troubleshooting issues.

Here are a few microservices logging best practices:

- **Use a correlation ID**  A *correlation ID* is a distinct value assigned to a request and exchanged among the services involved in fulfilling that request. In case of anomalies, tracing the correlation ID provided with the request allows you to filter the pertinent log entries without sifting through potentially millions of records.

- **Log structured information** A structured logging format such as JSON makes it much easier to search and analyze logs. Be sure to include enough context in your logs to understand the events that led to an error. This might include information such as the correlation ID, request URL and parameters, service name, user ID, time stamp, overall duration, and so on.

- **Use log levels** Using different log levels (error, warning, info, and so on) to indicate the severity of a log message speeds up your search for the most important issues while ensuring that you don't miss any significant but less urgent issues.

In addition to recording error messages, it is also advisable to log performance metrics like response times and resource consumption. This way, you can closely monitor the services' performance and pinpoint any possible concerns.

## Authentication and authorization

In a monolithic application, authenticating users can be as easy as checking their email and password against a proprietary database and issuing a cookie for successive access. Then, anytime the user logs in, the system can fully trust any request they issue. Authorization revolves around checking the user's claims (such as their role or feature-specific permissions) that are also tracked via the cookie. Cookies, however, work well only if the client is the browser.

A microservices architecture generally requires a different approach: using an API gateway and an identity provider. (See Figure 9-4.) Here, the client calls the API gateway and provides its own authentication token. If the token is invalid, the client is redirected to the identity provider for authentication. When authentication is successful, details of the identity are returned to the client in the form of a token. The token is then attached to every successive call to the API gateway directed at the various microservices.

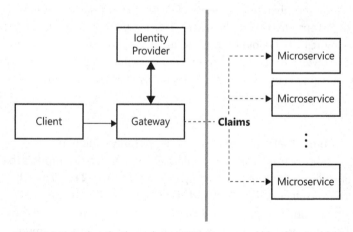

**FIGURE 9-4** Authentication using an API gateway and identity provider.

How can every microservice check the permissions of the requesting user? A reasonable option is to simply store all the user's permissions in the token as claims. That way, when a microservice receives a request, it first decodes and validates the token, and then verifies whether the user holds the necessary permissions for the action requested.

# Distributed transaction management

A *distributed transaction* is a transaction that involves multiple operations and changes to data in different systems. Ensuring the consistency and reliability of such transactions is a complex issue in distributed systems, and various techniques and protocols have been developed to effectively manage them in some way. Distributed transactions are not specific to microservices but, in a system made of many interacting parts, the chance for distributed transactions is much higher.

Managing distributed transactions is challenging due to factors like network latency, system failures, and the need to coordinate among multiple resources. Various protocols and techniques have been developed to handle distributed transactions, but the best option remains avoiding them in the first place.

I categorize this as a "gray area" because what might be a straightforward transaction within a monolithic system can readily transform into a distributed transaction when transitioning to a microservices architecture. The larger the microservice is, the more it can do internally without distributed transactions. At the same time, the larger the microservice is, the more things it may end up doing. In general, by appropriately breaking down the system into microservices, it's quite unlikely you would need to resort to distributed transactions. Moreover, the integration of eventual consistency, if acceptable for the application, would further decrease the requirement.

Various protocols and techniques have been developed to handle distributed transactions, including two-phase commit (2PC) and three-phase commit (3PC). The former is a widely used protocol that involves a coordinator and multiple participants. The coordinator ensures that all participants either commit or abort the transaction. It has some limitations, though, such as possible blocking and scalability issues. 3PC addresses these by adding an extra phase.

Another option for breaking down the inherent complexity of distributed transactions is to use the Saga pattern. Instead of trying to ensure all-or-nothing atomicity, this pattern suggests you break the larger operation into smaller, more manageable steps. Each step is a separate transaction, and compensation steps are defined to reverse the effects of completed steps if needed. Introducing the Saga pattern, though, has a relevant impact on the existing code and, even when coded in a greenfield scenario, requires advanced design and development skills.

> **Note** Eventual consistency assumes that data replicas may temporarily exhibit inconsistency due to network delays and concurrent updates. Unlike strong consistency models that enforce immediate synchronization, eventual consistency guarantees that all replicas will converge to the same consistent state, but *over time* and in the *absence of further updates*. This approach allows for high availability and scalability in distributed systems, as nodes can operate independently without the need for constant coordination. From a development standpoint, though, applications must be designed to handle temporary data divergence through conflict-resolution mechanisms.

## Data management

This is a huge topic with so many implications that it probably deserves a book of its own. First and foremost, no known laws currently prohibit the deployment of a microservices architecture on top of a single and shared database server. In my opinion, this is the best trade-off possible in terms of development costs and effective results. More importantly, this approach saves time spent grouping and joining data, possibly from multiple sources and heterogeneous storage technologies.

So, using a shared database is one option. Unfortunately, it is considered an antipattern. (This is an amply questionable point, but that's just it—if you advertise such a decision, be prepared to face a host of opponents who claim otherwise.) Why is a shared database considered an antipattern? A common (albeit somewhat abstract) answer is that tying microservices to a shared database can compromise microservices' fundamental characteristics of scalability, resilience, and autonomy. The alternative is the database-per-service approach, whereby each microservice has its own database. This ensures that services are loosely coupled and allows teams to choose the most appropriate database technology for each service's specific needs. Table 9-1 and Table 9-2 present the pros and cons of both patterns.

**TABLE 9-1** Benefits of microservices database patterns

| Database-per-service | Shared database |
|---|---|
| Services are loosely coupled and independent. | There's no need to resort to distributed transactions. |
| Each service can have the best data storage technology for its particular needs (or sometimes just the developer's ego). | The entire dataset is fully constrained and well structured, with integrity preserved at the root. |
| There is clear ownership of data. | Sophisticated GROUP and JOIN operations can retrieve data from multiple tables simultaneously. |
| Changes to the database schema or data of a given service database have no impact on other services. | There is reduced need for data duplication and redundancy. |

**TABLE 9-2** Drawbacks of microservices database patterns

| Database-per-service | Shared database |
|---|---|
| Each microservice can only access its own data store directly. | The database is a single point of failure |
| Each microservice must expose an API to exchange data with other services. | Ownership of data is unclear. |
| A circuit-breaker layer of code is needed to handle failures across service calls. | Changes to the database schema or data may hit multiple services. |
| There is no simple way to execute JOIN queries on multiple data stores or to run transactions spanning multiple databases. | Microservices lack complete independence in terms of development and deployment because they are interconnected and operate on a shared database. |
| Data-related operations spanning multiple microservices could be hard to debug in the event of a problem. | |

Notice that the drawbacks associated with the database-per-service pattern stem directly from the initial pattern choice. Moreover, you can mitigate them only by introducing complexities like circuit breakers, data APIs, and data aggregators (for example, GraphQL), and embracing eventual consistency.

**Note** A *circuit breaker* is a software design pattern used in distributed systems to enhance resilience and prevent system failures caused by repeated attempts to access an unresponsive service. It functions like an electrical circuit breaker, monitoring service calls. When failures reach a certain threshold, the circuit breaker temporarily halts requests to the problematic service, preventing further damage. It then periodically checks if the service has recovered. If so, it closes the circuit, allowing requests to resume. Circuit breakers improve system stability, reduce latency, and enhance overall fault tolerance in modern applications and microservices architectures.

What about the drawbacks of the shared database approach? Looking at Table 9-2, it becomes evident that skillful programming techniques and the judicious use of cloud services can reduce the effects of the first two points. Interestingly, these measures also indirectly alleviate the other two sore points.

There are several established strategies to prevent the database from becoming a single point of failure, including primary/replica sync coupled with manual or automated failover, clustering, and high-availability solutions. All these strategies are designed to diminish the potential for downtime. Supplementary actions like data backups and load balancing can also preempt problems that might ultimately lead to a breakdown.

Regarding data ownership, you can act at the code level by constraining each service to exclusively use the specific tables it requires. You can achieve this using Entity Framework by employing multiple DbContext components, each focusing on a particular set of tables. Or, in cases where your data allows for it, consider database sharding. This divides your data into smaller, more manageable pieces, with each shard potentially residing on its own server. This approach not only lessens the repercussions of a single-server malfunction but also imposes limitations on service access.

What's the bottom line? In my experience, if a shared database appears to be the most suitable solution for a microservices project, you might not need to use microservices at all. In such cases, a well-implemented monolithic architecture could be a more appropriate choice. Typical reasons to choose a shared database within a microservices application include the need to retain existing data tables or if the existing data access code is highly valued. Another critical factor is when efficient transaction management is of utmost importance.

## Operational overhead

Despite its apparent beauty, massively modular architectures have hidden wrinkles in terms of managing and maintaining the system. By design, an independent service lives on its own server and is good at one specific task. So, complex business operations must orchestrate interactions and communication among multiple services. This can lead to issues such as network latency, message delivery failures, and the need for robust error-handling and recovery strategies.

The overhead of inter-service communication—especially in a networked environment—can also affect performance. Efficient communication patterns and optimizations are required to mitigate this issue. In this context, gRPC becomes a viable option, often preferable to HTTPS, which is tailored more for public-facing web APIs.

> **Note** gRPC is an open-source remote procedure call (RPC) framework developed by Google. It enables efficient and high-performance communication between distributed systems by using Protocol Buffers (Protobufs) for data serialization and HTTP/2 for transport. gRPC is used for building fast and efficient APIs in various programming languages, making it ideal for internal microservices communication and scenarios requiring high performance.

Operational overhead is not limited to runtime. While testing a single microservice may be easier, end-to-end testing and debugging of multi-service operations can be challenging and may require sophisticated testing strategies and tools.

As part of their design, microservices inherently bring significant overhead in various areas, including communication, testing, and deployment, as well as discovery and version management. Notably, the financial aspect cannot be overlooked. In this regard, microservices also entail a substantial overhead. While they can offer cost savings through resource optimization, the initial setup and management of microservices infrastructure can be costly—not to mention the costs associated with the necessary shift in mindset when transitioning from a monolithic paradigm to a microservices approach.

# Can microservices fit all applications?

Designing a microservices architecture requires architects to undergo a notable shift in their approach to handling requirements and transforming them into cohesive and interoperable components. The transition to microservices presents complex challenges and the potential for substantial costs. Thus, it *should be* imperative to thoroughly evaluate the project's precise business needs before proceeding. Yet, many software managers have an unhealthy passion for silver bullets—especially when they are coated with a thick layer of technical jargon. As a result, microservices have garnered a reputation for being a universal remedy for all software-related challenges. Is that reputation truly well-deserved?

## The big misconception of big companies

The dominant message today is that microservices are good for all applications because several large companies use them. If it works for them, managers and architects say, then all the more reason it will work for us; after all, we are smaller and less demanding. This viewpoint is overly simplistic.

In fact, many large companies *do* run a software architecture whose description closely matches the definition of an abstract microservices architecture—a system broken down into small, independent, and loosely coupled services that communicate through APIs. And representatives of these companies rightly tell the world their success stories (even if sometimes those stories are bittersweet). People hear these stories during conference talks or read about them in articles and interviews, then go back to the office and say, "Let's do it too." But partitioning an application into independent services only *seems* like an easy task. It's challenging when you have an existing monolith to compare to; it's a true leap in the dark when you use it for a new application.

Large companies like Amazon and Netflix have contributed significantly to the evolution and fame of the microservices approach. I vividly recall the industry-wide impact when Amazon adopted an SOA around 2004. Netflix, however, is the iconic example of a company that has embraced microservices. In any case, Amazon and Netflix did not one day spontaneously decide to divide their existing applications into independently operating microservices. It occurred naturally within a broader evolutionary journey.

## How Netflix discovered microservices

According to Adrian Cockcroft, who led Netflix's migration to a large-scale, highly available public-cloud architecture around 2010 before joining Amazon as VP of Cloud Architecture Strategy in 2013, the original Netflix back end was essentially a monolith founded on an Oracle database. The business need that triggered the first crucial move toward microservices was to give each user their own back end.

The thinking was that the company's extensive and growing user base—each with a lengthy history that required frequent updates—could potentially overwhelm any relational database. So, the team at Netflix decided to denormalize the data store and move to a distributed key-value NoSQL database. The team also reviewed its data access code and refactored complex queries to optimize scalability. Finally, the team transferred all user data—previously handled via sticky in-memory sessions—to a Memcached instance, resulting in a stateless system. As a result, users interacted with a different front end during each visit, which fetched their data from Memcached.

Breaking up the monolith yielded various consequences. One was that it defined clear boundaries between parts, adding logical layers of code. Another was that it necessitated the replacement of existing chatty communication protocols between components with chunky protocols to proficiently handle timeouts and retries.

The Netflix team implemented these changes incrementally, developing new patterns and technologies and capitalizing on emerging cloud services as they went. Ultimately, the company transitioned from a monolithic architecture with a centralized relational database to a distributed, service-based stateless one. But this architecture didn't really have a name— that is, until the industry began calling it *microservices* in the early 2010s. This name would eventually be used to describe an extremely modular system in which each component is autonomous and features a well-defined service interface.

**Note** For a retrospective of the Netflix microservices story, you can read the transcript of Cockcroft's talk at QCon London in March 2023. It's located here: *https://www.infoq.com/presentations/microservices-netflix-industry.*

## SOA and microservices

Are you using a microservices architecture to build a global-scale system serving hundreds of thousands of users? Or are you simply using microservices to build enterprise line-of-business applications with a moderate and relatively constant user base and linear traffic volumes? Put another way, are you sure that what might be pompously defined a microservices architecture isn't simply an SOA with a lot of unnecessary infrastructure?

SOA is a traditional architectural style that focuses on creating reusable, loosely coupled services that communicate through standardized protocols (for example, REST or SOAP). These services are designed to be independent but can also be interconnected. SOA promotes interoperability and is suitable for complex enterprise systems.

Microservices represent a more recent architectural approach that decomposes applications into numerous smaller, self-contained services, each responsible for a specific business function. These services communicate through lightweight protocols like REST and gRPC and can be developed and deployed independently. Microservices emphasize agility, scalability, and ease of maintenance, making them well-suited for rapidly evolving applications.

The key difference between them lies in their granularity. SOA typically involves larger, coarser-grained services, while microservices are finer-grained, focusing on individual features or functions. This affects how changes are managed. With SOA, updates may require the coordination of multiple services, whereas with microservices, changes can be isolated to a single service.

## Are microservices a good fit for your scenario?

Improper use of microservices leads to more complexity and even higher costs. Determining whether microservices are suitable for a given application scenario depends on factors like scalability needs, state of the infrastructure, and development resources. A well-informed decision considers the application's growth potential and the team's ability to manage distributed development effectively. This section contains a short list of key factors for determining whether a microservices approach is right for you.

### Assessing scalability needs

To quote Paul Barham, Principal Scientist at Google, "You can have a second computer once you've shown you know how to use the first one." Application scalability functions similarly. An application requires a more scalable architecture only if it is proven that the current architecture can't go beyond a critical threshold, and that this critical threshold is reached often enough to risk damaging the business.

An application's scalability requirements are not derived solely from the projected numbers in the vague and distant future promised by some enticing business model. More concrete actions are required to gauge these requirements. Specifically, you must:

- Analyze current and projected user traffic patterns.

- Recognize peak usage periods and trends through server logs and the use of tools such as Google Analytics.

- Evaluate the application's responsiveness under simulated high traffic scenarios.

- Monitor network, CPU, and memory usage under different loads.

- Listen to user feedback and address complaints about slow performance or downtime, which may be signs of scalability issues.

- Compare your scenario with that of your competitors to ensure you remain competitive in the market.

- Consider future growth projections.

Before switching your development mindset and practices, first confirm that your existing architecture has real bottlenecks and performance issues and can't effectively handle increased loads. And if it does have bottlenecks, make sure whatever different architectural style you are considering will address them.

Having said all this, back-office applications and even most line-of-business applications rarely face highly variable volumes of traffic and users. In these cases, justifying a scalable but more complex architecture becomes challenging.

## Ensuring infrastructure readiness

Hosting a microservices application requires a robust infrastructure capable of handling the specific needs and challenges that come with a distributed architecture. One approach is to deploy each microservice on a plain virtual machine (VM) on-premises. In doing so, though, you lose most of the benefits of the microservices architecture. A more advisable choice is to deploy each microservice to its own container in an ad hoc platform such as Docker.

Managing and deploying several independent containers at scale, though, is tricky. Here, orchestration tools such as Kubernetes and Docker Swarm come into play. Kubernetes (K8S) is particularly popular for microservices due to its rich feature set and ecosystem. In particular, K8S provides a service-discovery mechanism to manage communication between microservices. You also need load balancers (for example, HAProxy, NGINX, or cloud-based load balancers) to distribute incoming traffic to microservices instances, and an API gateway (for example, NGINX) to help manage and secure external access to your microservices.

In summary, if the current company infrastructure is predominantly on-premises with a surplus of VMs, you can still deploy a microservices application; however, you might not be able to fully harness its scalability potential.

## Evaluating the importance of technology diversity

Because of the high degree of granularity offered by microservices, combined with containerization, you can develop each microservice using a distinct technology stack and programming language, which many developers see as advantageous. Personally, I consider this advantage somewhat exaggerated. In my experience, the technology stack tends to be relatively uniform. Even in the event of an acquisition, an initial step typically involves consolidating and standardizing technology stacks to the extent feasible. So, while technological diversity has its advantages, I don't consider it a significant factor when deciding to switch architectures.

## Calculating costs

Many people claim that a microservices architecture reduces costs. But whether that's true or not depends on the calculations that make most sense for the specific scenario. The function cost has many parameters:

- **Operational costs**  Microservices typically involve more operational overhead than monolithic architectures. You'll need to manage and monitor multiple services, which can increase infrastructure and personnel costs. Container orchestration tools like Kubernetes might also require additional operational expertise and resources.

- **Infrastructure costs**  Running multiple containers or VMs increases your cloud or datacenter expenses. You could incur additional infrastructure costs, especially if you adopt containerization. Furthermore, implementing distributed monitoring, logging, security, and other necessary tools and services can add to the overall cost more than with a monolith application.

- **Human resources costs**  Microservices require a team with specific expertise in containerization, orchestration, and distributed systems. Hiring and retaining such talent can be costly.

- **Maintenance costs**  Microservices-based applications require ongoing maintenance, updates, and bug fixes for each service. These maintenance efforts can accumulate over time. You will also likely face higher costs associated with troubleshooting, debugging, and coordinating among teams.

What about development costs?

Adopting a microservices architecture might require significant effort at the outset as you decompose your existing application into smaller, self-contained services that must be orchestrated and synchronized. You'll also likely expend increased effort designing and developing inter-service communication and coordinated data access systems. Finally, integration testing becomes notably more intricate and, consequently, costly. However, you might be able to balance these extra costs by parallelizing your development process to achieve a more aggressive and beneficial time-to-market.

All these cost items add up in the final bill. Interestingly, though, what often receives the most attention is the ability to exert finer control over resource allocation, which can potentially lead to the optimization of costs. The bottom line is that although microservices bring higher operational and development costs, they also offer benefits like improved scalability, agility, and fault tolerance. The ultimate cost-effectiveness of a microservices architecture depends on your specific use case, long-term goals, and ability to effectively manage the added complexity. Conducting a thorough cost/benefit analysis before adopting a microservices architecture is more than essential.

**Note** In some cases, the benefits of microservices may outweigh the additional costs; in others, a monolithic or hybrid approach might be more cost-effective.

## The case of Stack Overflow

For high-performance applications, many people assume that a microservices architecture is the only viable option. After all, internet giants like Amazon and Netflix, not to mention companies in the gaming, betting, and fintech sectors, use microservices because they could not achieve their goals using a more conventional approach. These companies adopted microservices—as well as other modern methods, like CQRS, and event-driven design—because they needed to efficiently handle concurrent and continuous write and read operations from hundreds of thousands of users.

But what if you only need to handle read operations? In that case, you can achieve an efficient solution without resorting to microservices. A great example is Stack Overflow. Launched in 2008 by Jeff Atwood and Joel Spolsky, Stack Overflow—a popular question-and-answer website for programmers—is a monolithic application hosted on a cluster of on-premises web servers. It relies heavily on Microsoft SQL Server to meet its database requirements. SQL Server alone, though, is not enough to seamlessly serve thousands of requests per second without expert use of indexing, finely tuned queries, and aggressive caching strategies.

Despite experiencing a decline in traffic after the explosion of ChatGPT, Stack Overflow has consistently maintained its position as among the top 100 most-visited websites worldwide. The key to its remarkable performance is its extensive use of caching. Stack Overflow employs multiple caching layers, ranging from front end to Redis, to significantly reduce the impact on the database.

Over the years, the initial ASP.NET model-view-controller (MVC) application has undergone multiple rounds of refactoring, including the migration to ASP.NET Core. Although the fundamental structure of the application remains monolithic, its architectural design is modular. Essential functions have been strategically separated and deployed as individual services, thus enabling the optimization of tasks without introducing unnecessary complexity to the overarching architecture.

Ultimately, Stack Overflow runs a suite of monolithic applications. The successful use of this pattern hinges on three factors:

- **Predictable traffic**   Stack Overflow benefits from a well-monitored and well-understood traffic pattern, which enables precise capacity planning.

- **Experienced team**   Stack Overflow's team boasts a wealth of expertise in building software and managing distributed applications.

- **Overall low resource intensity**   Stack Overflow pages are fairly basic and demand little processing power and memory. So, the application's resource requirements remain relatively modest.

The lesson from Stack Overflow is that complexity is not a prerequisite for achieving scalability or success. Through the judicious use of appropriate technologies, you can achieve great outcomes without employing an extensively intricate architecture. However, it's also worth noting that although Stack Overflow hasn't embraced microservices, it has evolved significantly from its original straightforward ASP.NET monolith architecture and now features a notably intricate infrastructure.

For further insights into Stack Overflow, listen to episode 45 of the DotNetCore Show, which features an interview with Nick Craver, the company's chief architect. You can find this episode at *https://dotnetcore.show*.

**Note**   For a different perspective, consider a collection of applications I routinely manage. Collectively, they support and guarantee daily operations across various sports events and tournaments. These applications comprise a network of discrete services, but like Stack Overflow, none of them can be classified as *micro*. Instead, they are coarse-grained services implemented as straightforward layered ASP.NET applications or web APIs. Given their current traffic volumes, these services perform admirably and demand only minimal Azure resources to operate efficiently.

# Planning and deployment

The planning of a microservices application involves one crucial step: breaking down the business domain into small, independent services, each responsible for a specific business capability. The objective is straightforward to comprehend but proves quite challenging to implement in practice. Yet, the resulting set of independent services is key to plan deployment, and to put the whole microservices architectural style into a new perspective.

## How many microservices?

The prevailing view on microservices is that having more of them allows for improved scalability, localized optimization, and the use of diverse technologies. When seeking advice on gauging the ideal number of microservices for your scenario, you might encounter somewhat arbitrary recommendations, such as these:

- There should be more than *N* lines of code in each microservice.

- Each functional point calls for a microservice.

- Each database table owner calls for a microservice.

In reality, the ideal number is the one that maximizes cohesion among components and minimizes coupling. As for the formula to arrive at this number? Simply put, it's "Not too many and not too few, and each of them is not too big and not too small."

Admittedly, this does not provide much concrete guidance. If you're looking for something more specific, I'll simply say that to my knowledge—without pretending it's exhaustive—it is common to encounter more than 100 microservices in a sizable application. As for my feelings on the matter, however, this strikes me as a huge number.

Yet, deployable microservices live in the application space, whereas business capabilities they implement live in the business space. The analysis starts breaking down the business domain into bounded contexts, and each bounded context—a business space entity—into more and more granular blocks. Once you have enough business capabilities, start mapping them into new entities in the application space—actual candidates to become deployed microservices. This is what we called microscopic services in Figure 9-2—logical, atomic functions to implement and deploy for a sufficiently modular application.

The key lies in this functional decomposition. Once you've achieved that, whether to use microservices or another physical architecture becomes a mere infrastructural decision.

## Architectural patterns for a logically decomposed system

From the global list of microscopic logical components, you create the aggregates that you intend to assemble in the same code module. Figure 9-5 shows the various options (thick borders in the figure indicate a deployable unit). The number of deployable units required to establish the business functionalities within a specific bounded context varies based on the chosen architectural pattern.

With a microservices approach, it's essential to keep the unit sizes relatively small, because the goal is to break down the model into the smallest possible autonomous components. There isn't a predefined threshold that dictates when to halt the decomposition; it's a matter of discretion. However, in most cases, you will find it advantageous to delve quite deeply into it. The SOA pattern shown in Figure 9-5 reflects essentially the same approach, with one distinction: The decomposition is halted earlier, yielding coarser-grained components. These are referred to as *monoliths* to emphasize that they aren't single-function modules. Finally, Figure 9-5 shows a monolith as a unified deployable unit that encompasses all functions within a single process.

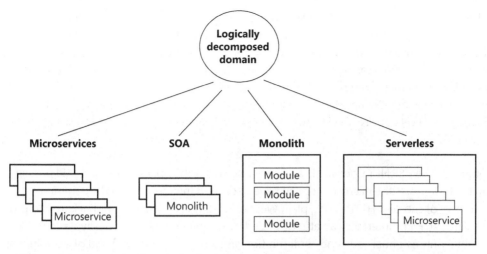

**FIGURE 9-5** Architectural options for implementing a logically decomposed business domain.

## Deployment options

When outlining a deployment strategy, your DevOps and development teams must make three crucial decisions:

- On-premises or cloud

- Processes or containers

- Whether to use orchestrators (for example, Kubernetes)

- Whether to go serverless

The golden rule is to build and deploy microservices within the cloud instead of relying on a conventional on-premises IT infrastructure. The cloud plays a pivotal role in facilitating the acclaimed benefits of scalability, flexibility, and optimization.

Hosted in-process on a server or VM, a microservice acts as an individual operating system-level process. It's probably the most lightweight approach in terms of resource use because it doesn't require the additional runtime overhead of containerization. However, the operational burden of setting up a VM should not be underestimated.

Containers offer stronger isolation than processes. Containers ensure that each microservice has its own isolated runtime environment, preventing any possible conflicts. But the crucial benefit of containers is portability across various environments, from development to production. Furthermore, building a container is generally easier than setting up a VM. And containers are well suited for orchestration platforms like Kubernetes. This simplifies scaling, load balancing, and managing microservices in a distributed environment.

When deploying applications to Kubernetes, you typically create a set of resources that define components, configurations, and how they should run within the Kubernetes cluster. Pods are the smallest deployable units in Kubernetes. They can contain one or more containers (for example, Docker images) that share the same network namespace and storage volumes. The main concern with Kubernetes is the steep learning curve. Using Kubernetes involves numerous concepts, components, and YAML configuration files, which can be overwhelming for beginners. To address these issues, organizations often invest in external expertise, implement best practices, and use other tools and services to simplify management and monitoring. Managed Kubernetes services from cloud providers (for example, Azure Kubernetes Service) can also alleviate some of these challenges by handling cluster-management tasks.

 **Note** On the ASP.NET Core stack, a microservice is a web application or web API project. In the latter case, the microservice can have dedicated middleware for the communication protocol of choice—HTTP, gRPC, plain WebSocket, SignalR, GraphQL, or background processing. An HTTP interface can also be coded with a minimal API specifically designed to require only essential code and configuration and to remove the overhead of a traditional MVC setup. If desired, an ASP.NET microservice can be containerized using Docker. This enables you to deploy and scale using an orchestration platform like Kubernetes.

## The serverless environment

Recently, another option has gained acceptance and popularity: deploying microservices within a serverless environment. In this case, you don't worry about processes, containers, and servers; instead, you run code directly in the cloud. With a serverless approach, your operational overhead shrinks to close to zero.

Serverless computing is a cloud computing model in which developers deploy and run code without managing traditional servers. Instead of provisioning and maintaining server infrastructure, serverless platforms automatically allocate resources as needed, scaling seamlessly in concert with demand. In the billing model adopted by many cloud providers, users are billed only for actual code-execution time, making it cost-effective and eliminating the need for infrastructure management.

Cost effectiveness is not a constant, though. In fact, cloud providers may have pricing models that become more expensive at scale. For example, certain pricing tiers or constraints may apply when dealing with numerous invocations, concurrent executions, or resource usage. Even with flat pricing, having more functions may lead to extra managing and coordination calls between various components and subsequently to additional costs.

Using a serverless platform such as AWS Lambda, Azure Functions, Google Cloud Functions, or Apache OpenWhisk, you package each microservice as a function. Each function is triggered by events such as HTTP requests, database changes, or timers. The serverless platform automatically handles resource allocation, scaling, and load balancing, eliminating the need to manage servers. Developers simply upload their code and define event triggers.

The effectiveness of the serverless model stems from lowered infrastructure costs and the ability to make rapid and precise updates to individual microservices to meet evolving application needs. Are there any drawbacks? Well, yes. The sore point of any serverless solution is potential vendor or platform lock-in, be it Azure, AWS, or Google Cloud.

More than a decade ago, IBM began development of an open-source serverless computing platform, which they donated to the Apache Software Foundation in 2016. The main strength of the platform, called Apache OpenWhisk, is its cloud-agnostic nature. In other words, it can be deployed across multiple cloud providers, including Azure, AWS, and Google Cloud, thus reducing vendor lock-in concerns. Furthermore, using OpenWhisk, developers can write functions in various programming languages and seamlessly integrate them with external services and event sources.

Whether to use an open-source solution or buy a commercial package is clearly a delicate business decision. Open-source software is typically free to use, whereas commercial packages come with a cost. If the open-source code does not fully meet your needs, you customize it at will (assuming you have the time and expertise to do so), whereas commercial packages typically come with professional support and service level agreements (SLAs), which can be crucial for critical applications. And, of course, any commercial package represents a form of vendor lock-in, although it is generally less binding than being tied to an entire platform.

> **Note** An interesting commercial platform built on top of the Apache OpenWhisk code base is Nuvolaris (*https://nuvolaris.io*). If you use microservices and intend to run your FaaS serverless application across multiple clouds, including on private or hybrid infrastructure, it is definitely worth a look.

## Modular monoliths

As outlined in the section "The big misconception of big companies" earlier in this chapter, the microservices approach originated from the organic evolution of specific large-scale platforms that were initially constructed using more traditional patterns. This evolution was spearheaded by top experts at leading companies. This is quite different from obtaining a round of investment, assembling a team of developers overnight (half junior and half part-time seniors), and expecting to use microservices to turn a tangled mess of ideas into an enterprise-level, high-scale application, as is often the case today. There are two prerequisites for successfully implementing a microservices architecture. One is deep knowledge of the application domain, and the other is the participation of a team of real experts—ideally with a powerful sense of pragmatism.

What could be a smoother alternative?

A modular monolith is a software architecture that combines elements of a monolithic structure with modular design principles. In a modular monolith, the application is organized into distinct, loosely coupled modules, each responsible for specific functionalities. Unlike legacy monolithic applications, a modular (just well-written) monolith allows for separation of concerns and easier maintenance by dividing the application into manageable, interchangeable components. This approach aims to provide the benefits of modularity and maintainability while still maintaining a single, cohesive codebase. It represents a much more approachable way of building modern services.

> ## The ghost of big up-front design
>
> Big up-front design (BUFD) is a software development approach that emphasizes comprehensive planning and design before coding. It aims to clarify project requirements, architecture, and design specifications up front to minimize uncertainties and changes during development. While BUFD offers structure and predictability, it can be less adaptive to changing needs. Agile methodologies emerged just to contrast BUFD and make the project adaptive to changing requirements.
>
> Approaching any new development with a microservices architectural mindset generally involves two main risks: getting a tangle of poorly designed endpoints and ending up with some BUFD. The first risk stems from a deadly mix of unclear objectives and the need to bring something to market as quickly as possible. It evokes parallels with the memorable conversation between Dean Moriarty and Sal Paradise in Jack Kerouac's groundbreaking novel, *On the Road*:
>
> "Where we going, man?"
>
> "I don't know but we gotta go."
>
> This dialog captures the spirit of adventure and improvisation typical of the Beat Generation—two qualities that do not align seamlessly with the field of software development:
>
> "What we coding, man?"
>
> "I don't know but we gotta code."
>
> To mitigate the potential for a chaotic and unwieldy web of minimal endpoints—which can be challenging even to safely remove—the team must perform an in-depth initial assessment, based primarily on assumptions, as to how a system might develop in a future that remains largely unpredictable. This initial assessment closely resembles the infamous BUFD. Worse, the BUFD will likely involve stabbing in the dark to identify highly dynamic requirements.

## The delicate case of greenfield projects

Considering the widespread popularity and proven success of microservices, you might reasonably wonder whether they are appropriate for every new project. My response is, no, initiating a project with microservices is not advisable—even if the application may eventually need to accommodate a substantial volume of traffic and experience unexpected peaks.

Microservices inherently introduce additional complexity in terms of managing a distributed system, inter-service communication, and deployment. This necessitates a highly skilled team. If your team lacks direct experience with microservices, not only will there be a learning curve, but there will also be a significant amount of trial and error involved. So, going against the mainstream, I say that if you want to develop your solution quickly, and you want your solution to be adaptable as requirements change, you should *not* start with microservices.

> **Note** Project Renoir, discussed in Chapters 4–8, is an example of a modular monolith.

## Outlining a modular monolith strategy for new projects

So, what would be a serious alternative? Well, the answer is a monolith. By monolith, though, I don't mean a collection of tightly interconnected classes—quite the opposite. Instead, I mean a *modular* monolith, which is essentially a well-designed monolithic application that can be reasonably transitioned to a microservices architecture should the need arise.

Monoliths are simpler to develop and deploy but may struggle with scalability and fault tolerance. Microservices offer greater scalability and fault isolation but come with increased complexity and operational overhead. Still, in general, there are too many unknowns to make microservices the right choice at the start of a new project. For the sake of budget and target goals, I strongly advocate a more cautious approach.

### Why not use microservices right from the start?

Why is a new project more likely to fail if you start with microservices? Ultimately, it comes down to two factors: inherent operational complexity and unclear boundaries.

Architecturally speaking, an application based on microservices is a massively distributed system, and according to the notorious "Eight Fallacies of Distributed Computing," articulated more than 20 years ago by software engineers Peter Deutsch and James Gosling (the father of the Java language) at Sun Microsystems, distributed systems exist to unsettle assumptions. (Three of the truest and most hard-hitting of these fallacies are "the network is reliable," "latency is zero," and "bandwidth is infinite.")

Beyond the inherent operational complexity of microservices, a trickier problem relates to erecting stable, well-defined boundaries to separate services. Defining accurate boundaries can be a daunting task, even when dealing with a well-known business domain. This is the primary reason teams sometimes resort to a BUFD approach.

Together, the complexity of microservices and the difficulties associated with defining boundaries makes refactoring between services considerably more intricate compared to a modular monolith architecture.

## The KISS principle

Not coincidentally, this approach aligns perfectly with a core software design principle: Keep It Super Simple (KISS). KISS is a design principle that encourages developers to keep solutions as simple and straightforward as possible. The KISS principle suggests that simplicity should be a key goal in software design, and that unnecessary complexity should be avoided. Keeping things simple doesn't mean ignoring potential future needs, however. It's often better to start with a simple solution and iterate on it as requirements evolve rather than trying to predict all possible future scenarios up front.

## Software architecture is the means

The goal of software investment is to create a successful application—*not* a successful microservices architecture. So, as a software architect, you should not chart a path to success for the microservices architecture but rather for the entire project.

Many microservice success stories advance through several well-defined stages, like the growth of a majestic tree. They begin with the establishment of a robust monolithic foundation—the actual roots of the system. Over time, the system expands until its size and complexity become unwieldy and overwhelming. As with a grand tree, this is the season for careful pruning, in which the original monolith is broken up into a constellation of microservices that can thrive independently while maintaining harmony within the ecosystem.

In the end, the success story of a modern application unfolds in three basic stages:

1.  Build of the initial monolith.

2.  Grow the monolith according to business needs.

3.  If, after a time (perhaps a few years), the monolith becomes unwieldy, consider migrating to a more distributed architecture, such as a microservices architecture.

## Traits of a modular monolith

The term *monolith* is sometimes unfairly demonized as something obsolete and dilapidated. As stated, such a strong repulsion can be justified when in response to legacy monoliths whose code base is full of hidden dependencies, untestable, poorly documented, and resistant to changes. It cannot be justified, however, for a freshly developed modular monolith, built from the ground up and inspired by the guiding principles of separation of concerns.

Modular monoliths exhibit several intriguing qualities:

- **Single code base**  Although the entire application is built as a single code base, it's organized into loosely coupled modules. You can think of these modules as self-contained units of functionality. An application, built as a single code base, is generally quick and easy to deploy using a DevOps CI/CD pipeline or even manually through publish profiles.

- **Testing and debugging**  Both testing and debugging are straightforward in a modular monolith because everything is in one place. Also, tracing and logging pose no additional issues.

- **Performance** Modular monoliths can perform better than microservices because in-process communication is significantly more efficient than inter-service communication. In addition, latency is reduced to a bare minimum, and data remains consistent by design (unless you deliberately opt for a CQRS data architecture with distinct data stores).

- **Development velocity** For smaller teams or simpler projects, a modular monolithic architecture can result in faster development because there's less overhead in managing multiple services. Furthermore, you don't need to manage the complexities of a distributed system.

On the downside, scaling a modular monolith can be challenging. Because it's a single deployable unit, you can't selectively add resources only where they're really needed. You can, however, give more power to the underlying database (most of the time, this will suffice) or spin up multiple instances of the application under a load balancer.

> **Note** To safely run multiple instances of the application, it is imperative that no shared state exists, such as global static data or in-memory caches. If session state is used, then sticky sessions must be enabled.

### Loosely coupled modules

In software design, coupling refers to the degree of independence and interconnection between modules at various layers of abstraction (e.g., classes, libraries, applications). In other words, low coupling means that each component can function and evolve without relying heavily on others.

What about communication? Communication between loosely coupled components occurs through a well-defined interface or contract that comprehensively sets a service boundary. Physical communication is carried out through APIs, messages, or events, depending on the abstraction layer—often without needing detailed knowledge of each other's internal workings.

You might recognize some of the points in the list of benefits brought by microservices. Quite simply, microservices apply loose coupling at the service level, whereas in a modular monolith, it takes place at the level of constituent libraries. A successful modular monolith is generally built using the guidelines of DDD layered architecture, as outlined in Chapters 4–8 and exemplified by Project Renoir.

## From modules to microservices

A highly emphasized statement like "applications composed of loosely connected microservices can be swiftly adjusted, modified, and expanded in real-time" contains a sacrosanct truth but overlooks a crucial aspect: One can adjust, modify, expand and power up *existing* microservices. The statement doesn't point out the cost associated with determining the optimal microservice boundaries through trial and error. In contrast, starting with a monolith allows you to experiment with different boundaries at almost no cost.

## Logical boundaries first

With the monolith successfully in production, you have a valid topology of logical services packaged into a single deployable unit. You can still expand the monolith to address new business requirements and any changes that become necessary. For example, if you need more horsepower, you can scale horizontally through replication or vertically through the addition of more resources. This doesn't offer the same granularity and flexibility as microservices, but it might be more than enough.

When additional requirements arise, these logical boundaries serve as the perfect foundation for the microservices architecture. At that point, the next step is to transform these logical boundaries into physical ones. As a practical exercise, suppose you want to convert the logical boundaries of Project Renoir into physical boundaries hosting independently deployable services. The starting point would be the monolith shown in Figure 9-6, an ASP.NET Core solution inspired by a DDD layered architecture blueprint.

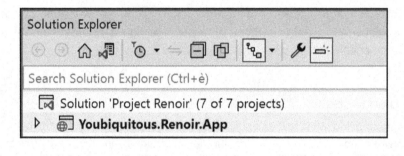

**FIGURE 9-6** The monolithic Project Renoir Visual Studio solution.

## Extracting boundaries in Project Renoir

Deriving physical boundaries from a simple monolith relies on the selected technology stack and your willingness to embrace more or less radical architecture changes. For instance, assume you have an ASP.NET Core stack and don't want to deviate very far from it. The initial step is almost indisputable: separating the presentation and application layers.

The presentation layer is now the front end and may remain an ASP.NET Core web application. The application layer is the entry point in the back end and becomes a standalone web API project. In the presentation layer, controllers retain the same job, except now they no longer call application service methods in-process.

The communication between the front end and the back end can take various forms, depending on your scalability needs:

- HTTP endpoints

- A homemade (or cloud-provided) API gateway

- A message bus

Ideally, HTTP calls go through resilient clients capable of coping with transient network faults. To handle transient faults, developers often resort to retries, implement circuit breakers to temporarily halt requests when failures occur, set timeouts to avoid waiting indefinitely, and provide fallback mechanisms to maintain essential functionality during faults. (In .NET Core, an excellent (and open-source) framework that takes care of all these tasks is Polly. You can check it out at *https://www.thepollyproject. org* or on the NuGet platform.) The front end can optimize essential requests by using faster communication protocols like gRPC and web sockets, while user interface updates are commonly managed through SignalR.

After the initial step, you have only two blocks and a single back-end service to maintain full references to the persistence layer. The various services in the infrastructure layer are all good candidates for decomposition. Deciding whether you decompose, though, is an application-specific decision.

There is further potential to break down the application layer into smaller components. Ideally, the application layer is organized around vertical slices of functionality built based on business features. Each feature has the potential to evolve into one or more individual microservices as needed. Depending on requirements, one or more features could also be implemented as serverless components. The database can remain unchanged (for example, a single shared database) or undergo changes such as migrating specific data partitions to separate stores managed by dedicated microservices. Additionally, you can encapsulate common code components—particularly the persistence and domain models—as NuGet packages for convenient sharing among microservices projects. (see Figure 9-7).

**Note** In Figure 9-7, the presentation is condensed into a block and given the abstract label of "Front End." One effect of decomposing a monolith into distinct services is that the original ASP.NET web application (including view models and Razor files) becomes a standalone front end that connects to other parts via HTTP. This opens a whole new world of opportunity for the front end, ranging from ASP.NET client Blazor to JavaScript-based platforms. I'll discuss this in more detail in Chapter 10, "Client-side versus server-side."

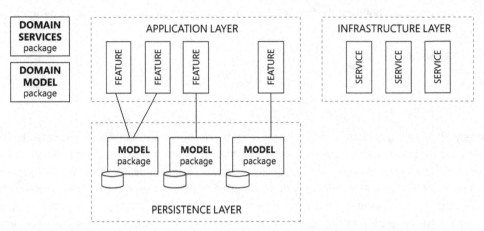

**FIGURE 9-7** Blueprint for decomposing a modular monolith like Project Renoir into a microservices architecture.

## Taking a feature-first approach

In a software application, a *feature* is a distinct and identifiable piece of functionality that fulfills a specific business requirement. Features are the building blocks of software applications; they're what make software useful and valuable to its users. In other words, features constitute the essence of the software, embodying the minimal complexity that no design or architecture can circumvent.

A feature-first approach to software development prioritizes the identification, design, and implementation of key features that directly address user needs or business objectives. This approach not only ensures that all pivotal components are built, it also subtly encourages development in modules with distinct and well-defined boundaries.

In a monolithic ASP.NET Core architecture, features are implemented within the application layer. These features can take the form of classes, with their methods being called on by controllers. Each method is responsible for a particular use case. At the project level, features are organized as class files neatly grouped within dedicated folders.

# Summary

The evolution of software is driven by a combination of user feedback, technological advancements, and the changing needs of companies and organizations. Software engineering also evolves to meet changing demands while remaining relevant in the technology landscape. Microservices are the latest development in the evolution of software architecture and engineering.

In the past decade, microservices have firmly established themselves within the IT landscape and are unlikely to diminish in relevance, even if they now have reached a point of stability. Compared to a more traditional software architecture, microservices introduce significant structural complexity from the outset. If your team cannot manage this complexity, the decision to implement microservices becomes a boomerang and strikes back. As usual, in software architecture, adopting microservices is a matter of trade-offs.

This chapter recounted the origin of the microservices architecture before outlining its benefits and gray areas. Ultimately, it concluded that microservices represent a significant evolutionary step in the life of a durable application when serious performance and scalability issues arise. However, starting a greenfield project with microservices is not necessarily the best path to success.

Microservices introduce deployment and infrastructure costs due to their distributed nature, containerization, and need for orchestration. However, these costs may be offset by benefits, such as improved scalability and faster development cycles. Monolithic applications, on the other hand, are often simpler and have lower operational costs but may lack the necessary level of scalability and agility in the long run. In summary, microservices don't offer a universal solution, and one should never underestimate the benefits and simplicity of a well-crafted modular monolith. Chapter 10 delves further into distributed application scenarios and explores challenges related to the front end.

# Client-side versus server-side

*Not all who wander are lost.*

—J. R. R. Tolkien, *The Fellowship of the Ring*, 1954

Chapter 4, "The presentation layer," summarized the presentation layer from a DDD perspective as the outermost layer of the application. Responsible for handling user interactions and displaying information to users, the presentation layer includes components like controllers and API endpoints. In web applications, what users ultimately see on their screens is the output of controllers.

Controllers may be designed to generate HTML on the server or to expose plain information (usually in JSON format) for client browser pages to invoke. This means there is a server presentation layer, which fits the description in Chapter 4, and a client presentation layer. The client presentation layer identifies the user interface and how information is visually and interactively presented to users. It encompasses design elements, layout, and user experience considerations, ensuring that data is displayed in a comprehensible and engaging manner. This layer typically includes components such as webpages, graphical user interfaces (GUIs), mobile app interfaces, and the use of technologies such as HTML, CSS, and JavaScript.

Today, the common idea is that the front end and back end should be physically divided, with different teams at work on each, using different technologies. Years of hype about client-centric technologies and frameworks and fervent emphasis on what is right and what is wrong have hidden the natural value of software elements. In relentlessly pursuing what seemed a great idea—client and server treated as separate applications—we ended up creating new problems each time that an idea proved problematic. Instead of having the courage to abandon the original idea, we added layers of new problems and new solutions, only to realize that, well, we ultimately need something much simpler and faster to write and to execute.

Yet, the most concrete act of change we perceive is self-deprecation, which leads to the use of the term *frontrend* and sardonic smiles at the tons of JavaScript files each front(r)end project needs to survive to deploy successfully. Web development has evolved, but the overall level of abstraction is still fairly low—as if back-end development teams were still using libraries of assembly code.

This is the digest of 25 years of web development. I have had the good fortune to live all these years on the front lines. For this reason—and only this reason—I now have a broad, non-tunneled perspective on the whys and wherefores of the evolution of the web landscape.

# A brief history of web applications

Web applications as we know them today began to gain prominence in the late 1990s and strongly consolidated with the advent of .NET and ASP.NET in 2002. One of the earliest examples of a web application was the Hotmail service, launched in 1996, which enabled users to access their email accounts through a web browser. Another notable early web application was Amazon.com, which launched in 1995 as an online bookstore and quickly evolved into a full-fledged e-commerce platform.

Until the early 2000s, technologies like JavaScript and XML (used for data exchange) played a role in making web applications more interactive and responsive. This era also saw the emergence of various web-based productivity tools and content-management systems, leading to the rich ecosystem of web applications we have today.

## The prehistoric era

As ridiculous as it may sound today, in the mid-1990s, a typical website was merely a collection of static HTML pages with very little style and nearly no JavaScript. Over time, however, that changed.

### Cascading style sheets

Cascading style sheets (CSS) became an official recommendation of the World Wide Web Consortium (W3C) in December 1996. It allowed for control over the basic style and layout of documents. A minimally usable version (by today's standards) arrived in 1998, introducing more advanced styling capabilities and positioning options. That was CSS Level 2. CSS3 followed shortly thereafter; to date, it remains the latest large release of CSS specifications. This is because the CSS group at W3C adopted a new release policy: no more large but infrequent releases. Instead, new features would be added independently to the CSS3 standard as soon as they were finalized and approved. The responsibility (and timing) of implementing support for each feature would still fall to the actual web browsers.

### JavaScript

In 1995, Sun Microsystems introduced the Java programming language. Shortly thereafter, Netscape—at that time the primary web browser on the market—declared its intent to incorporate Java into the browser. However, Netscape developers quickly realized that Java was too intricate for web designers to use; at the time, web development wasn't yet considered a core programming discipline. Consequently, Netscape opted to develop JavaScript, a sibling language that was smaller and easier to learn than its big brother.

Netscape presented JavaScript as a lightweight API, easy enough for HTML practitioners to learn, to script events and objects. Suggested use cases for JavaScript included checking for valid telephone numbers and ZIP codes in a form, playing an audio file, executing a Java applet (a small application written in Java running in the browser), or communicating with an externally installed plugin. Most of the time, though, JavaScript was employed to incorporate useless—if not annoying—features such as flashing images and scrolling messages in the status bar.

Although the groundwork for its use was laid, JavaScript had few applications until browsers exposed their internal representation of the page as a modifiable document object model (DOM).

## The document object model

A web browser is an application that points to a remote web server address and downloads files. An internal engine orchestrates all necessary downloads (HTML, images, scripts, and style sheets) and assembles the downloaded content into a viewable graphical unit. Underneath the visuals lies the document object model (DOM). The DOM is an in-memory tree that reflects the layout of elements in the HTML source for the page. The engine constructs the DOM upon loading the page.

The DOM is a standard established by the W3C in 1995 and serves as a standard interface to enable scripts to access and modify the content, organization, and appearance of a webpage. In particular, scripts can manipulate attributes and content of existing HTML elements, introduce new ones, and adjust their CSS styles. The initial DOM proposed by Netscape and approved by W3C was very basic and insufficient for serious real-world use.

## The browser wars

The race to achieve technological supremacy in the new world of the internet initiated what became known as the *browser wars*. The browser wars were an intense competition among web browser companies during the late 1990s and early 2000s. The main players in the browser wars were Microsoft's Internet Explorer (IE) and Netscape Navigator (often referred to as just Netscape).

Since the early days of the web, Netscape Navigator had been the dominant web browser, with a significant market share. Seeing the potential, however, Microsoft began bundling its brand-new IE browser with the Windows operating system. Users often found IE pre-installed on their computers, leading to rapid adoption. Both companies started adding new features and enhancements to their browsers, leading to a cycle of innovation and competition. This included support for HTML and CSS standards as well as JavaScript, and the introduction of proprietary features to gain a competitive edge.

The competition was intense, with each company releasing new versions in quick succession to outdo the other. This led to rapid changes in web technologies but also caused nontrivial compatibility issues for web developers. In the early 2000s, despite antitrust investigations in both the United States and Europe, IE's dominance became unquestioned and ended the war.

After the browser wars, new browsers such as Mozilla Firefox, Google Chrome, and others emerged, introducing competition and innovation once again. This new round of competition, though, also led to the gradual disappearance of compatibility issues between browsers.

# The server-scripting era

Server-side scripting is closely intertwined with the evolution of the World Wide Web (WWW) itself. In the early days of the web, websites were static and composed primarily of HTML files. The web was essentially a repository of static information, and user interactions were limited. So, serious programmers quickly dismissed it as uninteresting.

With server-side scripting, however, browsers began dynamically receiving HTML chunks, which were assembled upon each request. This new technology captured the attention of developers, highlighting the internet's potential and opening a whole new world of opportunities.

Server-side scripting unlocked the creation of dynamic content and data-driven websites for the dissemination of information. Server-side scripting also yielded web applications—highly interactive websites that enable user actions, processing of data, and delivery of dynamic content, often involving user registration, database interactions, and complex functionality for tasks like online shopping and social networking. Server-side scripting also made possible secure authentication and access control and the subsequent handling of sensitive operations. Finally, it raised the entire topic of application scalability.

Several server-side scripting languages and technologies were created over the years, all following the same pattern. These languages allow developers to embed code within HTML page skeletons that run on the server accessing databases, external services, local files, and libraries. The difference between them was mostly in the language (and frameworks) used to generate HTML. PHP, for example, is a programming language that relies on a cross-platform interpreter; Java Server Pages (JSP) uses Java snippets within HTML pages arranged following the model-view-controller (MVC) pattern; and Active Server Pages (ASP), developed by Microsoft, embeds code written in languages such as VBScript or JScript.

## ASP.NET Web Forms

ASP.NET Web Forms is a web application framework developed by Microsoft as part of the ASP.NET platform. It made its debut alongside ASP.NET 1.0. For approximately a decade, it was the preferred option for building web applications. However, around 2010, its prominence began to wane, as the natural progression of web development exposed certain original strengths of the framework as unacceptable shortcomings.

It was not an ordinary decade, though. In the decade during which ASP.NET Web Forms thrived, a huge number of developers and companies used it to build (or rebuild) the enterprise back end to pursue the opportunity offered by the internet. ASP.NET Web Forms was the ideal vehicle to ferry thousands of client/server, Visual Basic, and even COBOL developers to the web.

Five primary factors underpinned the success of ASP.NET Web Forms:

- It had an event-driven programming model, so it was similar to the way desktop applications were built.

- Its architecture was component-based.

- It offered deliberate, limited exposure to HTML, CSS, and JavaScript.

- It was offered along with a Visual Studio integrated visual designer.

- It supported automatic state management through the view state.

Altogether, these factors enabled rapid and effective development without a significant learning curve or intensive retraining. In particular, ASP.NET designers struggled to build a programming model in which JavaScript was used but, for the most part, was hidden to developers. The idea was to avoid scaring people with a non-web background (who at the time represented the vast majority) from developing web software.

A decade later, the same success factors turned into drawbacks. Specifically, the deliberate abstraction over HTML became a frustrating roadblock for competent web developers. Ultimately, limited testability and lock-in on the Windows platforms and IIS brought the ASP.NET Web Forms narrative to a definitive conclusion. Today, ASP.NET Web Forms is still supported and receives critical updates, but no more than that.

> **Note** I lack reliable statistics to pinpoint the zenith of ASP.NET Web Forms' popularity. But I do recall attending a conference in the early 2000s during which a Microsoft representative mentioned an audience of more than one million developers. Additionally, when conversing with component vendors, they consistently mention that a significant portion of their revenues still today originate from ASP.NET Web Forms controls.

## The model-view-controller pattern

Undoubtedly, ASP.NET Web Forms left an important mark. Competitors analyzed its weak points and attempted to provide a better way of building web applications. One weak point was that ASP.NET Web Forms oversimplified the issue of separation of concerns (SoC). Although the framework forced developers to keep markup separated from C# handlers of markup elements, further structuring within layers required the self-discipline of developers.

A handful of new web development frameworks introduced a stricter programming paradigm—based on the model-view-controller (MVC) pattern—that forced developers to separate an application into distinct components for better maintainability. The most popular framework was Ruby on Rails whose simplicity conquered the heart of developers; another was Django, which used the Python language; and yet another was Zend for PHP.

Microsoft introduced ASP.NET MVC as an alternative to ASP.NET Web Forms. It offered a more structured and testable approach to web development using the MVC pattern. It quickly gained popularity among .NET developers and is now part of the broader ASP.NET Core ecosystem. Today, the MVC programming paradigm is the primary way to build applications within the ASP.NET Core pipeline on top of the .NET Core framework.

**Note** Unlike Web Forms, MVC frameworks reestablish the central role of core web technologies such as HTML, CSS, and JavaScript, over (possibly leaky) layers of abstraction introduced to shield from them. To work with MVC web frameworks, a substantial understanding of core web technologies and HTTP is imperative. Historically, this demand for knowledge coincided with a period when such expertise was plentiful within the developer community—well over a decade ago.

## The client-scripting era

With web development more tightly integrated with the core elements of HTTP and HTML, the next objective became to minimize the server roundtrips required to refresh the page after any user interaction. Around 2010, it finally became possible to place remote calls from JavaScript without worrying about browser-compatibility issues. So, developers gave themselves a new challenge: Download plain data from the server and build HTML on the client.

### AJAX

Asynchronous JavaScript and XML (AJAX) is a set of web-development techniques that enables web applications to make asynchronous requests to a server and then update parts of a webpage without requiring a full-page reload. Even though the very first product to use this type of technique (before it was baptized as AJAX) was Microsoft Exchange, it was Google Gmail that elevated the use of AJAX to the next level. Gmail uses AJAX calls extensively to enhance the user experience and provide dynamic and asynchronous updates. For example, Gmail uses AJAX to show email in real time, to auto-save email drafts, and to integrate Google Chat and Google Hangouts.

Although Gmail is a web application, the user experience it provides is so smooth and fluid that it resembles a desktop application. This led developers to think that hosting an entire application within the browser had to be possible, and that all transitions could just be updates of the "same" DOM, much like in desktop applications.

The first step in this direction has been the development of client-side data-binding JavaScript libraries such as KnockoutJS and AngularJS (a distant relative of today's Angular, discussed in a moment). Client-side data binding is still at the core of what most JavaScript frameworks do: build HTML dynamically from provided data and given templates and attach them into the DOM.

### Single-page applications

Gmail and client-side data-binding libraries paved the road to the single page application (SPA) paradigm. An SPA is a web application that loads a single HTML page initially and then dynamically updates its content as users interact with it, with no full-page reloads required. SPAs use JavaScript to handle routing, fetch data from servers via APIs, and manipulate the DOM to provide a fluid and responsive user experience. An SPA approach is a good fit for any application that requires frequent updates and is highly interactive.

> **Note** Gmail is not an SPA in the traditional sense. It requests users to navigate between different sections (for example, Inbox, Sent Items, Drafts), each of which can be seen as its own SPA because it renders a basic HTML page that is modified further via AJAX calls.

Search engine optimization (SEO) has traditionally been a challenge for SPAs due to their reliance on client-side rendering. However, modern SPA frameworks have introduced solutions to enable server-side rendering (SSR), making SPAs more search-engine-friendly. With SSR, search engines can effectively crawl and index SPA content, ensuring that SPA-based websites are discoverable in search results.

## Modern JavaScript application frameworks

Today, new applications built on top of a server-side development framework such as ASP.NET are fairly rare. In most cases, the front end and back end are neatly separated. ASP.NET is still considered an excellent option to build the back-end API, but other, more popular options exist for the front end—in particular, rich JavaScript-based frameworks, including React and Angular.

### React

React is a component-based JavaScript library with a lot of extra features that elevate it to a full front-end framework for building SPAs. React—which originated at Facebook—is optimized for building applications that require constant data changes on the user interface.

In React, every element is regarded as a component, resulting in a web interface composed of numerous potentially reusable components. Each component is characterized by a rendering method that abstractly returns a description of the expected UI as a tree of elements. Internally, React compares the expected tree with the actual DOM and makes only necessary updates. This pattern is known as the virtual DOM pattern and is now commonly used by other frameworks as well.

React components are written using JavaScript or TypeScript. However, the framework's component-based nature calls for the use of JavaScript XML (JSX) or TypeScript XML (TSX) language extensions to simplify how each component declares its desired user interface. At compile time, both JSX and TSX markup are transpiled into regular JavaScript code that, once downloaded within the browser, creates and manages the DOM elements and their interactions in the web application. This effort, though, is not handled by the actual developer.

### Angular

Angular is a TypeScript-based full front-end framework designed from the ashes of AngularJS, which was simply a smart client-side data-binding library. Developed at Google and open-sourced, Angular is component-based and includes rich command-line interface (CLI) tools to facilitate coding, building, and testing. It also offers a collection of libraries that provide comprehensive functionality, including routing, forms management, client-server communication, and more.

An Angular application consists of a hierarchy of components. Each component is a TypeScript class with an associated template and styles. A template is an HTML file that defines the structure of the view associated with a component. It includes Angular-specific syntax and directives that enhance the HTML with dynamic behavior and data binding. Directives are instructions in the DOM that tell Angular how to transform or manipulate the DOM. Key Angular features include two-way data binding and dependency injection. Finally, its component-based architecture encourages code modularity and reusability.

Developing in Angular requires the use of the TypeScript language. It also means taking a component-based approach to architecting the front end, which is ultimately obtained by assembling potentially reusable components together. Each component expresses its own user interface via templates and employs two-way data binding to connect the application's data to visual elements. Dependency injection manages the creation and distribution of application components and services. Finally, Angular is supported by a vibrant ecosystem of libraries and a strong community.

# Client-side rendering

Client-side rendering (CSR) is a web development approach in which the rendering of the webpage is primarily performed on the client's browser rather than on the server. In the context of client-side rendering, the server typically sends minimal HTML, CSS, and JavaScript to the client, and the client's browser handles the rendering and dynamic updates.

The internet is saturated with posts, articles, and commercial whitepapers extolling the virtues of Angular and React. But that's not all: Their qualities and popularity are indisputable. Currently, Angular and React dominate more than 60 percent of the market.

Working with one of these frameworks offers new developers a great chance to kickstart their careers. Naturally, though, Angular and React will shape their understanding of the web—and that's a problem. Angular and React are designed to abstract away the inherent intricacies involved in harmonizing markup, styles, rendering logic, and data integration. But what they ultimately do is simply replace the natural intricacy of core web technologies with their own flavor of artificial complexity. So, most newer front-end developers have nearly no understanding of web basics and the rationale behind Angular and React's advanced rendering capabilities and build infrastructure. To combat this lack of understanding, the following sections dissect the layers and fundamental patterns of front-end development.

**Note** JavaScript is not the ideal tool for the jobs it currently undertakes. And yet it is used. Angular and React simply attempt to create order from a mess of poor language tools, complex applications, and rendering constraints. In the last 15 years, the industry let a great chance to redesign the browser pass, losing the opportunity to make it support languages more powerful than JavaScript. As long as JavaScript remains the primary and preferred way to run logic within the browser (WebAssembly is an alternative), a significant amount of complexity will remain necessary to write front ends.

# The HTML layer

At the end of the day, every web application produces HTML for the browser to render. HTML can be read from a static server file, dynamically generated by server-side code, or dynamically generated on the client side. This is what Angular and React do. Their work passes through two distinct phases: text templating and actual HTML rendering.

## Skeleton of a front-end page

Let's first analyze the structure of the entry point in any Angular application as it is served to the requesting browser. This entry point is often named index.html.

```
<html>
    <head> ... </head>
    <body>
        <app-root></app-root>

        <!-- List of script files -->
    </body>
</html>
```

The `app-root` element represents the injection point for any dynamically generated HTML. The referenced script files work together to generate the HTML. The exact list of script files depends on the application configuration. Those script files are ultimately responsible for composing HTML and modifying the browser DOM to make it display. React follows the same pattern.

## Text templating

Client-side HTML generation occurs in the context of a bare minimum page template downloaded from the server, like the index.html template shown in the preceding section. The process involves three main steps:

1. Retrieving data for display on the page

2. Understanding the schema of the downloaded data

3. Assembling the data within an HTML layout

Display data can be embedded directly in the downloaded template or fetched on demand from some remote endpoints. In the latter case, AJAX techniques are employed to download data in the background. Data can be expressed in several formats—most likely JSON, but also XML, markdown, or plain text. The invoked endpoint determines the format, and the downloader code adapts to it. The fetched data is then constructed within an HTML template.

In component-based frameworks like Angular and React, each component holds its own HTML template and is responsible for fetching and parsing external data. Typically, these frameworks provide engines to automate the assembly of HTML by defining templates with placeholders that will be filled with data.

# A minimal example of HTML templating

Angular and React templating engines are sophisticated code, but what they do boils down to what you can do with any independent templating library. Here's a minimal example of using the popular Mustache.js (around 10 KB in size) to render a template with some data. In addition to referencing the source of the library, the host HTML page includes one or more templates, as shown here:

```
<script id="my-template" type="text/template">
  <h1>Hello, {{ name }}!</h1>
  <p>Age: {{ age }}</p>
</script>
```

The template includes placeholders enclosed in double curly braces, like {{ name }}, where name is replaced with actual data. The syntax of the placeholder is a requirement set by the library. So, let's assume you have the display data shown here:

```
var data = {
  name: "Dino",
  age: 32
};
```

As mentioned, data can be statically part of the host page or, more likely, the result of an AJAX call. The following line of JavaScript code builds the final HTML ready for display:

```
// Get the template from the HTML
var template = document.getElementById("my-template").innerHTML;

// Use Mustache to render the template with data
var html = Mustache.render(template, data);
```

The library assembles the template and data into the following final piece of HTML:

```
<h1>Hello, Dino!</h1>
<p>Age: 32</p>
```

The next step is rendering the generated markup into the browser's DOM.

# Rendering HTML

The innerHTML property, exposed by DOM elements like DIV and SPAN, provides programmatic access to the HTML content of the element. When you read the property, it returns the HTML content of the element and its descendants serialized as a string. When you set the innerHTML property to an HTML string, the browser parses the string and re-creates the DOM structure within the element.

The property is a direct and convenient way to add, modify, or remove content from a webpage via JavaScript. Returning to the Mustache.js example, the following code completes the demo by inserting the dynamically composed HTML into the page DOM:

```
// Use Mustache to render the template with data
var html = Mustache.render(template, data);

// Insert the rendered HTML into a specific element of the DOM
document.getElementById("id-of-the-target-element").innerHTML = html;
```

There are a couple of points to note about the innerHTML property to advise against indiscriminate use. One point pertains to general security. Setting innerHTML with unfiltered user input can lead to security vulnerabilities like cross-site scripting (XSS) if the input is not sanitized or validated properly.

The other point has to do with performance. Although innerHTML is a convenient way to manipulate the content of elements, it can be less efficient than other methods, especially when used frequently to update large portions of the DOM. This is because it involves parsing and re-creating DOM elements, which can be computationally expensive. For better performance, consider using other DOM manipulation techniques like creating and appending new elements or modifying existing ones directly.

The DOM programming interface, based on innerHTML and direct DOM methods, is the only way to update webpages dynamically. Therefore, both Angular and React use the DOM interface under the hood of their customized and optimized API.

## How Angular and React deal with the DOM

Angular and React have different approaches to DOM changes and use renderers that follow different philosophies. Driven by the principle of two-way data binding, Angular originally architected the rendering pipeline to make direct changes to the DOM for the entire HTML fragment being touched by changes. In contrast, React implements a mediator pattern known as the virtual DOM.

The virtual DOM is a lightweight, in-memory representation of the actual DOM of a webpage. When data changes in a React component, instead of directly updating the real DOM, React first updates the virtual DOM, which is faster and less resource-intensive. Then, it compares the updated virtual DOM with the previous virtual DOM snapshot, identifying the specific changes that must be made to the real DOM. Finally, it selectively updates only the parts of the real DOM that have changed.

React's use of the virtual DOM minimizes the number of necessary low-level DOM operations. More recently, though, Angular introduced Ivy, a new rendering engine that supports incremental DOM updates. Basically, instead of completely re-rendering the entire component tree when data changes occur, Ivy updates only the parts of the DOM that have changed. (See Figure 10-1.)

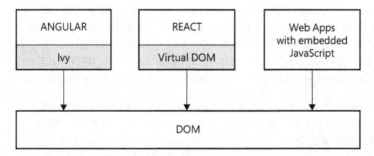

**FIGURE 10-1** Rendering pipelines of Angular, React, and generic web applications.

Aside from different implementation details, both Angular and React use optimized rendering engines based on the general mediator pattern, in which dedicated engines minimize the number of low-level DOM operations. Note that any web application that uses JavaScript to update the DOM (for example, via jQuery) dynamically applies its changes to the DOM without intermediation.

> **Note** Maybe you've heard of shadow DOMs. Although shadow DOM and virtual DOM might sound related, they are distinct concepts in web development. The virtual DOM is an optimization technique employed by frameworks like React to enhance rendering efficiency. In contrast, the shadow DOM is a standard established by the W3C to achieve component isolation and styling. It provides a way to scope CSS styles to a specific DOM subtree and isolate that subtree from the rest of the document.

# The API layer

In a client side-rendering scenario, such as an SPA, the front end is physically segregated from the back end. Whether written with Angular, React, PHP, or some other JavaScript-intensive framework, the front end is a standalone project deployed independently.

All front-end applications need a back end to handle data processing, storage, and business logic. The API layer acts as a bridge between the front end and back end, allowing them to be developed, function, and be maintained independently. The API exposes a fixed contract for the front end to call and represents a security boundary where authentication and authorization rules are enforced. Because HTTP is the underlying communication protocol, the back end can be built using any technology stack capable of exposing HTTP endpoints, regardless of the front-end technology in use.

## REST API versus GraphQL API

There are two main API architectural styles: representational state transfer (REST) and GraphQL. The main difference between these is in how data is transmitted to the client. In REST architecture, the client initiates an HTTP request and receives data as an HTTP response. In GraphQL, data is requested by sending a query command text.

A REST API is based on a predefined set of stateless endpoints and relies on HTTP methods such as GET, POST, PUT, and DELETE to perform operations on target resources. Data can be exposed in various formats, including plain text, CSV, XML, and JSON. More often, what is labeled as a REST API consists of a collection of public URLs accessed through HTTP GET and sometimes HTTP POST. Each of these endpoints features its own unique syntax, specifying input parameters and the data it returns.

There is an ongoing debate (which will likely continue indefinitely) as to whether a fully REST-compliant API is superior to a set of basic RPC-style HTTP endpoints. Many would agree that a plain HTTP endpoint is sufficient for simple tasks. However, as the complexity and functionality of an API grow, transitioning to a RESTful design may offer some benefits in terms of maintainability and developer experience, along with the potential to reduce the overall volume of API calls.

## Aspects of REST that GraphQL overcomes

The challenge with a REST/RPC API is that the client application has no control over what the endpoints return. This is why the GraphQL API approach came into existence. GraphQL allows clients to request precisely the data they need, thereby preventing both over-fetching and under-fetching. Clients send queries specifying the data structure they desire, and the server responds with data matching that structure. This flexibility empowers front-end developers, as they can request all relevant data in a single query, reducing the number of round trips to the server.

> **Note** A REST/RPC API doesn't let the client application exercise control over what the endpoints return. Rather, the endpoints themselves expose features to let callers tailor the desired response. This capability is called *data shaping* and consists of adding to endpoints additional query string parameters (the selected syntax is entirely up to the API implementors) that the API code uses internally to filter returned data.

The GraphQL query language for APIs was developed by Facebook and released as an open-source project in 2015. Facebook resorted to GraphQL to mitigate the inefficiencies of a REST API in its very special scenario. Facebook's data model is highly interconnected, with complex relationships between different types of data (for example, users, posts, comments, and likes). Facebook engineers needed a way to query such relationships efficiently—hence the development of GraphQL.

Here's a simplified example of a GraphQL query you might use to fetch a Facebook user's name and recent posts:

```
{
  user(id: "123456789") {
    id
    name
    posts(limit: 5, orderBy: "createdAt DESC") {
      id
      text
      createdAt
    }
  }
}
```

The query fetches data about a given user but returns only id and name properties. Furthermore, the query requests a maximum of five recent posts ordered by date. Each post contains id, text, and a timestamp. To execute the query, you would send an HTTP POST request to Facebook's GraphQL endpoint. The request would include the query in the request body, and the caller would receive a JSON response containing the requested data. (See Figure 10-2.)

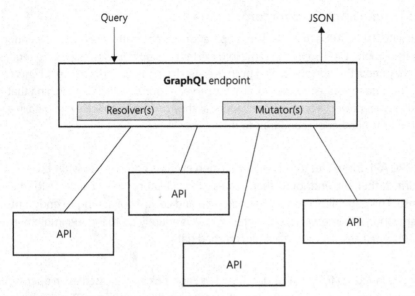

**FIGURE 10-2** Working schema of a GraphQL endpoint.

GraphQL isn't a magical solution. It requires real back-end code to make calls to APIs or database endpoints for executing queries and updates. Resolvers are dedicated modules that know how to selectively query an API. In contrast, mutators are components that modify data. In other words, the GraphQL runtime parses incoming queries, figures out which resolvers and mutators to use, and combines the fetched data to match the desired output. Resolvers and mutators must be written and deployed separately.

GraphQL exposes a single endpoint to access multiple back-end resources. In addition, resources are not exposed according to the views that you have inside your app. So, changes to the UI do not necessarily require changes on the server.

## Aspects of GraphQL that REST overcomes

GraphQL is not a magic wand that returns any data the client application wants. You have a single, flexible endpoint, but constrained resolvers and mutators underneath it. Those resolvers may be performing complex queries and may need caching. The amount of queryable data is restricted by the amount of data that resolvers can retrieve without negatively impacting performance and scalability.

For complex queries or updates, a plain REST API might be easier to design because it would give a distinct endpoint for specific needs. GraphQL's ability to request precisely the data you specify can also be achieved with a REST API by designing the HTTP endpoint to accept a list of desired fields through the URL.

Furthermore, an open protocol called OData provides an alternative. OData facilitates the creation and consumption of queryable and interoperable REST APIs in a standardized manner. OData equips you with a robust set of querying features. OData must be integrated and enabled when you implement the API, in much the same way you must set up resolvers in GraphQL.

The bottom line is that GraphQL was developed to address the specific needs of Facebook, which are relatively unusual compared to most other applications. Although GraphQL offers several advantages, many of these can also be addressed using a simpler HTTP REST API.

# Toward a modern prehistoric era

The rise of SPAs took the web-development world by storm. It marked a significant shift, challenging long-standing foundations of the web (JavaScript, HTML, CSS) that had intimidated an entire generation of developers. The prevailing message was to abstract the web and move away from direct HTML coding. Angular and React emerged, initially positioned as JavaScript libraries but ultimately expanding to replicate essential browser functions such as HTML rendering, routing, navigation, form handling, and cookie management.

In recent years, every new developer has faced choosing between these two camps. Consequently, many of today's younger web developers lack a fundamental understanding of how the web operates and perceive web programming solely through the abstractions provided by all-encompassing frameworks like Angular and React. Ultimately, although the quality of these frameworks is indisputable, they raise questions when it comes to the day-to-day practical experience of constructing web applications.

## Drawbacks of rich frameworks

While large frameworks like Angular and React provide a structured approach to development—which, in the case of large teams, may be a phenomenal argument in their favor—they're not immune from a few substantial flaws:

- **Performance overhead**   These frameworks require a specific project structure and the configuration of build tools and dependencies. It's quite common for projects to accumulate directories filled with gigabytes of JavaScript packages and configuration files, which can be bewildering to anyone involved. Consequently, it's not just the bundle you need to download that is sizeable, but the abstraction layer is too—resulting in longer loading times, especially for initial page loads.

- **SEO**   Angular and React use JavaScript to generate HTML within the browser. The content is fetched and rendered after the page is loaded. Hence, search engine crawlers, like Googlebot, initially see an empty or minimal HTML structure. In addition, the dynamic nature of JavaScript-intensive applications, including the possible use of client-side routing to navigate between different views or pages, makes it harder for crawlers to understand the site's structure and content and to index it properly.

- **Accessibility**   Web accessibility relies heavily on semantic HTML and ARIA attributes, which may not be inherently assured in pages generated entirely with JavaScript. Moreover, when content is dynamically added to the page, users employing screen readers or keyboards might lose their context and even remain unaware of new content. Developers therefore must diligently ensure expressive HTML, maintain proper keyboard navigation, and manage focus to uphold accessibility standards.

**Note** When speaking of Angular and React, one often highlights performance optimization as a benefit, as they tend to alleviate server load and minimize data exchange between the client and server. However, this advantage becomes apparent only when the application is up and running. So, the immediate obstacle to overcome is understanding how to set up a project in the first place.

To tackle SEO issues, speed up initial page loading, and enhance accessibility, Angular and React have introduced server-side rendering (SSR) as an additional layer of functionality. The adoption of SSR ensures that the initial server response contains fully rendered HTML content, making it easier for web crawlers to index the page and faster for the browser to load the page. Furthermore, discernible HTML on the server simplifies the process of tweaking it for accessibility. While SSR is possible in both Angular (with Angular Universal) and React (with Next.js), it does add one more layer of complexity to an already convoluted development process.

## Back end for front end (BFF)

Back end for front end (BFF) is a relatively recent term that indicates the presence of a dedicated back-end service designed and tailored to meet the specific needs of a front-end application. The idea is to have a back-end service that serves as an intermediary between the front end and the various APIs that make up the back end.

Consider a scenario where your back end provides APIs for use by the front end. The data returned to the front end might not precisely match the required format or filtering needed for representation. In such instances, the front end must incorporate logic to reformat incoming data, potentially leading to increased browser resource usage. To alleviate this, a BFF can be introduced as an intermediary layer.

The BFF acts as this intermediate layer, allowing some of the front-end logic to be shifted, enhancing efficiency. When the front end requests data, it communicates with the BFF through an API. One might wonder, can the desired BFF behavior be integrated directly into the back-end API? This integration approach has been common in countless web applications for many years. However, the BFF pattern is particularly beneficial in microservices applications where isolated APIs operate independently and lack awareness of the broader context—a scenario where BFF emerges as a valuable architectural pattern.

## The Svelte way to HTML pages

The idea that SSR helps make Angular and React better frameworks is devastatingly revolutionary. To make a bold comparison, it's like you're a vegetarian, and then you discover that to be a *stronger* vegetarian, you must eat meat. In fact, a growing number of developers are welcoming a simpler, back-to-the-basics approach to web development.

This counter-revolution is heralded by a new open-source JavaScript framework: Svelte. What sets Svelte apart from other popular frameworks like React and Angular is its compilation model. Rather than shipping a large runtime library to the client and interpreting code in the browser, Svelte shifts much of the work to compile-time.

The core idea is that during development, you write high-level, component-based code, similar to other frameworks. However, instead of shipping this code directly to the browser, Svelte's compiler transforms it into plain JavaScript code. So, at runtime, there's no need for a heavyweight framework library; your application is smaller and faster to load.

With Svelte, you don't write plain HTML directly. Instead, you write .svelte files—compositions of HTML with additional attributes, CSS, and JavaScript, and you add an explicit compile step that physically turns these files into deployable units. After compilation, the Svelte app will consist of HTML, JavaScript, and CSS files ready for production deployment.

In summary, you get much faster live pages, and a much simpler and cleaner development experience than with Angular or React. But Svelte still requires quite a bit of project configuration, a Node.js development environment, and build tools. An ad hoc development server (svelte-kit) helps keep the whole thing at a manageable level of difficulty and annoyance.

## Static site generation

Static site generation (SSG) represents a somewhat radical response to the desire to move away from client-side rendering. SSG refers to the combined use of a development tool and a JavaScript framework to turn a dynamic web application into a static website. A static site is essentially an unembellished assembly of predetermined HTML pages, where the content remains constant rather than being dynamically generated in response to user actions or real-time data requests.

All websites created in the 1990s were static websites. The difference with SSG is that the pages of a modern static website are not manually authored one by one; instead, they are automatically generated, starting with the source code, written using a server-side JavaScript-based framework.

Popular SSG frameworks are Next.js and Nuxt.js, tailored to work on top of React and Vue applications, respectively. (The next section briefly discusses the Vue framework.) The operational method is the same. For example, when you initiate a new project using the Nuxt.js CLI, it sets up a conventional project structure comprising directories for managing assets, components, plugins, and pages. A Pages folder is populated with the source files of the parent framework, be it React or Vue. Before deploying, the application must be compiled in a collection of static HTML pages. The compile step is typically integrated in a build pipeline.

In the event of changes to the server source, the entire website must be rebuilt. For this, many SSG tools employ a technique known as incremental static regeneration (ISR). This approach enables the dynamic updating and regeneration of specific pages within a static website, either during the build process or at runtime, without the need to rebuild the entire site.

**Note** ASP.NET experts will find SSG conceptually analogous to compiling Web Forms and Razor pages to classes. When compiling into classes, a DLL is generated, but every incoming request still dynamically generates HTML for the browser. (Caching the dynamically generated HTML is an optional feature that can be enabled and configured on a per-page basis.) In contrast, with SSG, the result of compilation is static HTML that is immediately usable.

## The Vue.js framework

In addition to Angular and React, there is Vue.js, an open-source JavaScript framework for interactive UI and SPAs first released in 2014. The unique trait of Vue is that it is designed to be incrementally adoptable, meaning you can start using it in your project at any level. For example, you could easily integrate it in an ASP.NET Core server application as a client-side data-binding library at the sole cost of injecting a single JavaScript file and adding some boilerplate code to trigger it. Vue is also component-based, making it suitable for building a full-fledged application with client routing much like Angular and React. Born as a plain data-binding library, Vue still retains a declarative syntax for defining the UI's structure and behavior, making it straightforward to understand and work with. Unlike Angular and React, Vue requires no mindset shift.

## The evergreen option of vanilla JavaScript

There are two different and largely incompatible meanings for the word JavaScript. The modern meaning refers to JavaScript as a sort of full-stack language. The original meaning refers to a simple tool to script changes to the page DOM.

**Note** Vanilla JavaScript refers to the fundamental core of the JavaScript language, devoid of additional libraries or frameworks. It is the native, browser-supported scripting language used to create dynamic and interactive web content. Vanilla JavaScript allows developers to manipulate the DOM, handle events, and perform various operations within web applications. Although modern frameworks like React and Angular raise the abstraction level of web development, mastering vanilla JavaScript is essential for obtaining a foundational understanding of the web and for effective troubleshooting.

Those who advocate full-stack JavaScript use the same language for both the front end and the back end. Specifically, JavaScript is used with feature-rich frameworks on the front end and as the basis for Node.js applications on the back end. (More on Node.js in a moment.) Adopting JavaScript as the exclusive language produces a relentless proliferation of new frameworks and tools that eradicate any sense of stability in mid-term and long-term projects. Moreover, JavaScript is a flawed language. It is single-threaded and lacks strong typing. TypeScript is a better option, but it's still JavaScript in the end.

In Angular and React applications, JavaScript is regarded as a full-fledged programming language, serving as the driving force behind the functionality of the frameworks (which are also authored in

JavaScript). But the core of the web is simply serving HTML to the browser with a bit of interactivity and style. In the end, all you need is a smart way to compose HTML dynamically and a way to surgically modify the DOM using JavaScript.

To achieve this, you don't strictly need an all-encompassing client-side framework. This explains why proponents of both Angular and React have begun to recognize the advantages of server-side generated content. However, the development process remains somewhat intricate, involving an additional layer of tools and code—albeit primarily for the purpose of compilation.

### The Node.js environment

Full-stack JavaScript? Enter Node.js. Node.js is a widely used open-source runtime environment for executing JavaScript outside of a web browser. It's built on Chrome's V8 JavaScript engine and represents a versatile choice not only for server-side web applications but also for development and networking tools. For example, you need Node.js installed on your development machine to build Angular, React, and Svelte applications, even when those applications are deployed as statically generated websites.

Node.js is cross-platform, running on Windows, macOS, and various Linux distributions. So, it is highly accessible to developers across different environments. It also supports modern JavaScript features and modules, making it compatible with the latest language standards. Furthermore, it has an extensive ecosystem of packages and libraries, thanks to its package manager, npm. And it is supported by a thriving community and a wealth of documentation and resources.

Node.js itself is not a web server, but it can be used to create web servers. Exposing Node.js endpoints typically involves creating routes using the built-in HTTP module to handle incoming HTTP requests. Alternatively, you can use a web framework like Hapi.js or Koa.js to simplify the process of handling HTTP requests, routing, middleware, and other web-related tasks.

> **Note** To expose endpoints from a Node.js environment, you just need to write the HTTP action handler. This characteristic inspired Microsoft to create Minimal API in ASP.NET Core. If you compare Minimal API ASP.NET endpoints and Node.js endpoints, you will see virtually no difference.

# Server-side rendering

Server-side rendering (SSR) is a web-development technique that involves generating webpage content on the server and sending the fully rendered HTML to the client's browser. This contrasts with client-side rendering (CSR), where the browser loads a basic HTML template and relies on JavaScript to assemble and display the page content. SSR offers clear advantages, such as faster initial page loads, improved SEO (because search engines can index content more easily), and better support for users with slower devices or limited JavaScript capabilities.

As you have seen, CSR frameworks have recently turned to SSR to mitigate SEO and performance issues. They couldn't cancel their client-side nature, though. So, SSR support has been implemented through additional frameworks like Next.js for React and Nuxt.js for Vue. But of course, CSR frameworks were developed in reaction to traditional SSR practices used since the early days of the web by server-side frameworks such as PHP, ASP.NET, Java Server Pages, and Java servlets. In those days, developers created endpoints to receive HTTP requests and templates that mixed HTML with server-side code to dynamically generate webpages ready to serve. Is this approach impractical today? I wouldn't say so. ASP.NET, for example, continues to be highly suitable for web applications with extensive back-end functionality—specifically, line-of-business enterprise applications.

# Front-end–back-end separation

CSR frameworks showed us that having distinct stacks (front end and back end) is possible and in many ways convenient. It's not a matter of separating concerns or improved security, though, as both are fundamental prerequisites in any piece of software. It's more a matter of wanting to address technological diversity, creating the conditions for multiple front ends (for example, mobile and web) and leveraging specialization of roles and related expertise. Finally, separating front end and back end enables more work to be done in parallel.

## Separating the front end and back end

Physically separating the front end and back end offers several advantages:

- It makes it easier to scale different parts of the application independently—crucial for handling increased user traffic.

- Teams can work in parallel on front-end and back-end development, reducing project timelines.

- Front-end and back-end developers often have different skill sets and expertise, with front-end developers focusing on user interfaces and experiences and back-end developers handling data management, business logic, and server-side operations. So, separation of the front and back ends allows teams to specialize in their respective areas, leading to more efficient development.

- You can use different technologies on the front end and back end, as long as they communicate via well-defined APIs (for example, REST or GraphQL). So, you can choose the best tools and technologies for each component independently.

> **Note** It is not uncommon today for applications to feature an Angular front end and ASP.NET Core or Node.js back end.

## Separating data and markup

A physically separated front end brings up the problem of obtaining updates from the server as the user interacts with the interface. Ultimately, within a web application of any kind, any update is simply data coming from a server endpoint in response to a request. Data can be returned as structured text (for example, JSON or XML) or markup (that is, data laid out in a graphical template). If the endpoint returns an HTML fragment, then the amount of data that travels over the wire is larger. However, the update is nearly instantaneous and, more importantly, can be managed with plain vanilla JavaScript.

If the endpoint is part of a web API and returns JSON, then the data must be parsed on the client and composed into an HTML fragment to attach to the DOM or turned into a list of update operations on the same DOM. Optimizing this process requires client-side templating engines and the implementation of some virtual DOM algorithm.

## Single web stack

ASP.NET is a classic server-side framework that manages web development from start to finish. Combined with some vanilla JavaScript, it represents an effective choice for line-of-business applications.

In my opinion, a single stack (for example, ASP.NET) should always be the first option to consider for combining flexible markup definition through the Razor markup language and API development. ASP.NET is typically based on controllers—the presentation layer discussed in Chapter 4—but can be also further simplified through page-specific endpoints (Razor pages) or even UI-less minimal API endpoints.

> **Note** Of course, there are compelling reasons to deviate from a single-stack approach. However, such decisions should be rooted in project-specific considerations rather than blind adherence to tech trends.

In terms of sheer simplicity and efficiency, it's hard to deny that a single stack like ASP.NET, combined with little more than basic JavaScript, is one of the most lightweight yet effective solutions. Still, the definition of *complexity* can be relative. For example, I've been working with ASP.NET from the start, and I know quite a bit of it. So, it doesn't seem complex to me at all. Similarly, all the younger developers currently employed at my company have used ASP.NET from day one and have become extremely familiar with it over the years. So, anything beyond it—such as React or Svelte—might initially seem more complex than it truly is, simply because they are unfamiliar with it. Similarly, developers who have spent three years on Angular may no longer view it as complex but might be bewildered by a server-side rendering engine or even more traditional technologies like jQuery or plain vanilla JavaScript.

# ASP.NET front-end options

When opting for a single ASP.NET stack, there are a few options to consider for building a highly interactive front end, as modern applications require.

## Razor and Vanilla JS

Razor is a templating engine used within the ASP.NET framework. It enables developers to combine server-side C# or VB.NET code with HTML. A well-thought-out Razor page receives a view model object from the controller with all the data it needs to render the view. So, it doesn't need to run any other business logic code. At the same time, the Razor syntax allows you to embed chunks of any sort of C# code.

Unlike some other data-binding frameworks, Razor doesn't impose strict syntax for attribute binding. Rather, it gives developers the freedom to programmatically generate strings within the markup. Essentially, the Razor engine functions as a plain HTML string builder, allowing for the seamless injection of JavaScript code wherever it is required.

## Razor and Svelte

The flexibility of ASP.NET Core and Razor make it possible to combine Svelte with Razor—an interesting scenario. With this approach, you create Razor views (or pages) as HTML templates, which you can then enrich by embedding Svelte components.

The ASP.NET project incorporates a few Svelte-specific folders for source files, tooling, configuration, and the output of builds. Any final view is a Razor template with either a single Svelte component or a component surrounded by other markup. The configuration of each Svelte component indicates the injection point in the DOM, whether the root body or a child DIV element. A Svelte component is referenced in a Razor view through a dedicated `<script>` element that points to the component's output JavaScript file. The deployment takes place the usual way via Visual Studio, but you do need to integrate the Rollup module bundler in the .csproj file to compile Svelte files on every build.

## Razor and Vue

Integrating Razor with Vue.js is even easier. All you do is download the library from a content delivery network (CDN). In this case, no setup, no bundlers, and no other tools are needed. The host page remains fundamentally an ASP.NET Core Razor page—there's just a new embedded script file that adds a bit of interactivity to the visual elements. The only requirement is that each Razor view that requires Vue must incorporate a bit of boilerplate code, as shown here:

```
<!-- Vue from CDN -->
<script src="https://unpkg.com/vue@3/dist/vue.global.js"></script>

<!-- CSHTML template enriched with Vue snippets -->
<h1>BEGIN of TEST</h1>
<div id="injection-point">
    <div>{{ message1 }}</div>
    <div>{{ message2 }}</div>
</div>
<h1>END</h1>
<!-- Vue bootstrapper -->
<script>
  const { createApp } = Vue
  createApp({
    data() {
        return {
            message1: 'First message!',
            message2: 'Second message!'
```

```
        }
    }
}).mount('#injection-point')
</script>
```

The `#injection-point` string identifies the injection point for any output under the control of Vue.js. The `data` function returns the object model to which Vue elements have access, and the object model is typically fetched from some remote source, which could include an endpoint of the same ASP.NET application.

## Razor and HTMX

In Razor, the most prevalent use case for vanilla JavaScript is retrieving content from the internet and seamlessly integrating it into the current page layout. Some developers are not particularly fond of using endpoints that furnish pre-rendered HTML because it could disrupt the clear separation of concerns between the markup and the data within it. I have a different view, however. While I acknowledge the importance of maintaining separation, I am willing to compromise it slightly on the presentation layer to reduce the complexity of JavaScript logic on the client.

If it is acceptable to use HTML endpoints, then you'll find yourself repeatedly employing the same vanilla JavaScript code to initiate an HTTP request, retrieve the response, handle potential errors, and subsequently update the DOM. While it is possible to write your custom routine for this purpose, it is often more efficient and elegant to use a compact library that facilitates this process with a clear and declarative syntax. This is where the HTMX JavaScript library comes into play.

With HTMX, developers use attributes like `hx-get` and `hx-post` to specify which server-side endpoints to fetch data from or send data to when certain user interactions occur, such as clicks or form submissions. These attributes can also dictate how the server's response should update the DOM, allowing for seamless server-driven UI updates.

Look at the following rich markup from a sample Razor page:

```
<button hx-get="/download/data"
    hx-trigger="click"
    hx-target="#parent-div"
    hx-swap="innerHTML">
    Refresh
</button>
```

The result is that clicking the button triggers an HTTP GET request to the specified URL. The returned content (ideally, HTML) will replace the inner HTML of the element designated by the `hx-target` attribute.

 **Note** HTMX enhances the user experience at a very low cost while preserving accessibility and SEO-friendliness.

## ASP.NET Blazor

Yet another option for an ASP.NET front end is Blazor. Blazor is a web application development framework with two hosting models:

- **Blazor WebAssembly**   This runs on the client side, in web browsers. It compiles C# and .NET code into WebAssembly bytecode, which can be executed in modern web browsers without plugins or server-side processing. Suitable for building front-end SPAs, Blazor WebAssembly has a component-based architecture with a Razor-like syntax.

- **Blazor Server**   This runs on the server side. With Blazor Server, the application's logic and user interface are executed primarily on the server rather than in the client's web browser. This approach relies on real-time communication between the client and the server to deliver interactive web applications. Blazor Server uses SignalR to establish a persistent connection between the client and the server. This connection enables instant updates and interaction without requiring frequent full-page reloads. For a server-side ASP.NET application, Blazor integration means an interactive user interface obtained without the use of JavaScript.

# ASP.NET Core versus Node.js

Both Node.js and ASP.NET Core are technologies used in web development. However, they serve different purposes and have different characteristics.

Although both platforms offer ways to build web applications, their architectural differences may make one more suitable than the other in certain use cases. It's also not uncommon for developers to choose one or the other based on personal preference or familiarity. In general, there are very few scenarios where one significantly outperforms the other.

## Node.js

Node.js is a runtime environment that allows you to execute JavaScript and TypeScript code. JavaScript applications within Node.js can be run anywhere—on desktop computers as well as (cloud) servers. A common use case for Node.js is creating command-line tools to automate tasks (for example, code compilation, minification, asset optimization), data processing, and other system-level operations. ASP. NET is not at all a competitor here.

The Internet of Things (IoT) is another use case for Node.js. In this context, Node.js is used to build server components to interact with devices and handle sensor data. Note, however, that this use case is not exclusive to Node.js; ASP.NET Core can also be used for the same purpose.

The versatile nature of Node.js makes it suitable for executing JavaScript code in a serverless environment such as AWS Lambda and Azure Functions as well as the backbone of Electron. Electron is a framework for building cross-platform desktop applications using HTML, CSS, and JavaScript. Electron includes a customized version of the Chromium browser (the open-source project behind Google Chrome). It also leverages Node.js (and a vast ecosystem of plugins) to access the underlying operating system and perform tasks like reading and writing files, making network requests, and accessing system resources. Ultimately, the Electron core sits between the JavaScript on the web front end and the

JavaScript in Node.js on the back end. With Node.js, you can bring a web server environment wherever you need.

> **Note** I have fond memories of a project in the late 1990s, in which I adapted an existing ASP website to run without modifications on a CD-ROM—essentially an early version of today's Electron. To achieve this, I crafted a bespoke browser using the WebBrowser component from Internet Explorer and the Scripting Host component from Microsoft. This customization allowed me to tailor the browser's scripting engine to handle ASP web references such as `Session`, `Response`, and `Request` within a self-contained and customized environment. Node.js did not arrive until several years later, in 2009.

## ASP.NET Core

ASP.NET is a well-established server-only technology. The version of ASP.NET called ASP.NET Core can be used to develop web applications that run not just on native Windows platforms, but on Linux servers too. ASP.NET Core uses full-fledged programming languages such as C#, F# and Visual Basic.NET.

ASP.NET Core was designed from the ground up to build web applications, ranging from small websites to large-scale web applications and even web APIs. ASP.NET Core is also suitable in IoT scenarios in cooperation with other frameworks in the Azure ecosystem. ASP.NET Core provides a seamless development experience. It offers coding tools, languages, and patterns to streamline the process of writing well-architected and maintainable code that also addresses cross-cutting concerns like security, logging, and error handling.

### Implementation of Web API

Both ASP.NET Core and Node.js can be used behind a web server to expose HTTP endpoints to handle various tasks. ASP.NET Core is incomparable for CPU-intensive tasks. But for I/O bound tasks, which tool will work better depends on your specific project.

Far too much literature emphasizes the overarching simplicity of Node.js endpoints and how little it may take to expose an endpoint. Here's an example that uses Express.js to abstract most of the details related to the creation of a web server that listens to a port:

```
const express = require('express');
const app = express();

// Define a route for the current time
app.get('/current-time', (req, res) => {
  const currentTime = new Date().toLocaleTimeString();
  res.send(`Current time: ${currentTime}`);
});

// Start the Express server
const port = 5000;
app.listen(port, () => {
  console.log(`Server is listening on port ${port}`);
});
```

This code belongs to a single file (for example, app.js) which is all you need in a Node.js environment to spin up a web server on port 5000.

As surprising as it may sound, it doesn't take much more to achieve the same in ASP.NET Core using Minimal API:

```
using Microsoft.AspNetCore.Builder;
using Microsoft.AspNetCore.Http;
using Microsoft.Extensions.Hosting;

var builder = WebApplication.CreateBuilder(args);

// Define a route for the current time
builder.MapGet("/current-time", () =>
{
    var currentTime = DateTime.Now.ToString("hh:mm:ss tt");
    return Results.Text($"Current time: {currentTime}");
});

var app = builder.Build();
app.Run();
```

Furthermore, with ASP.NET Core, you can perform much more sophisticated operations by introducing controllers to manage incoming requests. Minimal APIs are more lightweight in terms of resource use and potentially offer better performance for simple use cases. Controllers are tailored for complex routing requirements and large numbers of endpoints, allow integration with middleware and action filters, and support model binding and attribute routing.

 **Note** Model binding—that is, the ability to automatically map incoming HTTP request data to action method parameters based on their names and data types—is in Minimal API with ASP.NET Core 8 released in November 2023.

Essentially, the real debate about Node.js versus ASP.NET Core comes down to their ability to handle I/O bound operations. Node.js and ASP.NET have different architectures that affect how I/O bound operations can be handled. The winner—if there is one—is determined not by the number of amazing adjectives and superlatives in articles and posts, but by the context of a given project, including team preferences.

## The blocking/non-blocking saga

Node.js and ASP.NET Core take different approaches to handling concurrent connections and then improving the scalability of web APIs.

Node.js uses a single-threaded, event-driven architecture. This means it operates on a single thread, handling all incoming requests in an event loop. When a request is made, Node.js initiates the operation and continues processing other requests without waiting for the operation to complete. So, Node.js is always ready to handle new incoming requests, which minimizes the risk of a user receiving the infamous "503 service unavailable" error code. This behavior is referred to as *non-blocking*. In contrast, *blocking* refers to operations that halt further execution until the initial operation is complete.

## Processing a Node.js request

Node.js handles non-blocking calls by using callbacks, promises, and async/await operations to receive the results of these (asynchronous) calls when they are finished. This ensures that the event loop remains responsive and can handle a high concurrency of operations without blocking. Callbacks, promises, and async/await operations are not functionally equivalent, but they can be used to achieve similar outcomes when dealing with asynchronous tasks. The key differences lie in their syntax, read-ability, and ability to handle errors. Figure 10-3 illustrates in more detail the non-blocking, event-driven architecture of Node.js.

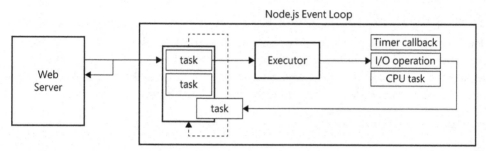

**FIGURE 10-3** Node.js event-driven architecture.

As you can see, everything starts when the web server places a request. As in the preceding code snippet, the request provides a callback to run at the end of the operation. Processing the request involves queuing it and returning immediately. The Node.js event loop scans the list of queued tasks and executes them.

A task is generally one of three types: a timer, an I/O operation, or some algorithmic task. In all three cases, at the end of the operation, the callback that was originally provided is added to the list of pending tasks to be resolved as soon as possible.

For timer tasks, the JavaScript engine records the expiration time and places the callback in the queue. For CPU-based algorithmic tasks, the single Node.js thread runs the code. The longer the task takes to complete, the longer the wait for all other pending tasks. For this reason, Node.js is ineffective for implementing algorithmic endpoints, which require a multi-threaded environment. But what about I/O-bound tasks?

## Processing I/O-bound tasks in Node.js

The strength of Node.js is its ability to perform tasks that do not engage the thread for too long. Reading files and querying or updating databases are potentially long-running operations but are accomplished by other processes. The JavaScript code just needs to wait for the operation to terminate.

In a single-threaded environment, what determines when the operation completes and adds a callback function to the queue? The answer is that in JavaScript, and particularly in Node.js, I/O operations use operating system-specific features. In Windows, Node.js leverages the operating system's I/O completion ports to efficiently handle I/O operations. On non-Windows platforms (for example, Linux and macOS), Node.js uses other mechanisms, like epoll on Linux or kqueue on macOS, to manage I/O operations efficiently. Node.js abstracts these platform-specific details for many I/O operations, such as file system operations, network operations, and other asynchronous tasks.

## ASP.NET multithreading

ASP.NET Core is a multithreaded framework. Each incoming request is typically handled by a separate thread from a thread pool. This allows ASP.NET Core to effectively handle concurrent requests. ASP.NET Core can leverage multiple CPU cores to process requests in parallel. This makes it suitable for CPU-bound operations in addition to I/O-bound operations.

How does ASP.NET process I/O-bound operations? The answer is, in the same way that Node.js does. However, you should note two important points. First, there is no alternative approach in contemporary operating systems to manage these tasks. Second, in ASP.NET Core, an optimization configuration for I/O-bound tasks is not automatic but is left to the developer. Here's an example:

```
public IActionResult LengthyTask()
{
    /* … */
}
public async Task<IActionResult> LengthyTask()
{
    /* … */
}
```

Of the two possible implementations of the same lengthy task, only the second is optimized for scalability, because it is marked for asynchronous execution. Let's review the code needed to call both URLs:

```
// Synchronous call
var response = httpClient.Send(request);

// Asynchronous call
var response = await httpClient.GetAsync(url);
```

In ASP.NET Core, you use the class HttpClient to place HTTP requests. All methods exposed by this class are asynchronous, with the sole exception of the generic Send method, added for compatibility and edge case scenarios.

When an ASP.NET Core asynchronous endpoint is called, ASP.NET Core selects a worker thread from its pool. This thread begins executing the endpoint's code and pauses when it encounters an awaitable operation. At this point, it configures a completion port (on Windows) and returns to the pool for potential reuse handling other requests. When the offloaded awaitable operation—typically file or network activity—is complete, the completion port triggers an internal ASP.NET Core callback. This callback adds a new task to an internal queue to finalize the original request. The next available thread, which may be the same thread or a different one, picks it up and generates the final response. Consequently, it's entirely plausible for a single request to undergo two distinct execution segments, managed by different threads.

The bottom line is that its multithreading nature makes ASP.NET Core much more suitable than Node.js for CPU-bound tasks. For I/O-bound tasks, both can be equally effective—although in ASP.NET Core, this requires the use of asynchronous controller methods or asynchronous Minimal API endpoints.

# Summary

This chapter revisited the history of web development, whose foundational principles have remained the same despite the continuous proliferation of new tools and techniques over the years. In the beginning, the web consisted only of super simple (yet nearly ineffectual) client-side code. Later, server-side frameworks like PHP and Active Server Pages (ASP) emerged, which evolved into ASP.NET over the new millennium.

Around 2010, the advent of single-page applications (SPAs) transformed the web-development landscape, giving rise to the present-day robust—and at times complex—frameworks such as Angular and React. A significant outcome of this shift has been the segregation of front-end and back-end development. This transition has prompted a renewed exploration of server-side rendering to address concerns related to slow page loads, search engine optimization (SEO), and accessibility.

Modern server-side rendering continues to entail the creation of a distinct front end, but it is now often compiled into static HTML during the build process. This begs the question: Why not just opt for a traditional ASP.NET application instead? Alternatively, should you consider using Node.js? This chapter concluded with a thorough examination of the architectural aspects of Node.js and ASP.NET Core.

In summary, a much simpler web is possible—although a much simpler web is probably not for every team and every application.

# CHAPTER 11

# Technical debt and credit

*A man who pays his bills on time is soon forgotten.*

—Oscar Wilde

In software terms, *technical debt* is a metaphorical concept that describes the consequences of taking shortcuts or making compromises in the development process. Although these shortcuts might be necessary to meet tight deadlines or deliver features quickly, they accumulate interest over time and can affect the long-term health and efficiency of a software project.

A less-explored but equally essential concept is technical credit. Whereas technical debt embodies the negative consequences of shortcuts and compromises, *technical credit* results from deliberate investments made during the software development process to yield long-term gains.

Both words—debt and credit—have Latin origins. Over the centuries, these words have evolved to their current meanings, which generally relate to finances. Debt signifies an obligation to repay, while credit describes the ability to take on new debt. In this context, debt plays a complex and sometimes contradictory role. When used judiciously to finance productive investments, it can contribute to expansion. However, excessive or mismanaged debt can lead to instability and hinder growth. In contrast, credit—essentially a trust-based arrangement—allows one to access services with a promise to pay for them in the future.

Technical debt and credit are similar to financial debt and credit. Incurring technical debt can help a team deliver features more quickly; meanwhile, technical credit conveys trust that any technical debt will be repaid to keep the software highly maintainable. High maintainability allows new debt to deliver more features more quickly in a virtuous circle of development. Unlike financial debt, though, technical debt is not intentionally sought but rather tends to accumulate organically.

## The hidden cost of technical debt

The term *technical debt* might be somewhat misleading. In essence, technical debt boils down to poorly written code. This encompasses a wide range of aspects, including coding practices, design choices, task breakdown, test relevance and coverage, code readability, and alignment with the latest versions of libraries and frameworks.

Poorly written code that just works isn't inherently problematic. The challenge arises when the code requires frequent or ongoing updates.

# Dealing with technical debt

In general, I believe that completely eliminating technical debt from software projects is an unrealistic aspiration. Dealing with it is necessary, though, and a pragmatic, rather than dogmatic, view helps considerably to achieve results.

## A pragmatic perspective

From a pragmatic perspective, technical debt is seen as an inherent characteristic of the system—a mere trade-off between velocity and quality. Keeping it controllable is just one of the non-functional requirements of the project. Overzealous attempts to eliminate it are destined to fail miserably because generating technical debt is in the mechanics of the software project. Much like entropy in thermodynamic systems, technical debt tends to move toward a state of maximum disorder.

All one can realistically do is monitor and proactively address debt before it becomes excessive, sometimes employing creative solutions as necessary. The root cause of technical debt is poor code quality, but it is not simply a matter of inexperience and lack of knowledge. There are many other factors that lead to debt. Yet, raising the quality of code is the only reliable remedy. Of the many facets of poor code, the following are more directly related to technical debt. Not all of them have the same relevance, but all do count. More lightweight and easier to address are:

- Inconsistent naming conventions

- Failing to apply standard style conventions

Both can be easily avoided, or just mitigated, with the use of code assistant tools, external to the IDE or just integrated. Any warning does matter, but often developers—especially juniors I'd say—tend to ignore warnings. More relevant issues are:

- Lack of comments and documentation

- Hardcoded values

- Insufficient modularity

- Large and verbose methods

- No unit tests

All these aspects of poor code have one common denominator—pressure to deliver features or releases quickly. In such cases, developers end up taking shortcuts or implementing quick-and-dirty solutions to meet deadlines, sacrificing long-term code quality for short-term gains. There are other factors, however, all linked together in a painful chain.

One common factor is lack of resources, whether time, budget, or skilled developers. Inadequate resources can force teams to make compromises, thus leading to suboptimal code and design choices.

Lack of resources is typically the result of poor project planning, insufficient analysis, or unclear specifications. When developers must make assumptions or guesswork in order to progress and deliver, accumulating debt is inevitable. Poor planning may also be the result of attempting to build overly complex or ambitious architectural solutions following technology trends rather than measuring the actual project needs.

## Reasons for creating debt

Overall, technical debt is a complex phenomenon that cannot be addressed either with the blunt force of aggressive schedules or with the resigned awareness that it cannot be entirely eliminated. It deserves attention and understanding. To start off, there are four distinct types of debt.

- **Intentional** This debt arises when a conscious decision is made to opt for a quick and rudimentary solution to fulfill a deadline or a given requirement, fully aware that it will necessitate future refactoring.

- **Unintentional** This debt happens when coding errors or shortcuts are introduced unknowingly due to a lack of knowledge or skills.

- **Avoidable** This debt occurs when it could have been avoided by simply adhering to established best practices, standards, or guidelines during the development process.

- **Unavoidable** This debt is caused by external factors such as shifting requirements, evolving dependencies, or changing technologies, which compel developers to adapt their code to accommodate these alterations.

Technical debt doesn't necessarily carry a negative connotation. In certain situations, it can be taken with a positive outlook, especially in the initial phases of a project when the ultimate direction isn't entirely defined. This might occur when you're coding for a potential throw-away prototype, a minimally viable product, or to validate a new business model.

An example of avoidable debt is the debt caused by the behavior of executives and project managers who, blinded by the glow of business, may disregard the inherent mechanics of software development. This often occurs when these managers lack prior experience in software development, or, even worse, when they have been developers but only at a basic level. They tend to regard every time estimate as excessive and view explanations for such estimates as indications of laziness.

Usually, as a developer you experience technical debt on yourself long before you learn its perverse mechanics and explore ways to tame it.

## Signs of technical debt

For instance, suppose you get to modify some existing code (which might even be code you wrote yourself months or weeks before) and you feel lost. You may feel lost because you find no valuable documentation except IntelliSense or sparse comments; because there are no automatic tests to ensure a minimally acceptable behavior; and because you find convoluted code flows in large and bloated methods. The most frustrating point, though, is when you start reading the instructions and find it hard to make sense of the logic because you find a lot of variables, methods, and classes with unclear and even cryptic names.

The technical debt of a software project is the sum of the technical debt that any single developer contributes. Being able to detect your own debt is just one of the most valuable signs of professional growth.

The first and most significant sign of an over-threshold technical debt is when even minor changes to the code become increasingly challenging and time-consuming. This complexity arises because it may not be immediately clear which directory or file to modify, or which specific lines need adjustment or removal, thus elevating the risk of introducing new errors or breaking existing functionality. This decreased agility can result in missed opportunities, delayed releases, and increased frustration.

Just like financial debt accrues interest, technical debt accumulates interest in the form of additional time and effort required for ongoing maintenance. As the debt grows, the maintenance burden becomes overwhelming, and valuable development resources are diverted from creating new features to fixing existing issues. Over time, these issues can compromise the software's stability, security, and performance, ultimately eroding user trust and satisfaction.

To manage technical debt effectively, development teams must adopt a proactive approach that acknowledges the existence of debt and allocates time and resources to address it regularly. Before everything else, though, a method for measuring the level of debt must be established. It can be a combination of automatic static code analysis run by tools like SonarQube and manual code reviews conducted by fellow developers. The outcomes of this assessment can populate a technical debt backlog, where identified issues are documented, described, and categorized. Each issue can be associated with an estimated cost to fix.

## Ways to address debt

Reducing the amount of technical debt is definitely possible. It is, however, a matter of engineering culture. The stronger it is, the greater is the awareness of technical debt as a serious issue to tackle. There are no best practices, though, let alone silver bullets.

Overall, there are only two possible ways to approach technical debt: as a separate project or side-by-side with the development of new features and releases.

### Separate the project

Projects exclusively dedicated to technical debt reduction are not commonly encountered. The rationale behind this is rather straightforward: these projects have no immediately visible business value. Consequently, they don't appeal to developers and represent a poorly understood cost for companies.

In contrast, a dedicated project can prove highly effective, as the team can operate without the constraints typically associated with side projects—notably, time limitations and the need to deliver new product builds. For a standalone debt reduction project to gain traction, it must address a well-recognized issue within an organization.

An excellent example is when a significant number of bugs are detected in production. Presenting a project that involves codebase analysis and the implementation of more automated tests has a great appeal to managers, as it pitches the potential to reduce the occurrence of production bugs and decrease the need for manual testing.

## Ship and remove

Most of the time, your focus is on system enhancements, and you work according to an often demanding timeline for releases. Is it prudent to allocate additional time to each task on the list to reduce technical debt while advancing? From a manager's perspective, this might not be the preferred approach. However, an effective compromise can be achieved by integrating debt reduction tasks alongside project-related tasks. A few times, I've observed team leaders with strong personalities and charisma subtly incorporating debt reduction actions into the standard to-do list, often without explicit authorization! They did their job and delivered the expected set of features in the context of a cleaner codebase.

The ship-and-remove strategy is also recommended for codebases where technical debt is present but in a relatively lightweight form. In such cases, it's essential to adhere to the golden rule of leaving the codebase cleaner than you found it.

## Inventory of debt items

For any actors involved in the project, taking a holistic view of the items within the backlog is helpful. There are situations where technical debt is managed in a separate container (a backlog other than the one that stores reported bugs and project to-dos), and this separation can sometimes hide debt from the view of product owners and managers. To enable the product owner to prioritize effectively, it is imperative that they have a comprehensive understanding and perspective of all the tasks and concerns at hand.

A regularly updated inventory of outstanding technical issues is essential for quantifying the potential impact of addressing each issue in the entire system. This process helps establish priorities. Take, for instance, the scenario of duplicated code. The straightforward solution involves moving the code to a shared library. However, what would be the ramifications of this move? What is the associated cost? Indeed, it would grow proportionally with the frequency of access to the codebase.

In general, for each specific issue (such as boilerplate code, insufficient modularity, naming conventions, long build time, automatic tests, or documentation), two values should be assigned: impact and reward.

> **Note** Technical debt directly impacts the business. As such, it should be regularly communicated to stakeholders not merely as a numerical metric but rather as a characteristic or, if it looks more appealing, as a prerequisite for planning new features. As emphatic as it may sound, a hidden war between teams and management is of no help to anyone.

## Agile techniques to tackle debt

To tackle technical debt, the initial step involves cataloging the outstanding issues that need attention. The next step consists in devising a strategy to seamlessly integrate these debt reduction tasks with routine development. There are three strategies commonly used to allocate time and resources for reducing technical debt.

- **Timeboxing**  A fixed amount of time is reserved within every development cycle just to tackle technical debt. For common two-week sprints, a common value is 20%. Because tasks are part of the sprint, this approach guarantees a dedicated focus on reducing debt in a structured manner.

- **Spikes**  Spikes represent a short amount of time explicitly dedicated to the investigation of a feature with the purpose of attaining deeper comprehension. Spikes are often used when the team encounters a technical challenge, a complex problem, or a piece of work that is not well understood. In this regard, a spike of one or two days can be spent to gain insights about the technical debt as a whole or just to start addressing specific items.

- **Slack time**  This is some extra time deliberately added to the timeline just to be ready to handle unplanned work that may arise during the development process. If no urgent issue arises, the team can use the slack time to address technical debt problems.

All these strategies allow development teams to balance the ongoing need to reduce technical debt with the demand for delivering new features and enhancements.

# Debt amplifiers

Time constraints, and subsequent pressure to meet tight deadlines, are the most common reasons for technical debt because they lead to quick-and-dirty solutions to deliver on time. Usually, this deliberate discount on quality comes with the commitment to fix it soon, already the day after the deadline. Unfortunately, this day rarely arrives.

## Lack of documentation

The first victim of time constraints is documentation. Tight deadlines mean that developers are focused on completing the core functionality of a project as quickly as possible and prioritize coding and testing over documentation to ensure that these features are completed on time.

Furthermore, some developers may perceive documentation as administrative overhead that doesn't directly contribute to the completion of the project. They may believe that their time is better spent on coding, which puts them in the spotlight more than writing documentation. In some organizations, in fact, developers are not recognized for writing documentation. If there are no clear incentives or expectations for documentation, developers may not prioritize it.

There's more to it, though.

Writing documentation requires focus and is time-consuming. Tight deadlines may also mean that there are limited resources available, including technical writers or documentation specialists who can assist with the documentation process. Without dedicated support, it is challenging to create comprehensive documentation.

Lack of documentation is not just a crucial part of the overall technical debt, but it is also the primary amplifier of it in the future. In the long run, poor or inadequate documentation leads to new errors, delays, and ultimately the accumulation of new technical debt. Factors other than time constraints, though, contribute to amplifying the amount and scope of the debt.

## Scope creep

The expression *scope creep* refers to the uncontrolled growth of the project's objectives and deliverables beyond what was initially planned. It occurs when new features and changes are introduced without proper evaluation and consideration of their impact on the project's timeline, budget, and resources.

Often, scope creep is driven by stakeholder expectations on the wave of allegedly changing market conditions. While addressing stakeholder needs is important, it must be managed within the project's constraints. When this doesn't happen, technical debt surges.

In an ideal world, project managers and teams establish clear project boundaries, define a well-documented scope statement, and implement change control processes. Change requests are thoroughly assessed for their impact on the project's timeline and budget before they are approved and implemented. Effective communication among project stakeholders ensures that everyone understands the project's scope and any proposed changes.

In the real world, scope creep is often the norm. However, scope creep is not per se the real sore point. Business-wise, expanding the scope of a project is often a great sign. The problem arises when the expansion is gradual and the impact on timeline, budget, and resources is not perceived as an issue to address. Hence, if corresponding time and resource adjustments are not implemented, the project becomes an automatic generator of technical debt.

## Rapid prototyping

Rapid prototyping is a product development approach that involves quickly creating a working model of a software application to test and validate its design, functionality, and feasibility. The primary goal of rapid prototyping is to accelerate the development process and reduce the risk of developing a final product that does not meet user needs or market requirements.

The key point is that a rapidly built prototype is neither intended nor designed for production use.

The misleading point for managers and stakeholders is that a prototype is a proof-of-concept and doesn't just lack the full functionality of the final application. It lacks many other invisible aspects, crucial for a solid, production-ready application.

Most commonly, it lacks robustness and may not be able to handle errors and exceptions without crashing or failing catastrophically. It is also not devised for performance, scalability, or efficiency, which are crucial factors in production systems. It commonly has security concerns. Worse yet, prototypes are typically not designed for long-term maintenance. Their code may lack proper documentation, may not adhere to coding standards, or follow best practices, making ongoing support and updates difficult.

Yet, in the ideal world of business, this code just works and can find its way into production environments with just a few adjustments here and there. In the real world, instead, transitioning from a prototype to a production-ready system typically involves substantial additional development, testing, and refinement to ensure the system's reliability, security, and performance.

Working on a project that was originally a prototype is a condition that works as a powerful amplifier of technical debt.

## Lack of skills

Whether or not the project was originally a prototype, it will face continuously changing requirements. I didn't spend all my career working day-by-day on software projects, but most projects I contributed were applications built with a customer in mind and then expanded to become multi-tenant applications. In such critical scenarios, all you receive are new, and sometimes contradictory, requirements to code as soon as possible.

It is viable to anticipate these changes, but only with deep domain understanding and sharp analytical capabilities. In these situations, if you fail to design the codebase to be flexible and adaptable, technical debt inevitably accrues as developers struggle to retrofit new requirements into the existing code.

It's not just the architect though. The quality of developers is fundamental. A lack of skills should be addressed while being aware that a six-hour online course, or even a three-day workshop, will not make the difference overnight. Technical debt is unavoidable in these situations. The sooner you start integrating technical debt in the development cycle, the better you keep the project moving.

 **Note** One more technical debt amplifier I have found is strong dependency on external libraries, frameworks, or third-party components. Especially in web applications, the extensive use of giant frameworks and component libraries creates a lock-in effect that over the years can hardly be fixed effectively, if not with a big rewrite. When I was purchasing my first house, my father advised me to contemplate how straightforward it might be to sell the same house in the years to come. Likewise, I warn against the adoption of a large library without first considering the potential challenges of removing it in the future.

# The hidden profit of technical credit

When used for business reasons, and not for mere laziness, and when reduced below a safe threshold, technical debt can be useful to growth. A proven record of recovered technical debt represents a credit for the team and an allowance to incur other technical debt in the future. The sore point of technical debt is not so much the quantity of it you have at a certain time, but how the team is able to manage it. Managing debt means knowing how to reduce it and knowing how to keep it to a minimum. This is the measure of the technical credit of a team.

## The theory of broken windows

As foregone as it may sound, technical debt accumulates more slowly when best practices of maintainability and readability are applied to the software being developed. This scenario appears to be an instance of the well-known broken windows theory.

The theory has its origins in the field of criminology and was first developed by a team of social scientists in 1982. According to the theory, in a community, visible signs of disorder and neglect, such as broken windows, graffiti, and litter, lead to an increase in crime and antisocial behavior. A broken window left unrepaired signals to potential offenders that no one cares about maintaining order and that criminal behavior is, in a way, tolerated.

To draw an analogy, when a developer writes code hastily and without due diligence, it sends a message to the next developer that code quality isn't a top priority and that taking shortcuts and writing messy code is acceptable. Conversely, encountering clear, readable, and well-organized code encourages others to uphold a similar standard of care.

In software, broken windows are coding practices such as duplication, large and bloated methods and classes, complex conditional statements, poor naming conventions, hardcoded values, code smells, and insufficient documentation. Refactoring is the technique to fix software broken windows.

### The time to refactor will never come

Some developers write code as it comes, linearly, without paying attention to readability, duplication, organization, and comments. Tight deadlines are only a mitigating factor, but not a complete excuse for neglecting these aspects. I have seen far too many developers delivering functional yet mediocre code with the promise to return to it, later, to clean it up.

Well, this later time to refactor the code will never come.

One thing is counting as technical debt rigid code that may not be easily extended with additional features. Quite a different thing is, instead, fixing poorly written code that is unreadable, packed with code smells, and excessively long and convoluted. A developer who knowingly produces subpar code with the intention of fixing it later fails to demonstrate proper project respect. Every developer should always strive to deliver the best code possible. The extra time to refactor will never come, and even if it did come, the result is that it took twice the time to produce well-structured code.

## Design principles are like hygiene

The world of software is full of nice acronyms sold as fundamental principles of coding. The list is long and includes at least the following:

- **DRY, or Don't Repeat Yourself**   This encourages developers to avoid duplicating code by abstracting common functionality into reusable components or functions.

- **KISS, or Keep It Simple, Stupid**   This advocates for simplicity in design and implementation to make code easier to understand and maintain.

- **YAGNI, or You Aren't Gonna Need It**   This advises against adding unnecessary features or complexity to the codebase based on speculative future needs.

The most popular, however, is SOLID, an easy-to-remember cumulative name for a set of five design principles. S stands for Single Responsibility Principle, O for Open/Closed Principle, L for Liskov's Substitution Principle, I for Interface Segregation Principle, and D for Dependency Inversion Principle. Overall, the principles offer valuable insights. Yet, it is naïve to think that failing them will compromise a project. A too-large class, or a too-long method, per se, will never jeopardize any project.

Rather than looking at SOLID and other acronyms as the tables of law, one should give them a relevance akin to that of personal hygiene. Just as maintaining personal hygiene is essential but cannot by itself cure or prevent any serious illness, these programming principles, if overlooked, may lead to issues but will never be the root cause of major problems in a project. Any system can well tolerate an amount of technical debt as long as the team masters the vision and techniques to reduce it.

Furthermore, these principles are often easy to grasp in theory but significantly more challenging to implement effectively. Simply taking a course on SOLID principles won't automatically make you a better developer. However, mastering SOLID principles reduces the likelihood that increasingly more technical debt will accumulate in your code.

## Agile doesn't just mean faster

That Agile methodologies make coding faster is a misconception that arises from a few reasons. First, managers often oversimplify the Agile principles and read terms like "continuous delivery" and "rapid iterations" as the guarantee of faster delivery of a product as a whole. In doing so, they miss completely the broader context of Agile.

Agile promotes efficient and effective development practices, but the primary focus is on delivering the right features rather than just working at a faster pace. The goal is to deliver a continuous stream of valuable, working software while maintaining a sustainable pace for the development team. Agile methodologies provide frequent releases and iterations, which can create a perception of rapid progress. This can lead managers to believe that the development process itself is faster because they can see new features being delivered more frequently. The point is that with Agile the final product is delivered piecemeal with the possibility of changing direction after each step.

This is great value, but it doesn't imply at all that coding is faster; in fact, it's quite the opposite! The frequency of releases might be greater, creating the illusion of speed. It's akin to breaking a marathon into a series of brief sprints. In the end, it may consume more time, but you can readily assess your progress at regular intervals.

It's therefore important for managers and teams to have a well-rounded understanding of Agile principles and practices. Agile is about delivering value, adapting to change, improving collaboration, and maintaining high-quality software. It's not (solely) about speed of development.

## Testability is more important than tests

A unit test is a piece of code typically written and executed by developers during the development process to ensure that small, isolated parts of the codebase work correctly. Unit tests are typically automated, meaning they can be run automatically by a testing framework. This automation facilitates frequent testing and integration into the development workflow.

Unit tests serve two main purposes: they help catch bugs early in the development cycle, and they provide a safety net for developers to refactor or modify code with confidence, knowing that any regression is detected quickly. Furthermore, unit tests are also the first form of documentation for how individual units of code are expected to behave.

One big sword of Damocles hangs over the head of unit tests: the relevance of the tests written.

The mythical 100% coverage means that every line of code in the unit of code being tested has been executed at least once during the testing process. This ensures that there are no untested or uncovered code paths, increasing confidence that the unit functions as intended. However, 100% code coverage doesn't guarantee at all that the unit is completely bug free or that all possible edge cases have been considered. It only means that every line of code has been exercised by the unit tests. It says nothing about which aspects of the method have been tested and whether they are relevant in the business case.

Unit tests do require code that lends itself to be tested. This aspect is known as testability. More than just having hundreds of unit tests for the sake of the code coverage magic number, I would aim at having high levels of testability in the codebase. Testability alone is not sufficient to reap the benefits of unit tests. At the same time, though, testable code makes it easier to write tests. And writing unit tests encourages developers to write clean, modular, and well-structured code.

# The power of refactoring

Refactoring is a fundamental practice in software development that involves restructuring and improving the existing codebase without changing its external behavior. Refactoring is not about adding new features or fixing bugs. Refactoring focuses on optimizing the internal structure of code to make it more efficient, maintainable, and understandable without altering its functional behavior.

Refactoring is closely related to technical debt. It is, in fact, a deliberate and systematic approach to paying down technical debt. When developers refactor code, they rewrite it to be more maintainable, readable, and efficient. This process mitigates the issues that contributed to the technical debt.

## Goals of refactoring

One decides to refactor to enhance the readability of the code or to simplify it. One refactors to restructure the code and give it a more manageable organization. Most of the time, achieving these goals is a matter of removing code smells.

Code smells are indicators of suboptimal code design. They consist of specific patterns or characteristics of the code that indicate potential problems or areas for improvement. Common code smells include long methods, duplicated code, large classes, complex conditional statements, deep nesting, lack of encapsulation, data clumps, and more.

There are several tools available to assist developers in performing code refactoring. These tools can automate repetitive and error-prone tasks and suggest refactoring actions to take.

## Refactoring as a learning experience

Ideally, refactoring is seamlessly integrated into the development process as an ongoing practice. There should be no need to call it out explicitly; refactoring should happen as a normal coding-related activity: you check-out a file to perform a given action and while there you review the code with different eyes and apply needed changes just to make it better.

In this way, refactoring becomes a true learning experience as developers can analyze the existing code, understand its intricacies, and identify areas for improvement. Overall, the process enhances their understanding of the codebase, the underlying design principles, and the overall system architecture. What's more, since refactoring often involves researching and implementing best practices, developers end up internalizing them.

In this way, refactoring evolves into a genuine learning opportunity for developers, enabling them to delve into the existing code and pinpoint areas for enhancement. This process ultimately makes developers more aware of the nature of the code, including the fundamental design principles and the overarching system architecture. Moreover, as refactoring becomes a regular practice, developers continually engage in research and the application of best practices, leading to the organic assimilation of these principles.

In the end, refactoring produces better code and better developers.

## The genesis of technical debt

When it comes to coding, making the perfect decision from the start may not always be feasible. It often requires time for thoughtful reflection, which can sometimes conflict with the natural pressure that moves projects forward.

Whether or not we embrace it, the prevailing mantra of modern times is the well-known "move fast and break things," which signifies a mindset focused on rapid innovation and development, even if it means taking risks and making mistakes along the way. The phrase was particularly associated with Facebook during its early years. But the early Facebook has very little to do with enterprise business applications that many write today. Applied outside the isolated cases of a (very) few devastatingly powerful unicorns, the "move fast and break things" mantra questions the actual objectives we should be pursuing. Do we really know the objectives we want to achieve so quickly?

As a result, teams are constantly busy and overwhelmed, in a perpetual state of stress, frequently delivering undesirable results. It's likely that only a small portion of the team's efforts are genuinely devoted to creating value, while the majority is expended on resolving issues arising from various factors, including skill gaps, misunderstandings, workflow inefficiencies, and even aspects of the company's culture.

This is how technical debt is born.

Technical debt, however, isn't necessarily a bad thing. When it arises from a deliberate choice, it can facilitate progress since it essentially involves deferring decisions. After deployment, at a later stage, you often have a better understanding of the code and are ideally positioned to devise a long-lasting solution for it.

This is how technical credit manifests.

# Do things right, right away

Technical debt encompasses not only code-level issues but also architectural choices that may have been made with insufficient planning or are based on short-term expediency.

For example, choosing a certain database, framework, or system architecture because it seems convenient in the short term but doesn't align with the long-term needs of the project is a clear example of technical debt. Such a questionable decision may require significant refactoring to address the resulting issues.

## The Zen of software architecture

Just as Zen Buddhism emphasizes simplicity and harmony, the Zen of software architecture links to the same qualities to help software architects make informed decisions about the structure and design of systems. So it happens that the seasoned expert often identifies just one solution whereas a junior may see multiple options to choose from. Yet another piece of popular wisdom that comes handy here is the old saying that "great minds think alike."

This is to say that even the architectural component of technical debt can be addressed from the start by expertise and domain knowledge.

In software architecture, critical decisions should be made as late as possible to take advantage of any single extra minute to reflect, but as early as possible to avoid building software on unstable pillars.

## The Zen of coding

A hard lesson I've learned over the years is that you will never have time to do it nice and clean later. Your only chance, therefore, is to write code as clean and simple as possible, as harmonic and thoughtful as possible, right away.

Nearly flawless code from the outset is possible, and all it takes is discipline and mindfulness. No developer gains such awareness of the coding practice for a given business domain instantaneously. That's where discipline and commitment, and tenacity and perseverance, arise. And a little help from powerful coding assistant tools such as ReSharper.

At the beginning of my career, I used to interview outstanding developers and book authors for a printed magazine. During one of these interviews, a notable author shared his approach to writing programming books. He emphasized the importance of presenting commercial-quality code in the companion examples and in printed listings. In fact, every code snippet he included was meticulously crafted, incorporating robust exception handling, uniform naming conventions, descriptive comments, concise methods, and showcasing an overarching commitment to elegance and simplicity despite the complex topics discussed.

## Raising the quality bar

For every developer, the objective is to elevate the standard of quality and produce superior code that surpasses the fundamental requirement of mere functionality. For instance, while a pair of nested IF statements may achieve the intended outcome, it constitutes suboptimal code, no longer aligning with the standards of today. Not convinced? Read on!

There are several reasons why excessive nesting levels can pose challenges. First, as nesting levels increase, it becomes increasingly difficult to trace and understand the logic and progression of the code. Furthermore, when changes are necessary, deeply nested code becomes more prone to introducing new bugs unless you are extremely careful and conduct thorough testing.

Moreover, writing comprehensive tests for deeply nested code can be intricate and time-consuming, and typically requires creating multiple test cases to cover different code paths. To address these issues, it's advisable to maintain strict control over nesting levels and, when necessary, refactor the code. This refactoring process often involves breaking down intricate code into smaller, more manageable functions or inverting the order of conditions tested.

Frequently, the IDE promptly signals nested IF statements that can be simplified with a simple click. However, even without an assistive IDE, whenever you encounter an IF-ELSE statement, take a moment to pause and consider whether there's an alternative approach to achieve the same result. When done as routine practice, it only requires a few additional seconds of your time. If it does demand more time, instead, be aware that such an additional investment contributes to a deeper understanding of the problem and the codebase, ultimately adding value to the project.

Put simply, strive to become a better developer, and write the best code you can right from the start. If there was ever a secret, that's the one.

# Summary

Technical debt refers to the accumulated cost of suboptimal decisions and shortcuts in software development. These choices, often made to meet deadlines or reduce immediate effort, can lead to increased complexity, reduced code quality, and future maintenance challenges. Addressing technical debt is crucial for long-term software stability and efficiency.

Paying back technical debt can be a nuanced process because teams typically can't halt their work, clean up the code, and resume. Instead, work on the recognized technical debt is often merged with ongoing development efforts. Agile methodologies offer several strategies to allocate dedicated time for these incremental refinements.

Not so popular as technical debt is technical credit. It is akin to making strategic investments in code quality, architecture, and development processes. These investments may involve allocating extra time and resources to ensure that software is not only functional but also robust, scalable, and maintainable. Unlike technical debt, which incurs long-term costs, technical credit may generate long-term profits by making the impact of technical debt much less harmful and minimizing the maintenance costs of a product.

As in finance, technical debt and credit run on the edge of the same razor.

By prioritizing clean code, relevant testing, and comprehensive documentation, you slow down the process but produce very lightweight debt. Furthermore, the quality of code is more than acceptable and can be adapted at a reasonable cost to whatever scenario the future has in store. At the same time, a team having technical credit makes it more palatable for a savvy manager to consider incurring new technical debt when no appealing alternative is available. On the other hand, offering credit to someone with a well-established history of payment is considerably more straightforward.

# Index

# X - Y

# Z